Can Schools Lea

Can Schools Learn?

PER DALIN and
VAL RUST

NFER-NELSON

Published by The NFER-NELSON Publishing Company Ltd.,
Darville House, 2 Oxford Road East,
Windsor, Berkshire SL4 1DF

First Published 1983
Reprinted 1987, 1988, 1990

ISBN 0 7005 0610 1
Code 8157 02 1

Printed in Great Britain by
Antony Rowe Ltd., Chippenham, Wiltshire

Contents

Foreword		viii
Chapter One	Strategies for School-based Educational Development	1
Chapter Two	Survey-guided Organizational Development	21
Chapter Three	Institutional Development Programme: Assumptions	44
Chapter Four	Institutional Development Programme: Process	66
Chapter Five	Institutional Development Programme: Practice	94
Chapter Six	Institutional Development Programme: Lessons Learnt	124
Chapter Seven	The Institutional Development Programme Consultant	156
Chapter Eight	Can Schools Learn?	168
Appendices		
Appendix A	Trends in Norwegian Basic Schooling and Teacher Education	179
Appendix B	A Case Study in an English School	186
Appendix C	Survey Feedback	190
Bibliography		195

To Astrid and Diane

Foreword

We have two major purposes in writing this book. Firstly, we wish to develop a conceptual framework for school improvement, and secondly, we wish to describe an actual institutional development programme that has been used in various schools and teacher-education institutions in recent years.

The book should be of special interest to educators who are located in schools and teacher education institutions, and who wish to improve the institutional settings within which they live and work. However, the book is appropriate also for school administrators at all levels, and support personnel such as school psychologists, counsellors, and teachers' centre consultants. It should be of interest, certainly to specialists who are involved with organization development, although its main purpose is not to serve as a tool-kit for specialists so much as to provide a conceptual and practical aid to those in the institutions themselves.

Because our orientation is towards the practitioner, we do not mean to imply that the value of specialists is diminished thereby. They play an integral role in the programme which we describe in the book. However, if genuine institutional improvement is to become a reality, those participants in the educational settings themselves must begin to play a central role in defining the types of improvements which are to occur.

The institution we are representing, commonly known as IMTEC, was established originally in the early 1970s as a project of the Organization for Economic Cooperation and Development (OECD) for the express purpose of coming to grips with the management of educational change. During this time, Per Dalin, Head of IMTEC, initiated the first broad-scale systematic international analyses of educational change, focusing at the institutional, regional, and central levels (OECD, 1973, a,b,c,; Dalin, 1973).

In 1977 IMTEC became independent of OECD, but it has retained much of its original mission of studying change and helping institutions and individuals in countries throughout the world define, initiate, and carry through educational innovations. Out of this work, IMTEC has evolved the Institutional Development Programme (IDP) which is the focus of this book.

The book is the result of an international team effort. Development work on the IDP started in 1974, and was followed by the international seminar 'Critical Processes in Educational Change', which was attended by researchers and practitioners involved in educational renewal. The first version of the diagnostic instrument 'Guide to Institutional Learning' (GIL) was tested in 18 teacher-training institutions in the United States, Canada, the United Kingdom, Belgium, and Norway in 1975–6. Several revisions have been made since that time. A comprehensive programme known as the Institutional Development Programme eventually came into being, which has now been implemented in about 100 elementary and secondary schools and teacher-training institutions.

We are indebted to several thousand teachers and students in these institutions, who have made a large contribution to this volume. Also, many colleagues have contributed significantly. Matthew Miles and Michael Fullan helped us in the design stages, Marvin Wideen and Reuben Richert served as Fellows to IMTEC during the early stages of development, Larry Kraft helped us to refine the GIL instrument and write the Users' Manual for the programme, Øystein Engeland and Birger Bertheussen did much work in adapting the programme to the Norwegian situation, and Wayne Flynn helped us to develop a training programme for consultants. The IDP would not have been developed without their help. And, moreover, this book would not have reached publishable form without the patience and skill of our editor, Heather Chisnall.

Finally, we could not have finished this volume without the professional and psychological support of the Norwegian IDP consultants who had to live with uncertainties, and our limitations, for so long. We do hope that what we have been able to reflect in this volume can be of help to them to some extent and to others who engage in the difficult and exciting work of organizational development in schools.

Oslo, March 1983

Per Dalin
Val D. Rust

CHAPTER ONE
Strategies for School-based Educational Development

There have been numerous attempts to 'develop' schools. In America, after the shock of Sputnik, attempts to compete with Russia led to major changes in school curricula. In Europe, Social Democrats tried to 'develop' schools by passing social reform legislation. In some cases, Research and Development institutions put together a number of 'packaged' solutions to educational problems. In England, teachers' centres tried to create a forum for teacher renewal.

This book argues a definite point of view with regard to educational improvement. It maintains that the individual school is the key organizational unit of formal education. The social and professional community of students, teachers, and support personnel is organized in the school unit, the fundamental ingredients of learning and teaching are centred in the school; even environmental factors which interact with education most clearly take definition as forces impinging on the individual school.

If the school is the key educational unit, it follows that the school also should be the basic unit for educational development or improvement. We support this point of view, not only because of the logic in it, but because we have found it to be consistent with much of the empirical evidence on educational change that has emerged in recent years (Goodlad, 1975; Fullan, 1983). We wish to put forward two propositions: the school as an organization must be both a primary force and the focal point of educational improvement.

The School as a Force for Change

The school itself must be a primary force or energy source for any genuine educational change. Genuine school renewal usually requires that those actually living and working in the school be directly involved in defining needs, setting goals, and participating in programme development. The pervasive attitudes throughout the Western world with regard to school participation have been quite the contrary. The schools typically have been victims of energetic reformists who have wanted to do something to them. Clearly, external forces are not inappropriate or unimportant. In fact, they are often of crucial importance but, ultimately, the school plays a vital role in any successful attempts to improve education.

Dalin has evolved a conceptual framework to explain this dynamic interplay between institution-based motivations and environmental forces for reform. He suggests that three factors come into consideration: first, schools possess differing potential for internal creativity; second, political, social economic, technical, and cultural dynamics in the environment result in differing levels of pressure on the school to change; and third, the interaction between school motivations and environmental pressures eventuate in a mutual adaptation process (Dalin, 1978, pp. 97–9). The three factors are elaborated below:

The Creative School: John Nisbet describes a school's creativity as 'its capacity to adopt, adapt, generate or reject innovations' (Nisbet, 1974: 10). A creative school has a desire and a capacity for thorough self-assessment of its values, structures, relations, and strategies for action. Further, it possesses the capacity to use this information as a basis for planning, implementing, and evaluating changes which are deemed important and feasible. It is commonly described as creative or problem-solving because it recognizes that if it fails to take initiative, it is likely that change will be imposed from without and its only opportunity will be to react rather than act in a way which is based on unique internal insights and knowledge (Institute for the Development of Educational Activities, 1970, p. 1).

The Innovative Environment: In spite of pockets of stability in the world, environmental pressures for reform are usually enormous. Charles Silberman reminds us that the United States has just experienced 'one of the largest and most sustained educational reform movements in American history' (Silberman, 1970: 158). Western European reform pressures have been so pervasive that there are some who maintain that educational, and especially school reform, must now be regarded as a permanent feature of the system (Frey, 1976, p. 80).

Schools reflect differing capacities to respond to these influences in a productive manner.

The Mutual Adaptation and Development Process: Typically, the mutual adaptation and development process implies that the creative school is not isolated from external innovations but is aware of and responsive to them. The most productive innovation climate involves a *dialogue* between the school and its environment. Any genuine dialogue eventuates in mutual adaptation and adjustment as a consequence of interaction. In the case of the school, research findings of International Movements Toward Educational Change (IMTEC), the Organization for Economic Cooperation and Development (OECD), the Rand Corporation, etc., are conclusive that institutions in Western Europe and America rarely adopt innovations from external sources, but successful innovation more often means that institutions are able to adapt and develop innovative ideas and practices, fitting them to their own needs and suiting them to their own purposes. This situation is most clearly evident in terms of experience being gathered from national Research and Development (R&D) efforts which have often failed because they have treated schools as institutions which need something to be done with them rather than operating with a mutual adaptation mode (Dalin and McLaughlin, 1975).

The capacity of the school to engage in internal reform activities and the capacity of the school to respond productively to external pressures for reform, are described graphically in Figure 1. Four extremes can be described as follows:

Figure 1: The Institution's Capacity to Implement Innovations

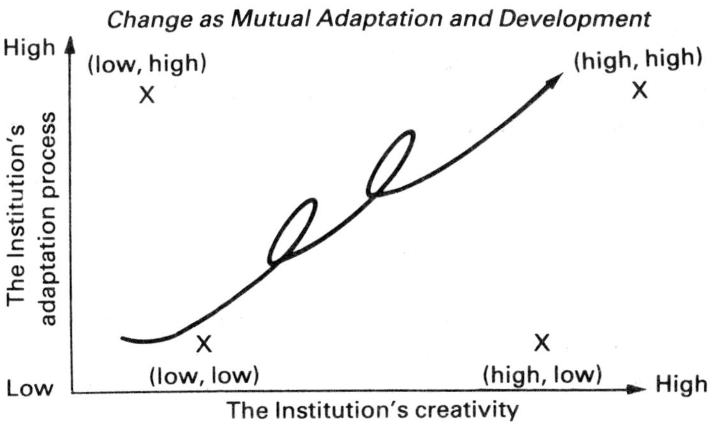

Position (low, low). The institution has an extremely low capacity both for internal and external innovation, and before both internal and external innovations are to succeed, major problems must be overcome. Time will be an important factor for the institution if changes are to take place. This position can be described as *maximum maintenance* of the *status quo*.

Position (low, high). The institution has a low self-awareness, a low degree of ownership of the innovation, a high dependency on external assistance, a high degree of adoption (not adaptation), and most probably a high congruence of values between the institution and external forces. This position can be called *maximum adoption.*

Position (high, low). There is high institutional awareness of innovative needs, low acceptance of external forces, little sensitivity to external policy decisions, high motivation within the institution, and a high degree of ownership of the innovations. This position can be called *maximum internal creativity.*

Position (high, high). The institution has a high capacity for both internal creativity, acceptance, and use of external ideas. The institution can manage changes over a short time, has high motivation, high ability for resolving conflicts within the institution and in the relationship to the environment, and uses a multiple set of strategies to cope with situations. In spite of the fact that there is a maximum acceptance of ideas from outside, the institution has a high degree of ownership in its practice. It is *not* assumed that compromise-solutions are the necessary result. This position can be called *mutual adaptation and development.*

Not only must the school unlock or unfreeze a reservoir of potential energy to be put to the service of educational renewal, but the school as an organization, institution, or system must be the focal point of educational development.

The School as the Unit of Reform

Any change effort is deeply conditioned by the system in which the change is intended to occur. Miles draws an image of Gestalt psychology to emphasize that, at least in America, 'specific planned change attempts have most typically been "in figure", occupying the focus of attention, while the organization itself has remained the "ground"' (Miles, 1965, p. 11).

Consequently, reform in schools has usually resulted in what might be called first-aid measures because they have dealt with educational improvement in such a manner that they have 'left the basic fabric of the schools unchanged' (Blumberg, 1972, p. 9).

Reforms which focus on factors such as teaching technology, curriculum, classroom instruction, various staffing arrangements, or school climate, have failed to consider the fact that educational institutions are made up of parts that are so interwoven with each other that fundamental change of one part requires adjustment of all parts (Dalin, 1978: 51–52). Attempts to improve educational dimensions such as teaching methods, or classroom grouping arrangements, are bound to be inadequate if they are not considered in the context of the entire school setting. According to Schmuck and Miles, 'school improvement efforts generally have failed because they have been piecemeal. They have not focused on the systematic features of the schools that enhance or retard innovative efforts' (Schmuck and Miles, 1971, p. 14).

Increasingly, however, the school itself has become the focal point of much education innovation activity. The capacity of the school to adapt and develop is coming to be regarded as one of the central factors in successful innovation (Bolam, 1977), and ample evidence is now available that schools, under certain conditions, are able to improve themselves (Schmuck and Miles, 1971; Goodlad, 1975; Fullan, Miles, and Taylor, 1980).

To accept the consequences of this evidence in terms of reform means that we must reassess the pervasive strategies for reform which have characterized both Western Europe and America. It is critical to review briefly what these strategies have been in order to place our point of view in adequate contextual perspective.

WESTERN EUROPE

It is difficult to make generalizations about historical European reform strategies because of the great cultural diversity which exists in countries such as Holland, Denmark and England which are in many respects more similar to the United States than they are to certain other European countries. In spite of this, all countries have struggled with certain historical conditions which have never existed in America. Louis Hartz reminds us that, in a dialectic sense, 'the feudal factor is the mother factor of modern life in Europe and has left a permanent and inescapable influence on its modern struggles' (Hartz, 1954, p. 5). With all their diversity, even today European social and educational institutions reflect this heritage. Also, the more fundamental liberal and revolutionary reform struggles of modern Europe can be characterized as reactions to this heritage.

In general, modern European educational reforms have focused on a single pervasive structural condition: its dualistic schooling tradition. Liberal forces in all modern countries during the past century have worked actively to break down this structure and replace it with a comprehensive, unified school. In Europe, commonly, it has been believed by liberal forces that social amelioration can be achieved, in part, by creating a common school structure. Throughout the 19th century, political parties and pressure groups worked to bring about some form of unitary schooling.

In the last quarter of the 19th century, specific legislative proposals for unified schools began to take shape, although Scandinavia was the only Western European area which was successful in institutionalizing some form of unified schooling before the turn of the century. In Norway, as early as 1869, the first three years of the primary school were informally perceived as being a common school. The *Folkeskole* Law of 1889 formalized this tradition, and, in 1896, the first five classes of all primary schooling were made common to all (Myrhe, 1976). The Swedish government actively engaged in discussions about a common school, and legislative bills were introduced as early as 1867. It was 1894, however, before a foundation school of only three years' duration was adopted (Paulston, 1968).

Germany, France, and England were not able to adopt legislation mandating the establishment of a common primary school until the second quarter of the 20th century. The first major breakthrough for a unified common school occurred in Germany, which, after the collapse of the monarchy at the end of the First World War, called a conference of 600 educators to design a comprehensive school-reform plan. The Education Law of 1921 was a consequence of this conference, and it stipulated that a common school was to *become* a reality by 1925 (Article 146:2). The Germans were also able to unify teacher qualifications since all *Volksschule* instructors were thereafter required to pass the leaving examination of the *Gymnasium*. However, National Socialism overtook the country before common schooling could be genuinely adopted. It was 1945, therefore, before all young people of Germany found themselves beginning school together at the age of six and remaining for four years before they separated into their dual schools.

The French also maintained complete separation between elementary and secondary schools until 1925, when some common primary schools were established; however, preparatory classes continued to dominate the scene until the mid-1930s when, through the efforts of Jean Zay, a common primary school law was passed. In 1937, a six-year common primary school became a reality, the last year serving as an observation class which would determine if a child was to go on to a classical, modern, or technical secondary school. In England a very similar programme was initiated in 1944; the primary school became standard for all children until the age of 11, when they were channelled to a secondary modern, technical, or grammar school.

At this point in time, the process of structural reform at the primary level in Europe has essentially been completed, and the major focus of political attention recently has been toward some form of lower-secondary integration, which has become commonplace in some parts of Western Europe. Sweden has maintained a nine-year common school since 1962. Norway, which established a seven-year common school as early as 1935, extended common schooling to nine years in 1969. France now provides a four-year 'cycle d'observation et d'orientation' above its five-year primary school, although children are still separated into loosely-defined general and practical sections based on ability. The socialist states of West Germany and the more liberal education authorities in England also are moving rapidly toward some form of lower secondary comprehensive structure (Rust, 1977, pp. 161–6).

Countries such as the Netherlands, Belgium, England, West Germany, Italy, Spain, and Switzerland are still dominated by the separation of children into different schools following primary school. All of these countries have political plans or policies which dictate future comprehensive education, and those countries which have already achieved lower-secondary integration are now struggling with the development of viable, upper-secondary programmes.

The strategy most Europeans have chosen to accomplish their comprehensive schooling aims has been to rely on political and administrative mandates. This has been necessarily so because the intent of the reforms has been less pedagogical than social. By that we mean that the reasons for educational reform have been the restructuring of society itself, in such a way as to reduce, if not eliminate, the dualistic, élite–mass social structure which was inherited from traditional feudal society.

Bennis, Benne, and Chin have characterized reforms that are played out in the political arena as Power-Coercive Strategies, because they take the following form:

> In general, power coercive strategies of change seek to mass political and economic power behind the change goals which the strategists of change have decided are desirable. Those who oppose these goals, if they adopt the same strategy, seek to mass political and economic power in opposition. (Bennis, Benne and Chin, 1969, p. 53.)

Labels such as 'power' and 'coercion' have pejorative overtones which might, for some, imply a breakdown in the democratic process. In the European context, however, nothing could be farther from the truth. It only means that the decisions, arrived at democratically, to restructure schools usually have been made external to the schools themselves. They are coercive in that the schools receive mandates from state authorities about what to do. Even this statement may be too extreme in some cultures. In Scandinavia, especially, a concerted effort has been made historically to include teacher groups in the development of local and national policy formation. In other words, teachers and other educators are not viewed by policy makers as simply technical implementers of policy but as contributors in a vital and often decisive manner to policy decisions themselves.

One should not minimize the importance of the establishment of law and other political mandates to enhance the greater social welfare, nor should one argue that little has been accomplished by the intense focus on external structural reform in Europe. These are now becoming commonly accepted as cultural values, but in the past this orientation has reflected a number of predictable pitfalls. Not the least among these is the inevitable lack of coherence between the intentions of the law and reality. Dalin has stressed that political strategies 'indicate procedures for the formulation and adoption of innovations but we are left with problems concerning the implementation of these policies'

(Dalin, 1973, 51). It often requires generations to translate law into reality. The giving of two different types of schools the same name, as we see in so many countries which have extended comprehensive systems, is a long way from creating a system in which children from different social classes are genuinely learning together. London, for example, defines all its post-primary institutions as comprehensive schools although in actual practice a large number of them remain essentially secondary modern or grammar schools.

The second major problem with the power-coercive strategy is that there is little mechanism for the participants inside the system itself to have a sense of ownership of the reform and they will usually resist it until they acquire such a sense. Because the reform measures in Europe have been so politically loaded, the participants themselves have failed to develop a unified professional community but have usually reflected the political biases manifest in the larger society.

Here, we might insert a personal value position and say that we believe structural reforms taking place in Europe are not only valuable but must become social imperatives. From a change vantage point, however, they reflect a basic flaw in that they are not perceived as a mutual adaptation and development process but rather as reforms requiring imposition of a foreign element into the school setting. That is, the school usually has no sense of ownership of the reform measures at issue and it reflects no value congruence with the reform directives. The principle of mutual adaptation and development continues to function even though it is not intended, with the consequence that, historically, the school has usually adopted the external reform in such a manner that it becomes compromised through internal adjustments. That is, the school reorganizes itself internally in such a way as to retain the social distinctions which it previously fostered externally, and, therefore, it fails often to ameliorate social class differences in any meaningful way.

In this section we have described what we feel is the pervasive historical orientation toward educational reform in Europe. It has been structural in nature and reformers have relied on a political-administrative or power-coercive strategy. It is important to note that strong tendencies for other modes are evident. A multitude of other strategies exist (see, for example, Taylor, 1981, 180–181). However, the above mode is so pervasive in most countries as to overshadow them in importance. We are able to find examples of power-coercive strategies in North America also, but these are overshadowed by a very different approach to educational improvement.

UNITED STATES

During the entire modern era in the United States, the school has been seen as a reinforcement of existing society rather than as a mechanism for fundamental social change. Even at the time of the founding of the American common school, the major opposition which common school advocates had to overcome was the claim that the Prussian *Volksschule*, which served as the model for reform, did not reflect the 'democratic' system of the American Republic, and that it was being used by the Prussians to strengthen the hold of despotism over the common man in Germany. The common school was only accepted in America when those involved in schooling were persuaded that it would not disrupt but would even support the existing social structure in America (Rust, 1968).

Significantly, at the time the common school was adopted, the élite *Gymnasium* was never considered in the reform proposals, and so the United States was able to bypass the dualistic phase of modern schooling, which, as we have seen, has dominated reform deliberations in Western Europe to this day.

Throughout modernity in America, a close working relationship between school and society has existed, though there have been protest movements when the schools were challenged to become instruments for social change (Counts, 1932). However, these have always remained 'protest' movements and have never reflected mainstream thinking in America.

Despite 'protests' such as that of progressivism, a remarkably stable relationship between school and society has remained in America. It is crucial, however, to point out that this stability is seldom seen as a static condition. Change, progress, and growth are now seen as a constant in the American way of life. In education, school reform is but a reflection of these changes and the term has now become almost synonymous with the proper management of education.

American education strategy toward reform and change has rarely been to alter directly fundamental institutional variables or social structures. It is commonly thought that since schools and society are made up of individuals, we can best improve both by changing the individuals who live and work in them.

Political reformers have usually defined their task as being an educational problem. Racial and minority groups have sought to redress disadvantage and discrimination by gaining access to more and better schooling. Social reconstructionists have sought to alleviate urban blight, poverty, and disease by providing educational programmes. Even those policy makers concerned with national security have defined their tasks as having important educational dimensions. The American response to Sputnik was the infusion of millions of dollars into special programmes in order to train teachers and upgrade school programmes.

It is also for this reason that American education, from its inception, has included provisions for the continual improvement of teachers through further education. America has never possessed a civil-service mentality which gave teachers occupational security in the same form as that which has existed in most European countries. Teachers have been expected to take evening and summer courses continually, and their status and salaries have reflected the degree to which this was done. Even teacher license renewal has depended on course credit accumulation. The assumption of this transition has been that the continual upgrading of teachers will ensure a high quality of schools themselves.

Human relations and group dynamics efforts, which characterize so much of conventional organizational development, also reflect the psychological orientation we have been addressing. The major conceptualizer of human relations, Kurt Lewin, had demonstrated during World War II that group methods were more effective in getting people to change their eating habits than relying on individual persuasion (Lewin, 1952). His students relied on these concepts to develop a movement which has penetrated industry, government and universities, but it remains a movement which, if effective, has its greatest impact on the individuals who participate in the process rather than on systemic features of the institutions where they work.

So pervasive is our commitment to changing individuals in an attempt to redress social ills in general that Cremin was once led to quip: 'In other countries when there is a profound social problem there is an uprising; in the United States we organize a course' (1965, p. 10).

In contemporary organizational development parlance, this major historical American strategy for institutional improvement resembles many elements of what Bennis, Benne, and Chin (1969) describe as *Normative Re-Educative Strategies*. It involves the changing of attitudes, skills, values, and human relationships because it is thought that a social system can be changed by releasing and fostering growth in the persons who make up the system.

This change orientation clearly assumes that the dynamics of society are linear and revolutionary in nature. That is, society is seen to develop in a stage-by-stage process and schools exist to serve as important building blocks in this continuous growth pattern. The orientation also reflects a consensus view since it assumes that society as a whole supports the growth that is taking place. Further, it is technical or means-oriented since the basic fabric of society is not at issue as much as are concerns for improving the delivery system and production process in existing society through education.

We would never disparage attempts to improve individual competence, because it contributes mightily to educational improvement. However, we agree with Katz and Kahn that

> 'the major error in dealing with problems of organizational change, both at the practical and theoretical level, is to disregard the systemic properties of the organization and to confuse individual change with modification in organizational variables' (1966, 390).

For example, even when in-service or human relations programmes are successful in changing individuals, they bring their new skills and insights back into the institutional environment, with its own norms, role expectations, and relationship patterns. These act as natural barriers to innovative efforts on the part of persons who wish to incorporate their newly acquired learning into the school programme. The expectation of colleagues is usually that the individual continues to behave the same way that he or she did prior to the experience, even if the changed behaviour has positive merit.

Occasionally, individual teachers do have an impact, but organizational studies have clearly demonstrated that this is an exception (Ness, 1977; Terry, 1977). The few cases in which individual change brings about institutional change occur, usually, where the person who alters his or her perspective is one of the powerful persons in the institution, such as the principal or head teacher. Fortunately, North America does have a tradition of continual professional development of administrators. There is strong evidence that school and district administrators rely on research and development information through informal channels, courses, workshops, and professional meetings (House, 1974; Havelock, 1969; Carlson, 1965).

Research and Development

In the last section, we described what we feel are the pervasive historical orientations toward institutional improvement in North America and Western Europe. It is important to note that strong tendencies for other modes are evident in both areas and these described approaches shoulds not be seen as clear-cut differences. A multitude of variations can be found, and our attempt has been merely to describe dominant tendencies. In both Europe and North America, new trends, especially in the last quarter century, have come to influence the thrusts which we described in the previous section.

Educators increasingly have come to advocate that educational reform should be based on empirically-grounded, technically-sound, and even 'scientific' findings. In conjunction with this trend, almost every nation state in these areas has established so-called Research and Development (R&D) centres. Although there is a good deal of interchange and some collaboration between the R&D centres, their individual purposes and methods remain highly coloured by peculiar cultural and historical orientations toward educational improvement.

In America, the prototype model developed by the major early formulators was a 'quasi-linear' design having the following components:

Figure 2

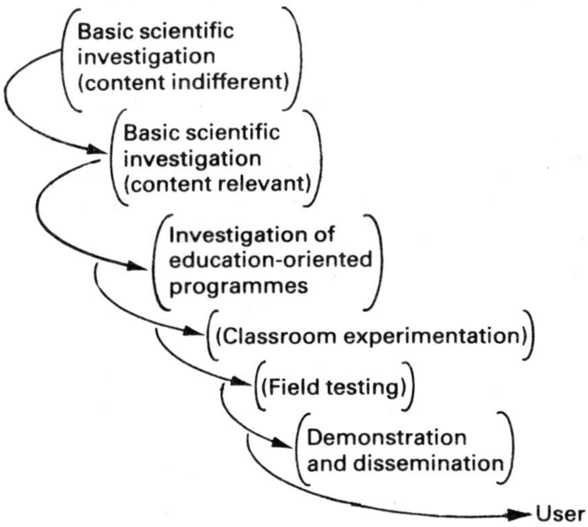

The model is linear in nature in that innovations are assumed to follow a sequence of basic and applied research phases. These are followed by a development phase which includes field-testing and evaluation. Finally, a demonstration and dissemination phase is attempted, which is intended to result in the adoption of the innovation in a wide variety of contexts (Clark, 1962).

We note that research was generally assumed to be the starting place of innovation. Much of this research was to take place in institutions of higher learning, while a large array of research and development centres as well as regional laboratories were established by the US Office of Education to help bridge the gap between basic research findings and actual practice. The research and development centres were intended to provide the applied research and development link between basic research and practice, while the regional laboratories were intended to adapt general findings to local needs.

The user of the research was seen as the educational practitioner in primary and secondary schools. It was taken for granted that he or she would 'assume a relatively passive role, and in most cases a resistant role, in the processes of implementation and dissemination' (Clark, 1962, p. 106). Once again, the problem of R&D centred on educating or reorienting the practitioner to new educational developments.

Although we refer to R&D as an entity in itself, from its inception, it actually has been seen as the first stage of a more elaborate model which includes the dissemination and implementation of educational research findings and development products. It should be described more accurately, therefore, as a Research, Development, and Dissemination (RD&D) model.

The early American conceptualizers of educational RD&D efforts drew on longer diffusion traditions in setting up their scheme. Agriculture (dissemination of new weed sprays, hybrid seed, fertilizers), medicine (dissemination of new drugs, vaccines, family-planning methods), and marketing (dissemination of new copper products, clothing fashions, appliances) served as these models. The agricultural extension specialist who would translate research findings and new products to the county agent, who would then expose the farmer to the product (usually by taking him on a visit to a farm already using it), provided the major stratagem for overcoming resistance to change on the part of the practitioner.

It is important to remember what the conceptualizers had in mind as to what was to be developed and disseminated. David L. Clark and

Egon G. Guba use the term 'invention', which refers to: (1) an idea or practice which departs from those generally prevailing among an aggregate of people who may be regarded as targets of change-directed effort; or (2) a change in technology (a material object with definitions of its use). (Clark and Guba, 1967, p. 115)

The 'inventions' mentioned above are seen to be largely technological in nature. Inevitably, a problem facing the RD&D enterprise becomes a technical issue and is dealt with by inventing some product or technical practice to resolve the problem. A good illustration of this prevailing attitude is seen in *A Diffusion Casebook* published by the Far West Laboratory. In this casebook, a selected number of project case studies are examined to demonstrate how R&D projects succeed. Only one project under discussion was not product-oriented and the authors explain apologetically that it 'stretches to the limit our definition of an educational product', as if that orientation represented an inherent weakness in the project itself (Turnbull, 1974, p. 21).

It is understandable why this model would originate in America, in view of such a strong tradition that enlightened individuals are assumed to want to take advantage of better products and better approaches. According to Havelock, the model assumes the existence of 'a more or less *passive but rational consumer* who *will* accept and adopt the innovation if it is offered to him in the right place at the right time and in the right form' (Havelock, 1973, p. 161).

It is accurate for Havelock to describe the potential user as a consumer since the model assumes that an innovation passes through one link to the next in a chain until it reaches the stage at which it can be marketed. House observes that 'the RD&D paradigm puts the practitioner immediately in the position of a consumer who is going to be sold a piece of goods which he has the option only to buy or reject' (1974, 223).

In spite of the fact that the RD&D model has become a multimillion dollar enterprise, it is now clear that it has several severe limitations. A major limitation is the persistent perception that the outcome of R&D is a tangible product to be disseminated (Boyd, 1979). It is understandable that this orientation should persist because it is easier to develop and disseminate a product, and the agricultural, medicine, and marketing models usually did involve products. However, serious questions must be raised as to its appropriateness in educational settings, simply because of the dynamic interrelationship of all dimensions of the educational process. In other words, even the adoption of a product has implications for other aspects of the educational process, which must be taken into account if any proposed innovation is to succeed.

The notion of the practitioner being a passive consumer presents an even more critical issue. Goodlad points out that the present model is really more an R&D than an RD&D activity. He maintains that in the present situation, an R&D product is actually diffused in such a manner that it is 'more or less adrift, requiring some other force to pull it into close juxtaposition with persons who might have some use for it' (Goodlad, 1975, p. 16). Even when this occurs, the potential consumer often exercises his or her right to reject it. House points out that the choice not to buy has often been a wise one because the 'goods are often damaging to the child or himself in ways the developers cannot comprehend' (House, 1974, pp. 223–224).

This is a clear indictment of the lack of connection which the entire scheme has with actual practice situations. At best, it fails to take into consideration the contextual constraints which prevent teachers from adopting otherwise valuable programmes. The lack of connection with schools themselves is a consequence of the scheme which was set up in the first place. The research and development centres are clearly engaged in activities which cause them to function more like centres of higher learning than schools. Even the regional laboratories, which were designed to address regional interests, are clearly research based, giving them a close identity with centres of higher learning. The natural tendency of middle-ground institutions is to identify with the higher status partner. The end result has been that the early stages of RD&D in North America rarely have been linked in any fundamental way with the users. In recent years the major R&D focus in America has been to rectify this shortcoming and funds have been heavily invested in mechanisms designed so that R&D might have a greater impact on educational practice (Gideonse, 1981). To this point the RD&D effort has had little impact on the public schools though, possibly, this might be less true if the RD&D system functioned as part of an 'integrated social system' (House, 1974, p. 224). That is not now the case in North America, nor in any Western country, although certain highly centralized European countries, such as Sweden or Eastern Germany, have integrated their systems to the point that incentive structures and structural relationships between institutions facilitate innovation more than is the case in most other places. Even in the less-centralized countries of Europe, a slightly different perception of the role of RD&D from that in America is found.

Many European countries have developed beyond the scholarly tradition of academic freedom, which aims at the pursuit of knowledge for its own sake, and have evolved a model described more nearly as Planning, Research, Development, and Dissemination (PRD&D) (Dalin, 1978, p. 73). Since innovation strategies have been predominantly political-administrative by nature in Europe, the new strategies have integrated the entire RD&D process with national policy making processes. That is, in Europe RD&D has been inspired and controlled by the dominant political ideologies that existed in various countries during the 1950s and 1960s. This has been particularly the case in Scandinavia, the Netherlands, and the United Kingdom, though admittedly there has been great variance even in these areas. Heavy government funding to centres occurred in order to satisfy politically inspired goals. Consequently national planning usually has served as the major impulse for designating projects which were to be undertaken.

Case studies of European R&D centres show that their work was connected generally with political and administrative efforts during the decades after World War II. For example, the Department of Research and Development of the National Swedish Board of Education relied on legislation and regulations to determine which innovations were to be implemented (Dalin, 1973, p. 111). The National Council of Innovation in Education in Norway was established originally for the express purpose of carrying out national policy regarding the coordination between several types of lower and upper secondary school (Dalin, 1973, pp. 85–7). Even the Schools Council in England has been described as having a 'non-violent' power-coercive strategy because various interest groups such as Local Education Authorities and teacher groups have arrived at common agreement before a project could begin (Dalin, 1973, p. 110).

The Northern European model has been somewhat helpful with regard to contributing to the success of the structural changes which we mentioned earlier, but generally we are forced to conclude that the PRD&D model has not been much better than the American RD&D model, mainly because in both cases, the user has been treated as a recipient of programmes. This is not to suggest that some practitioners have not been involved at every stage of the processes. For example, Bolam points out that teacher collaboration usually exists in most phases of European RD&D with the exception of 'pure' research which is not so likely to take place at special centres anyway. In Europe, teachers and teacher-groups are especially active in the planning phase of innovation (Bolam, 1974, p. 31). It must be stressed, however, that although teacher input is important in ensuring the appropriateness of projects, it may be insignificant in the problem of gaining acceptance by the wide spectrum of teachers in the field.

The European PRD&D model has reflected a major virtue over North American programmes. In North America, all too often project success has been determined by conventional academic standards such as proper field testing, publication of results, and development according to standard academic procedures. In Europe, because RD&D efforts have been linked with planning efforts, their success or failure has been much more closely linked with the degree to which they have contributed to political planning criteria rather than to academic criteria. This, in itself, is not necessarily a good thing, and the Europeans soon found the PRD&D model had definite limitations.

It was quickly found, for example, that more often than not, the diffusion process did not lead to real reform, and when desired reform did occur, such a considerable time-lag between the research and development phases and the implementation phase existed that the reform measure was so out of date that it resulted in an over-all negative effect (Ramstroem, 1975, p. 1).

Various courses of action were taken to correct the situation. For example, researchers in the Netherlands discarded the notion that implementation would be the last phase of the innovation process and have built into their projects a client-centred learning and attitude process which has been geared to help teachers design new behavioural patterns required by the anticipated innovation (Woerden and Knip, 1974). A recent OECD survey of R&D centres in Europe arrived at the following conclusion:

> All countries are witnessing the development of a major trend, either as a result of deliberate policy or as the outcome of spontaneous social pressure, whereby R&D and its dissemination are seen as part of an on-going innovative process in which the clientele of R&D is called upon to participate. Thus, the importance of developing effective mechanisms for feed-back, especially from the local level, is significantly increasing. (Woerden and Knip, 1974, p. 8).

Even in centralized countries such as Sweden, radical attempts to localize innovation to the school itself have been undertaken. In Holland, also, the national centres are now giving priority to requests for assistance from individual schools, rather than to the undertaking of nationally-conceived projects (Rapport, 1975). In Great Britain, certain projects have even been undertaken to organize a series of teachers' research and development groups 'to carry out small-scale and simple pieces of research' (Taylor, 1973).

We do not wish to imply that Europeans have rejected the conventional R&D model out of hand. We do suggest, however, that even though many innovations are internally inspired, they are often based on unique or isolated needs and do not have transfer value. Some type of R&D model is deemed important as a complement to internal needs so that questions of a general nature might also be incorporated into research activities. (Gran and Marklund, 1975, p. 7).

Awareness of the shortcomings of R&D centres in the United States has come very late. This is so because they have been so loosely connected with the realities of the schools and because there is no national planning tradition. Recent studies of federally funded programs such as the RAND reports (see especially Vol. VII, Berman and McLaughlin, 1977), and change investigations (Dalin, 1973 and 1978; House, 1974; Goodlad, 1975; Pincus, 1973) have demonstrated many of these shortcomings and have begun to lead to a new awareness that innovation is most genuinely possible when linked in some way with internal institutional renewal efforts.

This awareness has recently led to a new national strategy of change involving interaction of a number of educational administrative levels. The Federal goverment (mainly the U.S. Department of Education) allocates funds to the fifty state departments of education to provide grants to local school districts, including schools and classroom teachers, who wish to undertake some innovative project. The most successful innovations are then picked up and disseminated by the state and Federal governments to other school districts which wish to adopt the innovations (McDonnell and McLaughlin, 1980).

We have seen that the recent R&D activities in the United States and Western Europe have distinct and unique orientations, but that they are tending toward very similar conclusions about how they might overcome their disappointing records (Nisbet and Broadfoot, 1980). The implementation strategies that have been applied in the past have been found to affect strongly their outcomes and continuation. RD&D is being complemented therefore by orientations which do not have as their starting point knowledge obtained from research and the academic interests of educational specialists but originate from experienced and expressed needs of the practitioners themselves.

In recent years a number of strategies have been put forth which claim to induce change at the local level. These include such approaches as Performance Auditing (Herbert, 1979), which is an audit, conducted by social scientists, of what is and what should be in the performance of school management. Still another approach has been put forward by Zaltman, Duncan and Holbeck (1973), who provide a model process by which change is adopted in an organization. This model, in turn, has been elaborated to provide guidelines for the management of any change or innovation in an organization. These are isolated examples of change, and the most active school of thought that has emerged which provides theory, research and practical thrusts for institution-wide efforts is Organization Development. In the following chapter we shall discuss Organization Development as a general change strategy.

CHAPTER TWO

Survey-guided Organization Development

Organization Development (OD) is usually thought of as a general strategy for organization improvement. It is more than a social technology, however, because the field has evolved out of a set of concepts and theories which are continually undergoing refinement. Even so, OD is a new and growing field of activity and, therefore, it has not yet been standardized in terms of how it is carried out, how it adjusts itself to different types of institutional settings, and what its outcomes will be.

OD has been in existence in schools since the early stages of the movement, which began in earnest in the early 1960's. Much of the theory has been developed as a consequence of studies in school settings. A number of excellent statements exist, which explain the nature of OD in schools (Schmuck and Miles, 1971; Schmuck and Runkel, 1977; Derr, 1976; and Fullan, Miles, and Taylor, 1980). In spite of great variation in this education literature, some common understandings prevail.

First, OD is an activity which relies on concepts and research findings from the behavioural sciences, primarily from social psychology.

Second, the purpose of OD is to improve the health and functioning of school organizations. In contrast to more conventional strategies for innovation, especially found in America, OD is holistic or systemic in that it concentrates on the organization more than on the isolated individual or practice. However, the system is not here interpreted to be the broad political and administrative superstructure, but the school organization, or the sub-organization in the case of schools of education which form a part of universities. Certainly, environmental systems are a vital aspect of any organization, and must be considered in any renewal effort, but they are not the focal point of OD.

Third, OD is a self-correcting, self-renewing process, undertaken by the members of an organization, although external support usually exists in the form of consultants or self-assessment instruments. The consultant rarely imposes solutions but assists the members of an organization in identifying for themselves what the strengths and weaknesses of the organization are and what changes shall occur in the organization. However, it is the members of the group itself who are ultimately responsible for the way the organization is to be transformed.

Fourth, OD involves a deliberate set of steps including self-assessment, diagnosis, problem solving, planning and action phases. These are conceptually quasi-linear in nature, but aspects of every phase might be involved at any one point in the process.

Fifth, OD is a continuous or long-term process rather than a one-shot exercise or a brief episode in the life of the school.

Sixth, OD is usually evaluated in terms of its ability to enhance an organization's effectiveness and health as an organization rather than specific output criteria such as student achievement.

A multitude of definitions of OD is available. Boss (1978, p. 496) claims that one of the most widely accepted definitions is by Beckhard:

> Organization Development is an effort (1) planned, (2) organizationwide, and (3) managed from the top to increase organization effectiveness and health through (4) planned interventions in the organizations processes, using behavioral science knowledge (Beckhard, 1969, p. 9).

One of the most comprehensive definitions of OD in schools comes from Fullan, Miles and Taylor. It attempts to incorporate the elements of definitions gleaned from an extensive review of the literature of OD, and it reads as follows:

> Organization development in school districts is a coherent, systematically-planned, sustained effort at system self-study and improvement, focussing explicitly on change in formal and informal procedures, norms or structures, using behavioral science concepts. The goals of OD include *both* the quality of life of

> individuals as well as improving organizational functioning and performance. (Fullan, Miles and Taylor, 1978 Vol. 5:9).

Their comments on this OD definition might serve as a guide for our use of the term as well:

> The requirement of *coherence and systematic planning* may be too normative, but does serve to distinguish OD from haphazard efforts casually labelled "OD", as increasingly seems to be the case in our experience. The emphasis on *explicitness* indicates that OD deals directly with organizational phenomena and their alternation, rather than inducing changes indirectly through some other vehicle. The inclusion of both *formal and informal* organizational issues makes for more thoroughness, and excludes simply "official" rearrangements. The emphasis on *quality of life of individuals* and on *organizational performance* highlight the dual goal of OD and potential problems in pursuing these goals in a balanced value-congruent way. The permissive inclusion of *educational content* acknowledges that such work is a primary task of school districts, but indicates that curriculum focussed work is not necessarily OD in the absence of the preceding qualifiers. The label "sustained" is perhaps best left unspecified, though the 18 month figure is probably useful as a guide, given the year-by-year planning often characteristic of school districts (Fullan, Miles and Taylor, 1978, p. 9).

Organization development, as any other change strategy, has experienced intensive evaluation and criticism. In industry, in particular, it has been criticized for its identification with *management*. Walton and Warwick, for example, raise fundamental issues regarding the use of OD by management related to power, freedom and professional responsibility. 'Is it fair,' they ask, 'that those who already possess power and control wealth have much more access in our society to the "social technology" of OD than do others?' (Walton and Warwick, 1973, p. 684).

Still a second criticism of OD is its apparent consensus ideology. The school usually is considered to be healthy when differences are eliminated and everyone is in agreement as to goals, structure, relationships, and strategies of the organization. Especially as OD has become internationalized, we have begun to recognize its peculiar

American bias. Europeans have long given credence to conflict in organizations (Faucheux, 1982). In recent years, Americans have also begun to recognize alternative views of organizations (Clark, 1981), and now the idea of loosely-coupled systems (Weick, 1976), organized anarchies (Cohen, March and Olsen, 1976), natural selection (Gouldner, 1959), and even Marxian perspectives (Heydebrand, 1977) are gaining some visibility.

If we combine a consensus orientation identification with management, OD clearly will be met with concern and scepticism by teachers. Positive social change, meaning the redistribution of resources and life opportunities, will not be well served by a consensus management-oriented OD activity.

We do not view OD as a change strategy to serve management alone, but rather it is a strategy that allows *everyone* in an organization to have an equal part in development. Moreover, we do not see OD necessarily as a consensus-making strategy; on the contrary, OD activities may provoke conflicts, dilemmas, and disagreements (Milstein). Furthermore, social injustice, class conflicts, and unequal distributions of wealth and human rights are central issues to any organization, and, to us, are fundamental to any question of development and/or education. We see such issues as essential components of educational development prior to any discussion of educational productivity.

We are persuaded by Friedlander, who argues that the values inherent in OD are actually contradictory or at least in conflict with each other. He claims the following to be the case with regard to OD value orientations:

> Rationalism pushes contemporary OD towards becoming more scientific, more theoretical and conceptual, more logical and mathematical; toward abstract models, toward building theories; toward understanding the determinants of our organizational, social and personal worlds. Pragmatism pushes OD in the direction of becoming more useful – how does OD increase effectiveness, performance, productivity . . . . Existentialism within OD pushes the organization to become more humanistic, more aware, more emerging, more person growth oriented (Friedlander, 1976, p. 18).

The combination of these three ideal types results in divergent perspectives and tensions.

> The rationalist's entry into the organization is with "pre-built" concepts and models, and his interest in taking away knowledge to build better models makes him seem abstract as well as irrelevant, and unconcerned about the organization, its problems and people . . . The pragmatist's entry into the organization – with designs, exercises, planned interventions, training programs, and evaluation instruments – frequently seems like an irrelevant intrusion . . . . The rationalist fears that the pragmatist will become the victim of "whatever works", a technique, a fad, a method that has always been used – with little knowledge of how these fit into a larger organizational scheme. And the existentialist is sorely suspicious that "whatever works" may turn out to be a mechanistic *manipulation* of the person . . . . In contrast, the existentialist is seen by the pragmatist and rationalist as slow, irrelevant to the organization, overly loose, unproductive, and sometimes simply mystique or therapy. (Friedlander, 1976, pp. 19–20).

Few OD programs have a 'balance' between the three orientations Friedlander describes. In practice we believe that much OD has tended to become organizational *training* rather than organizational *development* (human relations training related to existentialism), or, on the other hand, productivity-oriented developments usually through techniques like MBO (pragmatism).

With this brief introduction to OD work, we would like to provide a more complete picture of how OD might function by describing three examples which have actually been used in schools.

In-service Education OD Programme

In 1975 a consultant team from the University of Michigan entered into a contract with a small neighbouring school district to engage in an in-service programme based on OD techniques. (Naumann-Etienne, 1976). There were roughly 2000 students and 100 faculty* in the district's three schools – elementary, middle, and high school. The core of the programme was a two day visit to each school by university consultants followed by occasional later visits. A five-step sequence of activities was designed by the consultant team. This consisted of (1) *Relationship Building*: An entire day was spent in each school to explain the purpose of the project and establish a working committee

*'Faculty' is here used in the North American sense of 'staff'.

structure, (2) *Diagnosis of System Needs*: A consultant worked a second day in each school talking with teachers about 'problems in the school or in the district, the quality of interpersonal relationships, and any special interests teachers might have . . .' Answers to a prepared set of questions were pooled and a 24-item survey instrument was prepared. (3) *Survey of Teacher Concerns*: The questionnaire was administered to all faculty members, followed by a fantasy exercise about 'how the system might look a year from now'. (4) *Survey of Programme Priorities*: A second questionnaire with 60 items was formulated from teacher and related-agency input and teachers were asked to indicate which were priority items for them. (5) *Feedback results*: Data from the two questionnaires were summarized and interpreted in a written report which was presented the next autumn to the superintendent.

The prioritized results were then given to the administrative council, and all results were finally presented to representatives of the three schools. This was followed by dissemination of results to the teachers in a whole group. The teachers then broke up into school units to work on their particular data sets. Ultimately they came together to present to each other their analyses and plans for implementing priority items.

A second type of OD programme relies on human relations more than on survey techniques. It is described below.

Consortium of Schools

A five-county region in New York joined together in 1970 to help 'specific schools determine for themselves the nature and kinds of organizational and program changes that were appropriate and critically needed'. This was to be accomplished 'through training in plan ning, interpersonal skills and small group leadership skills' (Feitler and Lippitt, 1972, p. 34). The following steps were followed in the programme. First, the central office administrators and principals were invited to explanatory meetings. Those principals who opted to join the project were invited to bring a team of from five to ten volunteer teachers to a two-day introductory workshop in April where twelve teams eventually decided to participate.

Formal training began in August when each school sent a team consisting of the principal and a sample of teachers to a five-day workshop. The first day-and-a-half were devoted to team building. Training focused on interpersonal and group-leader member-skills. The second and third days were devoted to training in 'problem solving skills and concepts related to organizational change including organizational climates and behaviors' (Feitler and Lippit, 1975, p. 35). The fourth day was devoted to the development of strategies for inducing change in each team's school. Alternative strategies were entertained at the beginning of the process, and after the activity was completed, the teams tested their plans with other teams. The final day was devoted to the development of a working consortium including an assessment of the resources available in each school and the formation of the consortium organizational structure.

The individual schools then undertook their own development programmes. After three months, some schools had obtained special privileges from the central office and had devoted faculty orientation-time to large and small group work, problem identification, and analysis of communication problems in the faculty. Some had widened the base of authority in their schools and had adopted techniques such as brainstorming, decision-making by consensus, and setting agendas prior to meetings. One school had accomplished almost nothing.

During the year the consortium council grew into a strong renewing force and by the end of the first year, and during the second year, schools with common interests had joined together to share planning efforts and costs of outside specialists. The consortium also began to act as a vehicle for dissemination of new ideas and multi-district development. A second variation of human-relations programmes is outlined below.

Organizational Training

A 70-hour in-service training programme was conducted at a junior high school (grades seven through nine) in Oregon in 1967/68. It was intended to improve communication among faculty members in order to bring about wider participation at faculty meetings, develop new forms of faculty-initiated organization in the school, develop more productive working relationships among formal role levels, and improve classroom instruction (Schmuck and Runkel, 1970, p. 3).

Training began with a six-day training laboratory late in August, 1967, and was attended by 54 people including all but two of the teachers, all administrators, the head cook, the janitor, and the head secretary. 'The first two days were spent in group exercises designed to increase awareness of interpersonal and organizational processes.' The group engaged in exercises consisting of puzzles and group games including non-verbal activities which required collaboration and effective communication (Schmuck and Runkel, 1970, p. 5). The last four days were devoted to a problem-solving sequence. During the first morning, three significant problems of the school were identified. These included insufficient role-clarity, especially among administrators, failure to draw on staff resources, and low staff involvement in committee, area, and faculty meetings. Three groups were formed which followed a five-step problem-solving procedure with these issued. The steps were: (1) identification of the problem, (2) diagnosis of force-field analysis, (3) brainstorming for action to reduce restraining forces, (4) designing of a concrete plan of action, (5) trying out the plan behaviourally through a simulation activity involving the entire staff. The six-day training culminated with a general discussion of individual staff resources.

The consultants worked in the school during the fall as participant-observers and interviewed staff members to identify unresolved problems. These were found to be 'communicative misunderstandings, role-overload, and the lack of capabilities for group problem-solving' (Schmuck and Runkel, 1970, p. 6).

The second intervention was a one-and-a-half-day session in December to deal with the unresolved problems. Training included more communication exercises, problem-solving techniques, decision-making procedures and skill development in group observations and feedback.

In February, the third training intervention, which also lasted one-and-a-half days, took place. It focused on the evaluation of staff-progress with regard to the problems that had been identified during the six-day workshop. This was mainly conducted through large and small group discussions of the problem areas.

During the spring, the faculty continued meeting in small groups without the presence of the consultants who withdrew and allowed the process to proceed on its own.

OD Variations

From the examples just cited, it is clear that great variation exists with regard to OD work. In the first place, programmes extend from single schools, to districts, to consortia of districts. A second variation factor has to do with hierarchical considerations in working groups. Certain programmes regard everyone from the top administrator to the janitor and secretary as a single working unit. Smaller groups are determined along interest- and specific-activity dimensions rather than hierarchical placement. Other programmes give great respect to those in authority. We noticed, for example, that the Michigan programme fed information back to the principals who 'recommended' that it be given to the faculties. However, before this was accomplished the superintendent shared the report with his advisory council 'in an effort to seek their opinion about the potentially threatening impact of its contents' (Naumann-Etienne, 1976, p. 10).

The third realm of consideration to account for variations has to do with the consultants' view of those organizational variables which appear to be crucial. It is clear that most programmes, as shown in the three above, concentrate on what we have described as human-relations variables, such as communications skills and flow, institutional climate, interpersonal skills, intact sub-group processes, or leadership styles. This is to be expected because OD has largely grown out of the group-process tradition which is based on social psychology theory.

However, structural value, and environment questions also receive some attention. We noted that the Organizational Training Programme, which was conducted in Oregon, gave attention to structural factors such as role-overload and role-clarity, and we would have found that the In-Service Education OD Programme in Michigan identified several priority issues that had to do with value definition such as 'how to stimulate independent learning', 'humanizing education', and 'values clarification' (Naumann-Etienne, undated, p. 9).

A school in the New York Consortium had confronted an environmental constraint by gaining permission from the central office to waive participation in the city-wide orientation programme so that it could focus on its own development.

A fourth variation factor has to do with the manner in which problems are identified in the OD process. With some approaches the participants engage in exercises and simulations which often cue them toward specific realms of problems in their own institution. In other cases, a large number of potential problems are identified through interviews and other means and then sorted out as to priority. Another approach is for consultants to take a school right into problem areas which they have found to be typical. Very often, the process of general problem-identification begins with more concrete and specific problems which exist in an organization. These may have to do with specifics such as pupil discipline, a new regulation that has been imposed on the school, or grading practices. However, consultants usually use these problems to begin tracing back 'to the contextual fabric of the organization, and the dynamics of its interlocking programs' in order to help the staff of the institution begin to deal with more fundamental issues (Buchanan, 1971, p. 11). The conceptual structure which the consultant brings to the situation will define in many ways the nature of the issues which are identified. If, for example, a consultant has a high human-relations orientation, most problems will tend to take on a human relations focus.

In a recent comprehensive review of the OD literature, Friedlander and Brown (1974) found two major types of orientation. The most pervasive is the *human processual* approach which focuses on humans and their interactions including communication, survey feedback, problem-solving, and decision-making. The other approach is called *techno-structural* because it focuses on the technology (task methods) and the formal structure of institutions. This latter approach has also more recently been further subdivided to *technology-focused* and *structural-focused* approaches (Hellriegel and Slocum, 1980).

The more mature programmes are now tending to become more comprehensive and include elements of both general orientations (Ross and Deal, 1977). The reader will find the conceptual framework of the Institutional Development Programme outlined later in this book to be comprehensive in nature.

A fifth major realm to account for OD variations has to do mainly with intervention strategies. In fact, OD has not even arrived at a common set of strategies which could exhaust the sphere of possible interventions. Schmuck and Miles (1971), provide one of the longer lists of 'intervention' strategies:

1. Training or education: including lectures, exercises, simulations, and T-groups;
2. Process consultation: concentration on observing ongoing processes and providing feedback;
3. Confrontation: bringing together units or groups which have a history of poor communication;
4. Data feedback: involving systematic collection of information which is reported back to the organization;
5. Plan-making: dealing with planning and goal setting;

6. OD task force establishment: setting up *ad hoc* groups to provide structure for solving problems and carrying out plans;
7. Techno-structure activity: focusing on structural factors, work flow, and means of accomplishing tasks (Schmuck and Miles, 1971, p. 9).

We are inclined to define some of these more as phases in the OD process rather than as strategies. The first four items just mentioned are more akin to our perception of a strategy, and these are also very similar to those distinguished by Schmuck and Runkel (1977, pp. 21–3). McGill (1977) summarizes a list of seven discrete alternative approaches, which he calls (1) Survey Feedback, (2) Process Consultation, (3) Team Building, (4) Laboratory Training, (5) Packed Approacher, (6) Sociotechnical Systems, and (7) Transactional Analysis (1977). Bowers (1973) describes five strategies, all of which could also be incorporated into the Schmuck and Miles scheme. The Institute for the Development of Educational Activities (I/D/E/A) stresses quite a different strategy from those mentioned above. This it calls a 'peer-group' strategy. It involves the establishment of school networks which serve as a source of institutional support and outside assistance (Bentzen, 1974, pp. 201–3). The New York Consortium, described earlier, also relied heavily on network-building. We found that network-building among participating schools is perceived as an important follow-up phase of the IMTEC Institutional Development Programme.

In the more complex schemes, several intervention strategies are relied upon, and usually in such a way that they actually 'flow into each other and are not mutually exclusive' (Schmuck and Miles, 1971, p. 9). In fact some intervention strategies, such as data feedback, process consultation, problem-solving, or laboratory training might well take place in some form at every step in the OD process.

In the major international review by Fullan, Miles, and Taylor described above, *outcomes* of OD projects as reported by evaluation studies were analyzed. First it was found that most OD projects reported had limited evaluation components. In many projects, evaluation simply was not included. In the authors' discussion they make a distinction between the following types of outcomes:

1. *Impact* on the district as a system (including impact on students);
2. Positive *attitudes* toward OD, especially those which bear on

whether it should be used in schools more generally;
3. *Institutionalization* or durability of the OD effort.

(Fullan, Miles and Taylor, 1980, Vol. III, p. 21)

In terms of *impact* (expected and unexpected) they conclude:

> To summarize: We have found that the most frequently-reported positive effects of OD programs in schools, both expected and unexpected, and in and out of the classroom, lie in both task and socio-emotional categories. Student effects are more likely to be 'soft' rather than expressed in test scores. Socio-emotional aspects of the OD program itself are seen as the prime explanation. Negative effects are mentioned by nearly three quarters of the sample; these seem equally divided among negative attitudes, and direct negative consequences, such as increased levels of threat or work load. But these effects are largely irrelevant to the degree of positive impact noted. Finally, OD is credited with causing a good deal of change in these districts, in terms of instructional innovation.
>
> (Ibid, Vol. III, p. 25)

In terms of *attitudes*, school districts seemed relatively satisfied, and the authors continue:

> When we asked our respondents whether they thought that OD should be used more widely in this country's schools, 64% said they definitely thought so, 26% said "Yes, probably", 7% were not sure, and 3% passed. No one expressed doubt or definite disapproval.
>
> (Ibid, Vol. III, p. 26)

On *institutionalization*, the authors investigated whether OD was still going on in the district. As of the spring of 1977, 88 per cent said that it was, in fact, still going on. The primary explanations for continuance were:

> good results obtained (23%), the commitment and hard work of participants (15%), and the support of top management (14%)
>
> (Ibid, Vol. III, p. 26)

The authors relate the outcome-measures in the following way:

Figure 3 Outcome Measures of Organization Development

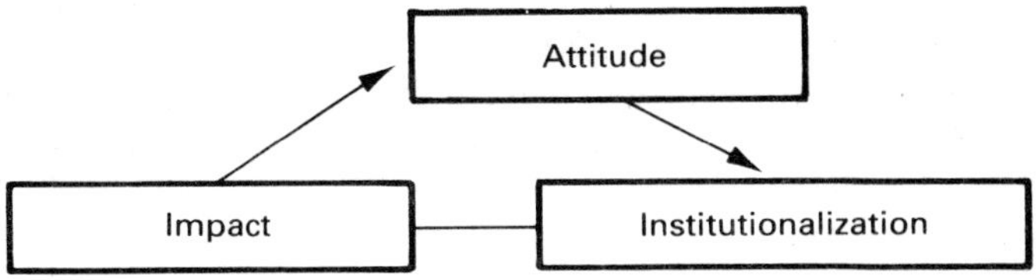

In other words, the hypothesis is that there exists a positive relationship between impact and attitudes, and between attitudes and institutionalization, and a neutral relationship between impact and institutionalization. In their general conclusion they state the following:

> A general summary of what we have found: The impact of OD programs in school districts is larger when more energy, resources and time are put in, when the approach is task-oriented, takes a structural, system-oriented tack, and is well supported with technical assistance. Attitudes supporting the spread of OD to other districts are stronger when the scale is large, when it is seen as useful for *educational* improvement, when structural and task emphases have been important, and when internal OD coordinators are in place. Finally, it seems likely that the institutionalization of OD programs in schools is likely for programs of moderate rather than large scale, those with an educationally-focussed emphasis – and a structural, system-changing approach. Technical support through manuals and materials helps. Excessive reliance on outside consultants seems to reduce ownership, hence institutionalization. (Ibid, Vol. III, p. 41).

Most OD programmes stress one intervention strategy more than another. This identification becomes especially crucial when the relative advantages and disadvantages of various programmes are assessed. At the time we began the development of the programme outlined in this book, the evidence was persuasive that survey feedback was an especially fruitful approach. We remain committed to its value although more recent evidence, which we shall discuss in

Chapter Six, has tempered our original judgement that it was far superior to other approaches.

Our intention in the section that follows shall be to discuss (1) the historical role of survey feedback in OD, (2) its various dimensions, and (3) why we were persuaded that it offers advantages that are not so readily attained in programmes which focus on other strategies.

SURVEY FEEDBACK

From OD's beginnings, specialists have relied on extensive use of data feedback in working with clients. Nadler (1977) points out that most data based approaches to organization development usually include some form of the following:

a. *there is some kind of systematic data collection*. Data may be collected through questionnaires, interviews, observations of behaviour, or examination of organizational records. Frequently this data collection is an integral part of the change agent's diagnosis of the system, but such a collection may have other uses also;
b. the change agent will *work with the data* to aggregate it, analyze, or interpret it. This may be done by the change agent alone, or in collaboration with members of the organization;
c. the change agent will in some way *give back the data*, perhaps with interpretations to organization members in a form in which they can make use of it. This process of feeding back data could be an immediate one, as when a process consultant gives feedback to a group on its behaviour, or it could be a long term process involving the computer processing of questionnaire data and the preparation of written reports.

Within the general framework just outlined, two distinct schools of thought can be identified (Bowers and Franklin, 1977). The first grew out of applied practice or clinical work and focuses upon normal, on-going activities rather than upon carefully devised and controlled situations. The single institution is usually the object of attention with less concern for comparative perspective, theory development, or general patterns. It concentrates mainly on interpersonal processes and considers the 'here-and-now' situation to be the major interest.

Historically, survey feedback within the context of human relations efforts has consisted usually of small specifically tailored questionnaires and interview schedules which have been constructed by the consultant during some phase of his or her work with an institution. These instruments have been intended to help the members of the institution collaboratively to identify potential problem areas, or to serve as a basis for helping the institution relate more adequately to already identified problems. The major rule of thumb for these devices has been that

> 'the client system is usually involved in data collection activities; members are often asked explicitly to develop questions for the survey, and to plan with the outside staff for data collection' (Miles *et al*, 1966, p. 458).

They have ranged from fairly elaborate instruments, as we noted in the Michigan project earlier, to almost spontaneous 'How are we doing?' exercises of a small number of items that are devised on the spot during the process of a workshop or meeting.

Parallel with the human-relations-oriented activities in OD is a different school of thought oriented towards the utilization of scientific knowledge and research to understand how complex organizations function. This originated

> 'not from the search by practitioners for more effective helping tools, but from the concern of organizational management researchers for better ways of moving new scientific findings from the producers (researchers) to the consumers (organizational managers)' (Bowers and Franklin, 1972, p. 43).

The major centre for survey feedback research endeavours has been at the Institute for Social Research at the University of Michigan, and it originated through the work of Floyd Mann and his colleagues. Their work was almost exclusively in industrial settings, and by the time OD entered schools, good survey feedback was already recognized as an important aspect of many OD programmes.

Survey research endeavours concentrate, on the one hand, on the development of more rigorous survey techniques in organizational settings, and then on devising a mechanism for making the research results more usable by management.

Hausser, Pecorella and Wissler describe three basic characteristics of an efficient survey. First, the survey should possess an optimal number of items or questions which measure the variables under consideration. This requires important research to determine the value of items in measuring the organizational situation, in assessing the responses, and in feeding data back to clients. Second, indices must be developed. An index is formed by grouping items together to form clusters, profiles or other facets of common domain of functioning. It is necessary to engage in extensive study to develop these clusters in some meaningful and reasonable way. Third, norms are eventually established on the basis of summarized data from several similar organizations (Hausser, Pecorella and Wissler, 1977, pp. 18–9).

Research skills are necessary not only with regard to survey construction and administration, but to the process of feedback which itself requires systematic testing and study in order to assess the potential value of various options that present themselves. Feedback-design must be developed in such a way as to facilitate organization-wide interpretation of the data, including discrepancy data between various types of individuals and groups in an organization. Bowers and Franklin remind us:

> Survey-feedback is not a sheet of tabulated data, nor is it the simple return of such data to some representation of the respondents. Instead, it is a relatively complex guidance *method* which draws upon the device of the questionnaire to upgrade and make more complete, rational, and adequate a process inherent in social organizations (Bowers and Franklin, 1974, p. 221).

The typical surveys of human-relations consultants have been problem- and institution-specific and, therefore, have had direct relevance to the renewal process underway at the institution. Because clients usually have participated in their construction, they have been easily accepted as having validity and reliability.

However, data-collection activities of human-relations consultants have run many risks. Such activities have rarely allowed for rigorous instrument development because of the immediacy of the problems and issues being considered and because the consultants usually have been more similar to the clinician than to the researcher. Their direct involvement with the institutions has required that they deal with normal on-going activities rather than with carefully devised and controlled situations. The single institution has been the usual object of their focus. This has limited their ability to obtain comparative perspective and general patterns.

Clinical working-skills and procedures are laudable, but in the case of survey-feedback, serious questions must be raised with regard to aspects of consultant work which requires the skills and orientation of the researcher. This is especially the case with survey-instrument development, administration, and interpretation. The construction of good instruments requires careful and painful procedures if they are to be credible. Clinically-oriented, human-relations experts rarely possess either the desire or the background to do this. Further, the situation they find themselves in rarely allows for pilot testing and standard statistical checks, because such efforts would contaminate the survey results.

We maintain that survey-research activity has been vital and necessary. Research is an important activity, but its ultimate value in terms of organization development is that it goes 'beyond the accumulation and expansion of knowledge into the use of that knowledge to solve social problems' (Neff, 1965, p. 24). A healthy combination of pure- and applied-research endeavours must exist if any data-feedback programme is to be effective.

The major potential advantage of survey data is that it provides input into the general picture of the institution which is derived from all institutional members. Human-relations-oriented consultants often obtain a distorted picture of the institution because they obtain their information from a biased sample. Those people in visible or powerful positions in the organization tend to dominate information sessions and it is mainly through surveys that a balanced, unbiased perspective is obtained.

Still another potential advantage of survey-feedback is that perceptions and feelings of school members are reduced to facts and figures, allowing for comparisons of differences and similarities between individuals and groups. Usually little claim is made that the data derived from the survey is infallible, but it serves to force institution members to deal with data rather than to accept only information that has supported prior preferences and feelings. However, we must look at actual empirical research to identify its actual advantages over other forms of OD.

Empirical Findings

Growing numbers of empirical studies have begun to clarify how to use data-based methods on institutional renewal as well as to catalogue the advantages and pitfalls involved. We shall undertake here to review some of the more significant survey-feedback* projects. Miles *et al* (1966) developed a project on organizational development in school systems in the 1960s. They report a particular programme in a small school system using a feedback system. School personnel themselves developed questions on particular aspects of the schools which were of concern and a plan for data collection, including some interview strategies. After the data was analysed, it was fed back to the personnel through 'work families' or groups which report to a common superior. These work-families were similar to the 'organizational families', which had been studied by Floyd Mann, who had arranged them to account for the task and authority realities of organizations (Mann, 1957). Feedback sessions in the Miles study took place at meetings which were also rated. It was shown that the group decisions were rated satisfactorily and that the amount of interaction in these meetings alone was equivalent 'to that occurring in six months' work on the job' (Miles, 1966, p. 464).

The schools also engaged in planning for action through 'task force' committees. There were definite changes in communication and interpersonal relations in the schools during the process, but the researchers were forced to conclude

> 'that the survey program represented a momentary perturbation in the functioning of a stable system, and that no fundamental shifts in information flow, power handling or normative structure had occurred' (Ibid, p. 467).

In 1971, Miles, who had worked on the project just mentioned, joined with McElvaney to report the work of a three-year survey-feedback project in a school district. Once again they were unable to observe quantitative statistical differences in the system as a consequence of the intervention beyond 'chance fluctuation' (Miles and McElvaney, 1971, p. 113). They did present qualitative evidences in the form of consultant reports which supported their hypothesis that survey-feedback would result in changes in organizational processes.

In 1972, Dave Brown published another study of a private-boarding-school intervention-effort which emerged following a two-day 'sensitivity training workshop to improve communication among faculty', which had been viewed as successful. A 15-month pro-

*The most recent general OD research review about schools can be found in Fullan, Miles, and Taylor, Vol. II (1978).

gramme of data-collection, diagnostic-feedback and discussion-meetings was arranged. Repeated questionnaires were administered which allowed for a time-series research design. A control measure was available since not everyone participated in the sessions. Positive ratings were obtained in terms of increased participant involvement in the system, not only for staff but for students as well. (Brown, 1977, p. 710).

Perhaps the most sophisticated attempt at evaluating the impact of survey-feedback in schools was undertaken by Coughlan and Cooke (1974) reported in a later work by Cooke and Coughlan (1979). They worked with four different experimental groups and tested the relative impact of various approaches. These included a complete survey-feedback activity, a problem-solving programme, a collective decision-making process and a more limited survey-feedback or data-handback process. Evidence was strong that the comprehensive survey-feedback process had significantly more positive results on changing decision-making structures, increasing organizational health, changing individual perceptions of decision-making processes and enhancing attitudes toward the work environment than did the simple survey-feedback process alone.

The number of survey-feedback studies in education which we can draw on is admittedly limited. Certain studies which have taken place in public-sector settings outside schools (Adams and Sherwood, 1979; and Davis, 1979) showed promise of the use of survey-feedback processes in identifying problem-areas and facilitating productive change. We would like to describe in some detail one study from industry, conducted by Bowers, because it gives some insight into the relative effectiveness of different intervention-strategies and supports the study by Coughlan and Cooke that survey-feedback without a more comprehensive approach to institutional renewal is of little value. Bowers collected longitudinal data from 14,000 respondents in 23 organizations in the state of Michigan. Four 'experimental' treatments were used which he named Survey-Feedback, Interpersonal-Process Consultation, Task-Process Consultation, and Laboratory Training, and he named two 'control' treatments: Data-Handback and No Treatment. The survey-feedback mechanism included extensive data collection and feedback as well as

> 'discussion of tabulated perceptions through a cataloguing of their implications, to commitment to solutions to problems identified and defined by discussion'. (Bowers, 1973, p. 24)

The Interpersonal-Process Consultation concentrated on helping the clients develop the capacity for 'forming and implementing their own change programme' but the focus was on human rather than on technical processes. Task-Process Consultation focused on the task objectives and dealt only with interpersonal processes that related to work-task situations. Laboratory training was a more conventional programme where a 'family group' withdraws to a secluded environment for from three to 14 days to engage in a series of experiential exercises.

Throughout the programme, Bowers repeatedly administered the Survey of Organizations questionnaire (Taylor and Bowers, 1972). The instrument focuses on 16 critical indices under major headings called Organizational Climate (6 indices), Managerial Leadership (4 indices), Peer Leadership (4 indices), Group Process (1 index) and satisfaction (1 index). In figure 4 we find pre- and post-treatment scores for all indices. It will be noted that a so-called 'capstone group' and a 'whole system score' is found. The whole-system scores refer to all respondents in an organization which was undergoing treatment. The capstone group scores are of those scores from the members in an organization who actually underwent the treatment. Even a superficial assessment of the table shows that the process which had a significant and substantial impact across most indices was the survey-feedback treatment. Some of the other treatments actually resulted in substantial negative change. For example, the laboratory training had a dramatic negative effect on organizational climate. Interpersonal-process consultation reflected significant positive change for the whole system on 7 of the 16 indices. Task-process consultation affected two capstone indices positively, while all significant changes of the whole system were negative. Survey-feedback of the capstone group showed positive and significant change for every index except managerial leadership and the whole system even showed significantly positive change in 11 of the 16 indices. It must be noted that mere data-handback demonstrated essentially no change for all but one index (managerial leadership).

We must caution against certain conclusions that may be drawn from the Bowers study. On the surface, survey-feedback appears to be highly advantageous over other approaches in improving organizational climate, leadership, group-processes and satisfaction. It must be pointed out that the study was conducted by one who is committed to survey-feedback, and the assessment instrument was most likely

Figure 4 Changes in Questionnaire Indices, from First to Second Survey Waves, by Variable and Change Treatment

Area-Measure	*Laboratory Training* Caps. Gps N = 116	*Laboratory Training* Whole Sys. N = 3417	*Interpersonal-Process Cons.* Caps. Gps N = 12	*Interpersonal-Process Cons.* Whole Sys. N = 3706	*Task-Process Cons.* Caps. Gps N = 38	*Task-Process Cons.* Whole Sys. N = 1047	*Survey-Feedback* Caps. Gps N = 85	*Survey-Feedback* Whole Sys. N = 3693	*Data-Handback* Caps. Gps N = 55	*Data-Handback* Whole Sys. N = 832	*No Treatment* Caps. Gps N = 51	*No Treatment* Whole Sys. N = 935
Organizational Climate												
Hum. Resources Prim.	−.42*	−.18*	+.10	−.02	−.04	−.17*	+.35*	+.15*	+.13	−.05	−.59*	−.61*
Communication Flow	−.19*	−.12*	+.10	+.12*	+.16	−.06	+.22*	+.15*	+.23*	−.12*	−.02	−.06
Motiv'l Conditions	−.13*	−.12*	−.22	+.02	+.03	−.04	+.24*	+.01	+.04	−.16*	−.09	−.09
Dec-Making Prac's	−.15*	−.13*	−.17	+.03	+.21*	−.14*	+.30*	+.17*	+.04	.00	−.32*	−.52*
Tech. Readiness	−.01	+.13*	−.25	−.07	+.02	−.11*	+.30*	+.05	+.02	−.08	NA†	NA†
Lower-Level Infl.	+.03	−.10*	−.23	+.05	+.11	+.03	+.26*	+.01	−.33*	−.18*	−.47*	−.23*
Managerial Leadership												
Support	−.10	−.11*	+.31	+.11*	−.11	−.19*	−.07	+.18*	+.18	+.01	−.16	−.32*
Inter. Facilitation	−.04	+.02	−.05	+.20*	+.07	.00	−.11	+.36*	+.27*	+.15*	+.21*	.00
Goal Emphasis	+.11	−.06	−.13	+.08	+.09	−.06	.00	+.17*	+.21*	+.06	−.11	−.11*
Work Facilitation	+.12	−.08	+.29	+.21*	−.09	−.05	+.17	+.27*	+.33*	+.15*	−.09	−.
Peer Leadership												
Support	−.20*	−.11*	−.24	+.02	+.17	−.13*	+.29*	+.06	−.01	+.03	−.19*	−.23*
Inter. Facilitation	+.09	−.04	−.07	+.12*	+.68	−.05	+.30*	+.20*	+.06	+.20*	−.04	−.11*
Goal Emphasis	−.05	.00	+.08	+.12*	+.22	−.02	+.21*	+.14*	+.15	+.12*	+.04	−.12*
Work Facilitation	+.07	+.03	−.17	+.15*	+.04	−.03	+.36*	+.19*	+.09	+.20*	−.02	−.03
Group Process	+.20*	+.27*	−.05	+.01	−.03	−.06	+.26*	+.21*	−.14	−.21*	NA†	NA†
Satisfaction	−.09	−.15*	−.04	+.04	+.32*	−.03	+.17*	+.09	+.07	−.02	−.07	−.23*

* Change large enough to be statistically significant at or beyond .05 level of confidence.
† Measures omitted in edition of questionnaire used in these sites.

constructed to be sensitive to variables which are influenced by that process.

Furthermore, as yet, scholars do not have a common conceptual framework for a general description and assessment of organizational effectiveness (Yuchtman and Seashore, 1967). Bowers chose to concentrate on various social-psychological measures as the criteria for effectiveness, whereas the logical measure of effectiveness for certain of the other approaches in his study might have been something quite different. For example, because task-process consultation focused on completing work tasks, or the ultimate products more efficiently, psychological measures would, therefore, be of less concern than the degree to which these were accomplished. In the school context, efficiency might be determined by choosing to concentrate on the health of the institution, the achievement level of the pupils or some other criteria, separately or in combination. This choice is crucial and must be spelled out before judgements as to efficiency can be made.

A final caution has to do with unintentional biasing of the experimental treatments. To explain we shall address ourselves to the different outcomes between laboratory training and survey-feedback. We recall that laboratory training had negative effects on evaluation measures, whereas, survey-feedback had highly positive effects. Reviews of T-group effectiveness in other studies show mixed results (Campbell and Dunnette, 1968); however, one generalization seems appropriate. Argyris points out that the organizational effectiveness of T-groups is contingent on follow-up 'changes in the organization, its policies, managerial controls, and even technology' (Argyris, 1970, p. 337). In other words, laboratory training must be conducted as a part of a broader institutional renewal programme if it is to be successful.

The Bowers study might be described as having unintentionally 'stacked the deck' against laboratory training in that it was conducted without being a part of a larger undertaking. Survey-feedback was defined as having these accompanying components, which proved to be vital in comparison with simple data-handback, which is obviously of little value in terms of institutional renewal efforts. It is likely that both laboratory training and survey-feedback can be effective, at least in terms of organizational factors, if they include extensive accompanying diagnostic, planning, and action programmes.

Our general conclusion from this brief review of the literature is that any single intervention device such as survey-feedback and laboratory training must be a part of a larger enterprise, and certainly an integrated change strategy focusing on school self-renewal must build close relationships to the environment – in particular, to the school district office.

All of the elements of an integrated professional and institutional renewal programme are already available, but they are rarely coordinated in some meaningful way. In-service activities, counselling, human relations, survey-feedback and organizational programmes have existed as isolated fragments of renewal, and have only on occasion been integrated to form a total, institutional development programme. The IMTEC Institutional Development Programme (IDP) represents a deliberate attempt to include these elements in a coordinated effort. Our task in the next two chapters shall be to describe its evolution and present state of development.

CHAPTER THREE

Institutional Development Programme: Assumptions

The IMTEC Institutional Development Programme (IDP) is an intervention strategy which is designed to help educational institutions undergo a comprehensive self-assessment and self-development process. It aims to help institutions diagnose their present situation, plan, implement, evaluate, and readjust themselves in order to meet internal and external requirements with increasing effectiveness. The focus of the IDP is on the educational institution as an organization. Our task in this chapter shall be to outline our basic concept of an organization and then to discuss the assumptions on which the IDP is based.

Because the focus of an institutional development programme necessarily must concentrate on the institution, educators interested in renewal must have some general conceptual framework for understanding its nature as an organization. A major task of the social scientist is to conceptualize the organization in such a way that it 'reduces and quantifies the system variables to manageable proportions' (Ruedi and Lawrence, 1970, p. 55). At the same time, it should not be so narrowly conceived that it eliminates crucial organizational factors. IMTEC has evolved a concept of the school as an organization which is systemic in nature, and includes the major elements of (1) the environment, (2) institutional values, (3) human relations, (4) organizational structure, and (5) development strategies (Dalin, 1978, pp. 48–52).

THE ENVIRONMENT

We define the environment as the persons and organizations external to any focal organization with which it must transact in order to survive (Derr and Orton, 1975, p. 237). Educational organizations carry on a responsive exchange with their external environments. Their boundaries are not only permeable, but they are also in many respects blurred in that they are formal parts of larger systems. They are formally linked with educational bureaucracies and public or private government and funding bodies. They are linked in a quasi-formal sense with parent groups, professional organizations and other schools which act as feeders and/or recipients for the pupils. They are also informally interdependent with a host of environmental economic, cultural, social, technological, and political forces.

INSTITUTIONAL VALUES

The value dimensions refer to variables pertaining to the fundamental beliefs (*Weltanschauungen*) of the members of the institution, especially as they are exemplified through philosophies, rituals, ceremonies, and symbols. This dimension refers also to the formally-stated purposes, goals or mission of the institution as well as the unstated norms and realities which influence the daily work of the school. Finally, it refers to the instructional goals of the institution both collectively and individually.

ORGANIZATIONAL STRUCTURE

The structure of an organization consists of its shape or configuration as it might appear in an organizational chart. It includes decision-making structure, task structure, and communications structure. It also consists of the institution-wide and classroom roles which exist, the type and flow of the task and time structures, the physical context and material resources available, and the regulations which are reflected in policies, rules, and formal guidelines.

HUMAN RELATIONS

The human-relations dimension has to do mainly with the interpersonal aspects of an organization as manifested in the communications system, the internal influence and power structure, the behavioural norms as reflected especially in meetings, as well as the general climate of the organization, including the degree of satisfaction, trust, and support which exists. We also define certain measures of individual effectiveness and feelings of personal commitment toward the institution as reflections of the quality of relations which exist.

DEVELOPMENT STRATEGIES

The strategy dimension pertains to the mechanisms and methods for managing and changing the school, the decision-making strategies, the reward and incentive structure, leadership styles and procedures for keeping values, relations, and structures in balance.

Assumptions of the IDP

Given this skeletal outline of organizational dimensions, we would like to give it life and substance by outlining several assumptions which relate to it and which have implications for the IDP. We understand assumptions to be those things which are taken for granted or taken to be true by IMTEC and the authors of this book. The major IMTEC IDP assumptions are as follows:

Assumption one: In spite of a much greater segmentation of organizational variables in educational institutions than exists in most industrial or commercial institutions, there remains a dynamic interdependence between most organizational variables.
Assumption two: Because the organizational picture possessed by each member of an institution is both unique and limited, all members have an equal right to provide input data about the real nature of the organization and what it ought to become.
Assumption three: An institutional renewal programme must be a collaborative effort involving as wide a scope of individuals in the institution as possible.
Assumption four: Conflicts are normal organizational events and constructively can be used to facilitate the institutional development process.
Assumption five: Institutional renewal usually requires some form of external support.
Assumption six: Even though the consultation process of the IDP is unavoidably not value free, the consultants attempt to remain goal-free in terms of anticipated outcomes in the institutional renewal process.

Assumption seven: Sufficient degrees of freedom in environmental frames exist to tolerate school renewal efforts.
Assumption eight: The effectiveness of the organization can be assessed only within a contextual framework.
Assumption nine: Schools can learn.

We shall now discuss each of these assumptions in some detail.

Assumption one: In spite of a much greater segmentation of organizational variables in educational institutions than exists in most industrial or commercial institutions, there remains a dynamic interdependence between most organizational variables.

Institutional change must account for both the interdependence and the segmentation of institutional variables. Organizational development conventionally has concentrated on the Gestalt notion that parts of an organism maintain their characteristics because of their relationships to the whole. This would imply that change in one part would necessarily require adjustment of other parts. We assume that organizational variables are interdependent. This can be plotted graphically in terms of our organizational construct in Figure 5. The degree of interdependence is, of course, a relative matter. Goodwin Watson suggests that

> 'school systems are probably less cohesive and integrated than most business organizations. A teacher has more autonomy than a sales-clerk or middle manager. Considerable change can take place within one classroom and have relatively minor effects on what other teachers are doing' (Goodwin Watson, 1969, p. 20).

In fact, the very segmentation of educational organizations has important implications for renewal efforts. Some scholars suggest that school systems are organized in many ways like the conventional modern factory in that personnel and tasks are differentiated into ever smaller and simpler cells which are then integrated again to produce large educational mills to process the raw material of society (Toffler, 1970, p. 400). Schools are subdivided into age grades, classes, disciplines, specialized departments and streams. The personnel are divided into specific roles which are highly individuated. Problems of teachers and others 'are usually dealt with on a one-to-one basis', and, once dealt with, the interaction terminates until the next problem arises. A problem that one teacher encounters in the course of his or

Figure 5 Organizational Interdependencies of a School

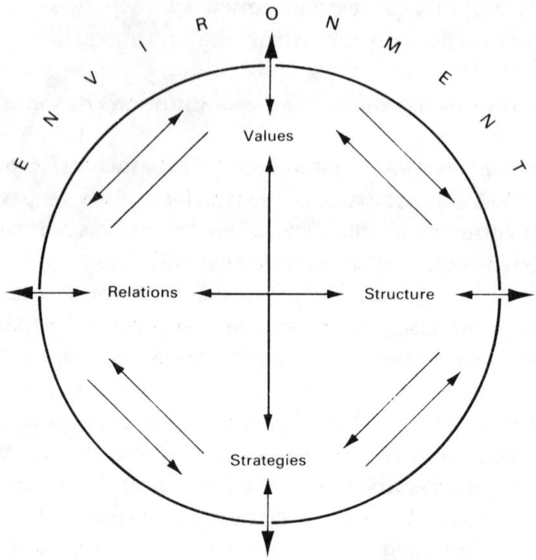

her work bears no necessary relationship to problems encountered by any other teachers.

According to Lortie (1975) school officials have avoided building systems with great interdependence so that space and teachers can be matched with a fluctuating clientele. Structural looseness permits the addition and subtraction of classrooms, streams, and schools as they are demanded. Teachers are also interchangeable so that they can be shifted according to administrative requirements.

The system described by Lortie does not exist exclusively because of administrative requirements; schooling has been so characterized for centuries. Teachers, especially, view their role in terms of what happens in their own classroom. They are accustomed to working in self-contained environments and often even accept isolation, alienation, and loneliness as a given feature of their profession. Fragmentation in educational systems is exacerbated by the existence of 'low vertical integration' between district administrators, principals or rectors, and teachers (Lortie, 1975).

Weick has described schools as loosely-coupled systems. Such a notion has disturbing connotations for behavioural scientists because organizational theory is based almost exclusively on the idea that organizations are rationalized and a great interdependence exists, but in educational studies there is a substantial unexplained remainder which cannot be incorporated into conventional organizational theory. This may be disturbing to some because 'just as scientists have special problems comprehending loosely coupled worlds, so too must the inhabitants of these worlds' (Weick, 1976, p. 18).

In spite of these qualifications, the schools remain dynamic organizations, many parts of which are strongly interwoven with each other. This should not be interpreted to mean that they are all directly connected at any one moment. Realignments of goal statements, for example, might not influence classroom practices immediately, but eventually they will affect each other in significant ways.

The interdependence of variables is especially crucial as changes are made in the organization, because change in any one variable will most likely result in some adjustments in the others. For example, if an institution were to alter its communications patterns, great adjustments would take place in other relations-variables such as norms in meetings, influence and power realignments, interpersonal effective ness and the general climate. The change would likely influence certain structural variables having to do with the shape of the organizational chart or certain roles. Elements of the time structure, such as who works when, might be affected and certain regulations might need to be altered. Strategy variables would also require alteration because a different communications framework would probably affect the leadership styles of certain individuals. It might also suggest different priorities in the incentive- and reward-systems of the institution. The value dimension would certainly need clarification. The communications structure reflects the basic attitudes of people in an organization and may require a reassessment of the fit between certain individual goals and the organizational goals.

The interrelatedness of an organization would reasonably imply that decisions to improve one variable might have side effects that are destructive in some other part of the organization. Teachers might decide, for example, that the administration should handle many more of the day-to-day decisions of the school only to discover that the school begins to function in a hierarchical fashion never intended. Of course, this assumption would also imply that decisions to improve one variable would likely have a large number of positive side effects. A decision to alter pupil-teacher relationships would likely lead to comparable adjustments in the teacher-principal as well as school-parent relationships.

Earlier in this book we mentioned that the failure of contemporary reforms was due largely to the fact that they were piecemeal and fragmented. In fact, major reform strategies, which pretend to work on general school improvement, often reflect but one dimension. R&D efforts which we discussed in Chapter One are overwhelmingly oriented to little more than the development of educational products and have largely disregarded the institutional settings where these products are to be utilized. We have also described the political reform measures in Europe which are dominated by structural concerns and fail to attend to values and human relations which flow into these structures. Teachers often think of reform only in the context of their self-contained classroom or their subject matter and fail even to think of reform as an issue involving broader institutional variables.

The IDP assumes that successful institutional renewal requires institution-wide adjustments even though the focus of renewal might well be on specific problem areas.

Assumption two: Because the organizational picture possessed by each member of an institution is both unique and limited, all members have an equal right to provide input data about the real nature of the organization and what it ought to become.

We maintain that each individual member of an institution has a narrow, limited, and restricted perspective of that institution. There may be a total organizational reality but each individual view of that reality is of necessity not only partial, but different. To illustrate, permit an analogy involving views of a valley surrounded by mountains and passes. People who approach the valley through the various mountain passes, or by air, or via the broader highway access routes, see the valley in quite different ways. The view varies depending on the position of the viewer.

Consider now the formal school. Many feel it is 'what it is' and some even think that it looks the same to everyone. But various constituents of the school deal with that institution with quite different methods, terminologies, concepts, and results. To expect the same description of that reality to emerge from the various perspectives is like expecting photographs taken from various approaches to the school to be identi-

Figure 6

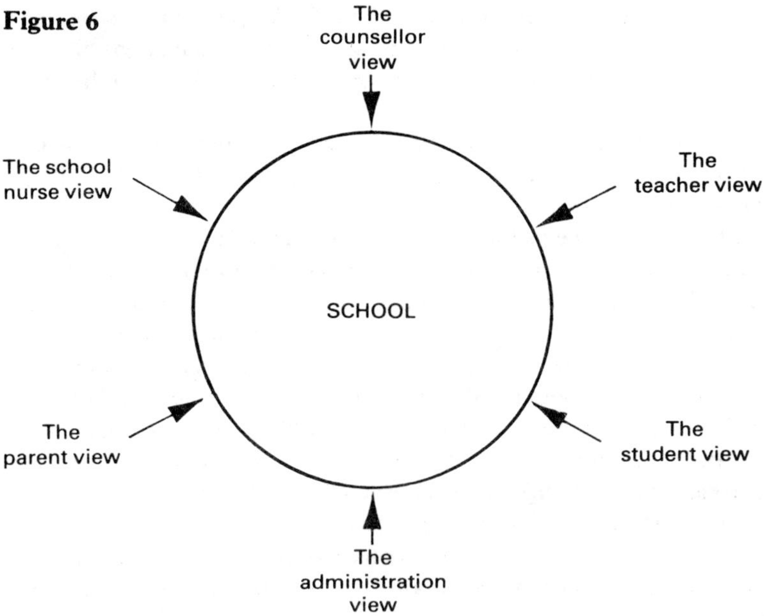

cal. Various views of the school, from different roles, are graphically illustrated in Figure 6.

The school reality takes on further complexity when we consider the variety of interests, values, and purposes of individuals and groups. The school might be something to be subverted by one student, conquered by another, and revered by still another. It might be a place of work to one teacher and an institution for the expression of another's highest ideals. It might be seen as a place to dominate by one principal and a place to exercise democratic leadership by another.

The difference among views of reality not only pertains to the school as a whole, but to different elements of the school and its programme. This is readily illustrated when different people look at, for example, student discipline. Students would have a much different perspective from teachers, while administrators might see it differently from either of these two groups.

If perspectives are unique for groups and individuals, it becomes imperative to obtain the views of as many people and groups as possible, in order to gain as complete a picture of the total school reality as possible. In this sense, reality becomes a composite of the collective perspectives represented in the institution. Under these conditions, if a few individuals control the types of data to be included in diagnosing an institution, it is a sign of poor institutional health.

Assumption three: An institutional renewal programme must be a collaborative effort involving as wide a scope of individuals in the institution as possible.

This is a logical extension of assumption two. Just as the institution is perceived differently by various members, plans for change can never be determined by selected segments of the school simply because the plans will be distorted by the peculiar perspective of the innovators. Further, a sense of ownership is only possible if the changes coincide with the desires and aims of all members. The Rand studies on innovation firmly concluded that projects which were adopted and continued by schools required that sense of ownership (Berman and McLaughlin, 1977 Vol. VII, p. 72).

An important review of the literature by Swierczek, where he examined evidence concerning collaborative intervention in sixty-seven change studies, demonstrated that collaboration is crucial in the process. Collaboration requires that an 'equal relationship between the practitioner and the organization, shared information, and participation' exists in successful change (Swierczek, 1980, p. 441).

Usually ownership is perceived to mean that teachers and administrators must feel the innovation belongs to them. We feel that important insights and directions can also come from representatives of parents and students as well as from non-professional staff members.

It must be recognized that even though participation should come from as many groups and individuals as possible, the change-goals and the strategies adopted to achieve these goals are political processes. They involve, necessarily, an interplay of forces which rarely will benefit all individuals in an institution equally.

Consequently, whatever decisions are made will rarely be done using a consensus mode. In most decision-making situations in the school, participants don't even share the same perspective and it is illusory to assume that they would, therefore, be able to agree on a single set of goals, structures and strategies (Manning, 1977). The process of goal-setting and problem-solving is ever shifting and vaguely understood under the best of circumstances.

We are, however, beginning to gain some ideas as to conditions that contribute to willingness on the part of teachers to develop a change-orientation. Jean Bartunek (1980) suggests that simple participation training can enhance the desire of teachers to participate in the school decision-making process.

Certain studies have indicated that teachers who reflect a high sense of efficiency are willing to engage in change processes (Edmonds, 1979; Cohen, 1980; Berman and McLaughlin, 1977). Judith Little's (1980) study of six urban schools is also instructive. She found that a school-improvement orientation is found where teachers 'engage in frequent, continuous and increasingly concrete and precise talk about teaching practice.'

Assumption four: Conflicts are normal organizational events and can be used constructively to facilitate the institutional development process.

Conventional OD stresses harmony and consensus relationships between groups in an organization and plays down conflict and disharmony as something to be overcome. The major historical reason for such a bias is that OD theory and practice has been dominated by Americans. The major social theory in America during the post-Second World War era has been structural-functionalism, which focuses on the maintenance of equilibrium in a social system. According to structural-functionalists, change is seen to occur through internal malfunction or external intervention, which disturbs the equilibrium of the system. Structural-functionalists believe that the system inevitably attempts to adjust itself when this occurs in order to return to a new stability. In other words, the ideal system should maintain stable equilibrium. We might recall that this frame of reference is consistent with the historical view of change in America which we described in Chapter One. It is consensus-oriented in that it assumes all members support the basic direction in which society is moving as well as the form of schooling which supports that movement. It is technical- or means-oriented in that fundamental issues are rarely questioned, while there is much discussion of how to improve the present system.

In contrast to the structural-functional point of view, which until recently has dominated in America, different competing schools of thought which view conflict not as a form of ill health, but as a constant condition, are found in Europe. Groups are viewed as being in a continual struggle to maintain or gain status and control (Dahrendorf, 1959, p. 162). The highest form of democracy can be described as the open and productive interplay of these conflicting groups.

We do not intend to champion conflict as better than equilibrium, but simply to recognize its existence. We define any process of change to include consensus-building as well as conflict-clarification and recognition of unclear preferences on the part of participants.

Assumption five: Institutional renewal usually requires some form of external support.

Even though the major responsibility for renewal must come from those individuals who are actually living and working in the institution, outside assistance in some form is usually necessary. The Rand study on innovation determined that projects which continued after termination of Federal support did not depend on continual financial support as much as on more qualitative attitudinal factors. The central administrative office was committed to the project and school boards considered it worthy of 'special protection' from typical bureaucratic regulations and scrutiny (Berman and McLaughlin, 1977, XII).

The question of outside support was investigated also by Fullan, Miles and Taylor (1978). Although large projects with high external support did have a positive impact on attitudes, these factors were negatively correlated with institutionalization. They found that high levels of *internal* commitment (district- and building-level coordinators and internal consultants) were positively correlated with *attitudes, impact*, and *institutionalization*. They conclude .... 'so the issue may be as much "ownership" as scale of the effort ...' (Vol III, p. 40).

Special external inputs can be found in organization development endeavours. We have identified three major types of external assistance in OD. First, some educators have encouraged the development of 'locally-based full-time experts on innovation' (Havelock and Havelock, 1973, p. 161). Such an expert would be similar to the farm extension agent who has existed for decades in the United States. This agent exists in the school system itself as a direct representative of the superintendent (Carlson, 1965, p. 4–5). So far this recommendation has not gained firm footing although it has been employed in the Louisville, Kentucky and the York, Ontario, Canada systems (Schmuck and Runkel, 1977, p. 526).

European countries, most of which have an inspector tradition, may be better off than the United States with regard to the employment of experts on innovation. Inspectors have gradually taken over the role of advisers and even consultants to school districts. Bolam and his colleagues at the University of Bristol (Bolam, Smith, and Cantor, 1978) surveyed fourteen English Local Education Authorities and found that 62 per cent of the advisers spent some time advising with a single school or college on the introduction of major organizational changes.

The most common source of external support has come in the form of organizational development consultants, who work directly with schools and school systems. Centres for the training of OD consultants and for conducting educational renewal programmes have become very prominent. Currently, the most active university centre is the Centre for the Advanced Study of Educational Administration at the University of Oregon. The University of Michigan has also been influential in the United States as have a few other institutions in Canada and Western Europe.

A third source of outside support is the forming of a consortium of schools to act as a support system for each other. We described a consortium project in Chapter Two (Feitler and Lippitt, 1972), but would mention here what we suspect to be the most publicized and researched education network in existence, called the League of Cooperating Schools. It was initiated in 1965 under the sponsorship of the Kettering Foundation and organized by I/D/E/A. It consists of 18 schools in 18 different school districts in Southern California. No fewer than seven books have been published on the League (Goodlad, 1975; Shiman *et al.*, 1974; Culvier and Homan, 1973; Bentzen, 1974; Williams *et al.*, 1974; and Tye and Novotny, 1975) and untold smaller publications have resulted. The League is essentially a direct attempt to act as an external stimulus for participating schools to help them define their situation more fully and to support them in undertaking a continuing renewal process.

We find some merit in all three support strategies although each has its own difficulties. The idea of locally-based experts on innovation is commendable, although we have grave reservations as to the appropriateness of the farm extension agent concept. Such an approach is reasonable in farming because the agent's task is to clarify such things as crop yield pay-off for a small additional investment or the erosion factor of certain irrigation practices. In general, schooling variables are much too complex, and 'change agents' are unable to concentrate on a few, selected variables as a mechanism of educational improvement.

There is yet another important issue with regard to locally-based consultants having to do with marginality. This concept has been defined, clarified, debated, and criticized in the literature for over 40 years (Wright and Wright, 1972). It centres mainly on the concept of a person, in this case the consultant, 'who stands on the boundary between two or more groups that have differing value systems, goals, and behavior patterns' (Browne, Cotton and Golembieuski, 1977), and who plays the role of broker, knowledge-linker, or interfacer of various elements in the organization (Lawrence and Lorsch, 1969; Mather, 1973; Sashkin, Morris and Horst, 1973). There are those who argue that consultants should come from within the system because the 'insider possesses intimate knowledge of the client system (and the power to legitimize) that the external change-agent lacks.' On the other hand the 'outsider consultant can provide the perspective, detachment, and energy so necessary to effect a true alteration of existing patterns' (Bennis, 1966, pp. 114, 155). Recent evidence has substantiated the intuitive wisdom that these differences are real in terms of consultant perceptions of their own marginality (Browne, Cotton, Golembiewski, 1977). However, there is such mixed evidence in terms of outcomes that distinctions between the two types of consultants may not be very crucial (Dunn and Swierczek, 1977, p. 143–4).

Fullan, Miles, and Taylor find that the use of internal, as well as external, consultants is important for outcomes. It is more a question of *scale*, how the two types of consultants are used, and how they interlink. The training of insiders may be the crucial factor. The authors conclude '. . . it seems likely that supplying training for inside change agents, and developing more linkage to other OD professionals could in principle enhance program impact and increase institutionalization' (1978, p. 50).

The league or network concept also provides a valuable model for peer support, but these rarely function well without some systematic organizational effort. The I/D/E/A/ project, for example, ceased funding the League of Cooperating Schools after five years. The schools decided to continue on their own, but soon thereafter the League ceased to maintain its momentum and is now essentially a memory.

The IMTEC program has drawn elements of all three support notions into the IDP, which shall be described in detail in the next two chapters. We actually train school-district and local personnel to act as organizational development consultants to schools in their own communities, which reduces or eliminates the expense of consultants from the outside. However, consultants from different communities work with each other and they are in constant contact with IMTEC staff, which gives them some assistance in remaining detached and retaining perspective of the situation. We also build support networks among IDP schools, teachers' centres and teacher training institutions as a part of the entire process.

Assumption six: Even though the consultation process of the IDP is unavoidably not value-free, the consultants attempt to remain goal-free in terms of anticipated outcomes in the institutional renewal process.

It is reasonable to assume that random selection of organizational structures is inappropriate, but there is little evidence to suggest which structure is the most appropriate for a given context. Of course, each reflective educator has made certain personal decisions. The authors of this book admit to having clear biases, but they also agree that it is inappropriate to impose these on others. Such an admission does not suggest a lack of wisdom or credibility on the part of educators. The nature of contemporary society and schooling is such that claims of holding a universally valid position are untenable. In contrast to industry and business, where at least the aim of a particular enterprise is commonly accepted, the goals and standards of education are no longer commonly agreed upon. 'Too little is known about the relative importance of the various processes to educational outcomes to assign priorities' (Crecine, 1977, 84).

It is for this reason that the IDP under discussion in this book attempts to look at a comprehensive array of organizational factors and takes care not to pre-select organizational outcomes. We assume that institutional conditions do and should differ from one another, and that the people most capable of deciding their ultimate form should be the participants in the educational settings themselves.

Inevitably, such a frame of reference will create value-dilemmas for the consultant. There is substantial agreement that all OD is value-laden (Huse, 1975). We agree that the IDP is based on many value-assumptions, and the consultants who work with schools will have values which will conflict with those of many staff members, parents and students. If schools make choices which the consultant finds distasteful, he or she is usually faced with a dilemma. There is no easy way out of this situation. Argyris (1970) has attempted to redefine the

OD process so as to avoid some of the more troublesome value-dilemmas consultants normally face. He maintains that the intent of organization development should be to help an organization gain valid information about how it functions. The system itself must then decide what to do with this information.

Such a point of view challenges the conventional OD practice of deciding that measurable change is the task of OD. Essentially, all research for OD projects looks for the 'change' it will produce in the organization. Donald Bowen reminds us of the fallacy of such an approach. 'A good doctor does not find something wrong with every patient, and OD professionals will experience fewer value conflicts if they define their functions so that they are not tempted to perform organizational surgery on every client.' (Bowen, 1977, p. 555).

The role of the IDP consultant is to aid schools in understanding themselves and giving them assistance in making judicious choices about their professional lives and environments. We call this 'goal free' consultation, because the outcomes of the process are not predetermined. The primary decision-makers are the groups in the schools themselves, not the consultant, IMTEC, or the school district office. One of the options open to schools is that if a school has been conscientious in assessing itself and it finds that its current situation is satisfactory, it may choose to continue existing practices.

In order to facilitate the consultant role, it is imperative that the consultant be as candid as possible with regard to his or her own values. If done in a sensitive manner, such openness should facilitate reciprocal value statements on the part of school personnel.

We have already mentioned the three underlying value-orientations of various organization development programmes conceptualized by Friedlander (1978). These are the 'space between rationalism, pragmatism and existentialism.' In order to be as candid as possible, we have asked consultants to indicate where they felt that the IDP is placed in this 'space' and where they would like the programme to be. The consultants, at this stage, feel that the programme is very much in the middle of these triangle dimensions as indicated in Figure 7. Most of the consultants, however, feel that the programme could be less rational, more pragmatic and more authentic and growth-oriented. The differences, however, are not very large and indicate more generally that the consultants are satisfied with the balance of the programme. The development phase of the IDP is somewhat dominated by Research and Development activities, including the development of surveys, evaluation of process and outcomes, etc. For the consultant practitioner, these activities are relevant only so far as they help him or her in the actual role. We see the response of 'decreasing the importance of rationality' as a reaction to the early IMTEC R&D activities.

Figure 7 Three Organization Development Values

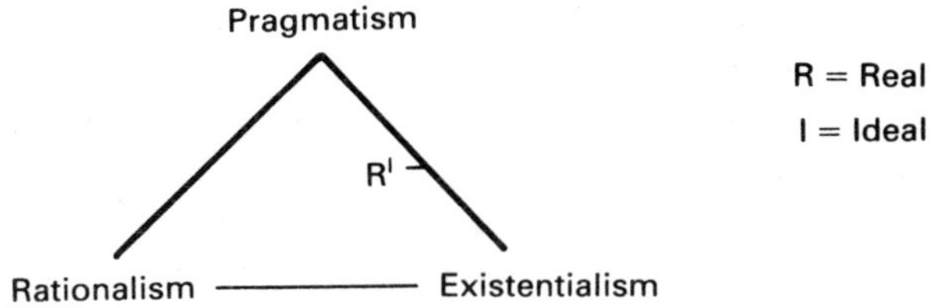

Assumption seven: There is enough freedom in environmental frames to tolerate school renewal efforts.

The press of environmental forces is sufficient to compel educational institutions to fit within rather strictly defined constraints. In fact, environmental relationships in public schools are so strong that Carlson has been led to describe them as 'domesticated organizations'. Schools are special types of service organizations because by and large, they do not exercise the right to select their clients, and because the clients are not free to accept or reject the service. This peculiar role in society places schools in a position of being 'protected and cared for' in the same manner as domesticated animals. They are not required to attend to all the ordinary demands of those organizations that must compete for clients or even for existence. In return, however, they are expected to conform to the social and legal norms imposed on them (Carlson, 1965, p. 7).

In spite of the established frameworks around educational institutions, we assume that there is a sufficient degree of freedom to allow for locally defined institutional adaptation and development, including freedom in terms of organizational, educational, personnel, and even economic choice. The degrees of freedom available differ according to the population and the culture under discussion. West Germany, example, has encouraged experimentation during the past decade. However, experiments which depart from the basic structure of the educational system require the prior recommendation of the Standing Conference of Ministers. In other words, experimentation takes place when school officials recommend that it takes place (Rust, 1973, p. 15).

The state is not the only constraining force. In Holland, the government is obliged by its constitution to establish and maintain schools under minimal state regulations. However, the pressure from the churches and the social ties of schools is sufficient to ensure that radically different schools are rarely found.

In Denmark, both government and cultural factors encourage a wide variety of educational programmes and types of institutions in the country. Their forms appear to be limited to a large degree by the imagination and resourcefulness of the educators themselves.

We would caution people against a naive tendency to make global value-judgements about the relative merits of the conditions just described. They are simple illustrations about how environmental constraints vary according to the culture under question and should not be interpreted as statements about which culture might prove best to facilitate a given innovation. In fact, it may be that IDP efforts in West Germany, which has many constraints, would prove to be very fruitful because school renewal programmes would be formally sanctioned by the state and the participating schools would be assured of adequate state support for such undertakings.

We are convinced that there is enough freedom in all western cultures for schools to undergo much needed self-renewal efforts. Many constraints are, in fact, self-imposed because educators often fail to use the legal and social freedoms granted to them as fully as they might. Professional educators have the space to improve their institutions. No one else can or should do their job for them. The IDP is but a mechanism to help educators learn more about themselves and their organizations; it is a tool which they can use in doing their job.

The IDP presents a challenge not only to schools, but also to school authorities where renewal efforts are under way. Because any creative school programme will call for redefinitions of established norms and expectations, it will be necessary for school authorities continually to re-think priorities, to adapt and further develop educational policies. We assume school systems are flexible enough to accommodate themselves to grass-roots innovation.

Assumption eight: The effectiveness of the organization can be assessed only within a contextual framework.

The range of choices available to institutions as they evolve organizational plans depends largely on the theoretical assumptions and ideological commitments which are acceptable to institutional personnel. The authors of this book hold to a point of view which closely resembles contingency theory found in industry. This theory derives from conclusions drawn from certain empirical studies. Galbraith summarizes this theory by making two propositions:

1. There is no one best way to organize;
2. Any way of organizing is not equally effective (Galbraith, 1973, p. 2).

Thus, we can find a wide range of effective organizations, but there are contextual factors which suggest that some organizations would be more suitable than others.

The first proposition represents a challenge to the technique ideology which has become so pervasive in mature modern society. No longer can we assume that one organization is better than another in an absolute sense. (Lorsch and Lawrence, 1970, p. 1). It can be judged properly only in a contextual sense. For example, Burns and Stalker observed 20 British and Scottish firms and found that those which were effective in stable markets tended to reflect a mechanistic organizational form while organic organizational forms were more effective in rapidly changing environments. In America, Chandler looked at 70 large industrial firms which ranged from a centralized to a decentralized multi-divisional structure. He found that centralized structures were highly effective if they were pursuing a growth strategy in a single industry. However, decentralized organizations seemed more suitable if the firm was engaged in product diversification (Chandler, 1968). A variety of other studies have confirmed still more contextual variations whose effectiveness was contingent on the specific nature of the industry and the task they were attempting to perform (Lawrence and Lorsch, 1967; Hage and Aiken, 1969; Duncan, 1972).

Having thus challenged the attempt to find a single best way of organizing, it does not follow that random selection of organizational form is valid. In the examples just cited, it would have been inappropriate to decide on a centralized structure if the industrial firm were committed to diversification. It would be ill-advised to adopt a mechanistic structure if the market were unstable and changing.

We have certain hints in the literature as to the appropriateness of certain educational organization structures that are more appropriate than others in given contexts. We shall illustrate this by looking at certain environmental considerations. Dalin, drawing liberally from Burns and Stalker (1961) and their studies of British industries, suggests certain general relationships arising from a matrix of simple and complex organizations that might exist in stable and dynamic environments.

Figure 8 Three forms of organization

	Simple	*Complex*
Stable		Mechanistic
Dynamic	Organic	Systemic learning

If, on the one hand, complex organizations exist in a stable milieu, they will likely tend toward a mechanistic form.

If, on the other hand, the environment is simple and dynamic, the organizations will tend to be simple and organic, or if they are complex, they will tend toward what Dalin describes as a systemic learning structure (Dalin, 1978, pp. 41–8).

These three types of organizations are described as follows:

Mechanistic organizations have hierarchical structures in which most rights and obligations are precisely defined. Tasks are specialized – only a few have control of over-all objectives, new knowledge is located at the top, and interactions are seldom horizontal but most often vertical;

In organic organizations, individual tasks are constantly redefined to keep them in harmony with the over-all objectives of the organization. There is a tendency towards collective 'ownership' of problems and innovations, a 'network structure' of control, authority and communication and advice rather than vertical instructions and decisions;

The term *systemic learning organizations* as presented here is a concept that attempts to take into account the complexities and nature of the educational task in an increasingly dynamic environment. It is a movement away from the alienation tendencies of the mechanistic tradition towards an organic organization that allows for democratic control of educational development in complex organizations.

Certain forms of contingency theory have concentrated on the relationship between particular environmental conditions to internal characteristics of organizations (Lawrence and Lorsch, 1967). Behavioural scientists have done this because they feel that the organization is compelled to fit its internal needs with these external forces, at least sufficiently to satisfy their basic requirements. Derr and Orton have adopted four environmental aspects from contingency theory which, they maintain, are crucial to the appropriate definition of educational organizations. They are: 'the degree of *change* within the environment, the degree of *uncertainty* in the environment, the *diversity* in the environment, and the extent to which there is a need for *interdependence* among the parts of the (educational) organization to perform tasks which are important to the environment' (Derr and Orton, 1975, pp. 237–40). If, for example, the environment is changing, it is likely that the school will cope with this condition most successfully by becoming decentralized and open. If there is great uncertainty about the direction of environmental forces, in all probability the successful organization will function more on the basis of contingency plans than plans which are established and inflexible. If there is a great diversity in the environment, it will be to the advantage of the organization also to be greatly differentiated and in such a way as to match up with the external counterparts (Ibid.).

The contingency relationships which we have drawn are couched in behavioural science language; the unwary might conclude that we are dealing with environments as clusters of neutral forces. We are, however, actually describing socio-political forces which are constantly at play in the educational process, and which might shift or become confused overnight.

It must also be kept in mind that the 'environment' is not of one piece. It includes decision-makers who have direct access to the direction of the school. It includes those who are entering and those who have left the institution. It includes those who provide funds for the institution. These may or may not be the same groups. One group might be changing, another diverse, and so forth.

The political nature of educational change causes us to be very hesitant about finding reliable factors in explorations of organizational change. A classical dilemma in the change process is that those who are involved in problem-identification, problem-solving and decision-making, and those who need to change their behaviour are often individuals and groups with different roles, expectations and interests. They often live and work apart from each other, *are members of different networks*, and seldom 'communicate'. (Dalin, 1978).

Figure 9 Relations in Educational Change (from Dalin, 1978)

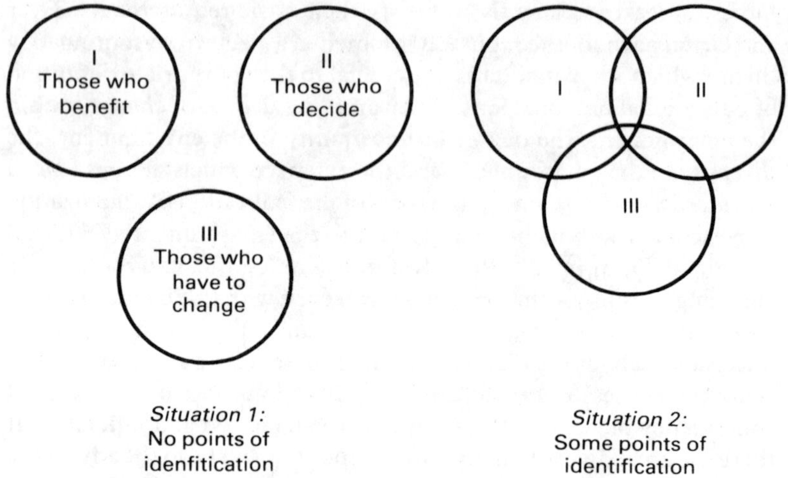

Even though some insights have been gained from industry as to the appropriateness of organizations, more advanced theories, which include open-systems theory (Katz and Kahn, 1966) and organic-adaption theory (Leavitt, 1974) intentionally avoid becoming too explicit as to the most appropriate factors or contingencies for examination. Such a position is even more appropriate with regard to educational settings than industrial. Certainly there is no single best system of education, and educational research is not yet able to make solid claims in terms of which internal states and processes of educational institutions are appropriate regarding given contingencies.

Assumption nine: Schools can learn. The most obvious assumption of the IDP is that all schools have some capacity to engage in organizational renewal. Schools, under certain conditions, can unlock or unfreeze a reservoir of potential energy which can be put in the service of organizational renewal.

This assumption, however, does not win universal acceptance. Several researchers and practitioners of organization development have pointed out the problems of schools as organizations in terms of their motivation for organization development. Derr (1976), for example, feels that owing to the lack of common indicators of performance and the nature of school environment, organization development may be inappropriate in schools. Figure 10 illustrates his point of view:

Figure 10 School Organization v. Organization Development

School Organization	*OD Concept Violated*
A. Lack of Common Indicators of Performance	A. Readiness —must feel a need for improvement —client system must sense its own problems in order to be committed to working on them.
B. Nature of School Environment —survival guaranteed —public relations orientation —crisis orientation	B. Improvement Orientation —it is worth time, effort, money, to improve —must continuously learn from experience (self-renewal) —long term effort
C. Autonomy Needs of Employees	C. Collaborative Theory and Method
D. Low Required Interdependence —don't have to work together	D. Systemic Orientation —also, collaborative values and methods in OD
—benefits of collaboration not greater than costs	—real incentives to stress opportunity costs of non-collaboration
E. Civil Service Mentality	E. External and Internal Capability, Improvement Orientation
—some goal displacement employment v educational systems	—must employ best internal OD specialists from whatever background
—job security conscious	—both external and internal OD specialists
—inbreeding	—roles and structure fluid and dynamic; choose best men or group for given job —norms of risk taking and improvement should prevail
F. Few Resources	F. Adequate Resources Necessary

(from Derr, 1976, p. 236)

This point of view, however, has been challenged by several others, who feel that the conclusions of Derr are 'extreme' and can be tempered by cautious and collaborative efforts between specialists and school personnel (Miles, 1976, pp. 249–50).

CHAPTER FOUR

Institutional Development Programme: Process

In this chapter we shall describe the steps a school goes through when it participates in the Institutional Development Programme. It should be made clear that even though the content of the steps is original in many respects, the steps themselves follow the sequence of events of other OD models.* The IDP has ten distinct steps which are as follows:

1. Initiation;
2. Contract between IMTEC and the school;
3. Data Collection: filling out the questionnaire;
4. Data Analysis;
5. Data Feedback and Dialogue: clarifying school characteristics:
   a. school's strengths: what does the school do well?
   b. school's weaknesses: what aspects of the school need to be changed in order to strengthen the school further?
6. Goal Setting:
   a. short term goals: what can the school or what must the school do immediately?
   b. long term goals: what are the more fundamental changes which the school must work toward?
7. Planning for Action: how are the goals to be accomplished?
8. School Development: the school undergoes change;
9. Networking: participating schools joining together;
10. Evaluation.

The steps are graphically outlined below. We might point out that the process often reverts to the data-collection phase at two major points. This is indicated by the dotted line in the graph.

* Kolb and Forhan (1970) may be considered typical of these models. For example, they describe seven steps: scouting, entry, diagnosis, planning, action, evaluation, and termination.

Figure 11 School Renewal Phases

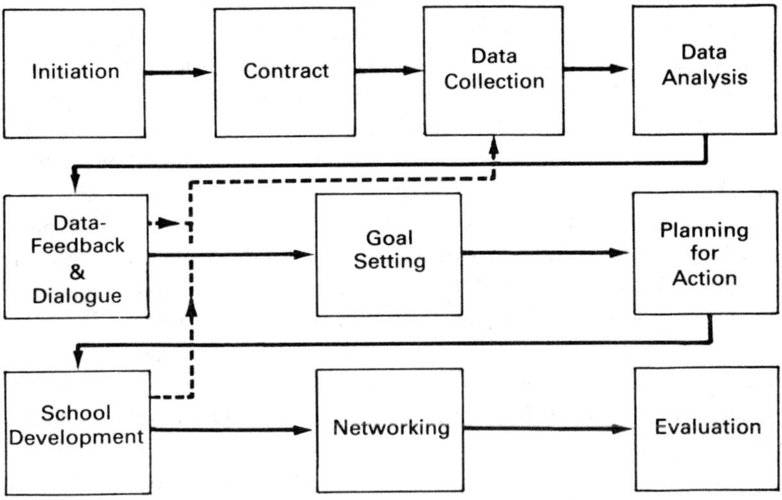

We must offer a caution that real-life events involving human beings never fall into a neat and orderly sequence. We have already described earlier in the book how aspects of most intervention sequences appear in some other sequence. Schein, for example, describes how certain aspects of the initiation phase provide important diagnostic data both to the school and the consultant (1969), while Nadler (1977) points out that data collection occurs at every stage in the programme.

In spite of the discrepancy between reality and the model, it does provide a map of the various activities that occur in the IDP. We shall therefore outline the IDP map in a general way in this chapter, and then give it a reality base by describing various case studies of the actual process in the following chapter.

1. Initiation Phase

The initiation phase involves the bringing together of IMTEC personnel with people representing educational institutions for the purpose of exploring the possibility of engaging in the IDP. IMTEC has developed many mechanisms for identifying institutions that are seeking support. These include newsletters, circulars, and articles, but the major reliance in information flow remains that of personal contact 'along the social networks of personal acquaintance' (House, 1975, p. 11).

The process is usually formally initiated with the visit of a consultant to the institution to gather preliminary data, and meetings with individuals from the school to clarify the process and distribution of information. The consultant is a member of the IMTEC network, usually an employee of the school district, who has undergone consultant training. Typically, the consultant is a representative of the local teachers' centre, school district office, or teacher education centre.

Institutions that enter into serious consideration of participation in the IDP usually recognize a need or express a desire to improve their organizational situation. Of course, healthy institutions engage in renewal efforts even though they have no severe problems. However, they usually recognize a large enough discrepancy between the state of affairs which exists, and that which they desire to have. This does not mean that renewal efforts must originate from within schools themselves. In fact, the empirical evidence for adoption of change is that externally initiated efforts are as important in terms of ultimate change as are internally initiated efforts (Dunn and Swierczek, 1977, pp. 145–6). However, we concur with Schmuck and Runkel that productive change is not likely to occur unless the members of an organization ultimately acknowledge the need for improvement and 'are reaching out for help' or 'exhibit other signs of readiness to profit from an OD effort.' (Schmuck and Runkel, 1977, p. 25)

IDP consultants are well aware of the complexities involved in this matter. Who represents 'the school' and 'the needs'? Are we talking about the staff, students or parents? Are their needs the same? What individuals constitute a school and how many are necessary to represent a need strong enough to get into an OD programme? What interests are served by bringing the IDP into the school?

Usually initial linkages with an institution are established with the administration or people in the system who exercise leadership of some kind. The initiation phase must, however, extend to all professional personnel of an institution at an early stage in the process. Otherwise, detrimental working patterns become the norm and these are difficult to redirect once the process has moved to a new stage. It is especially important that the consultant develop a rapport with the entire school such that he or she is accepted as a legitimate and valued source of support and stimulation.

Schmuck and Miles stress that 'beginnings tend to foreshadow much of what follows'; things begin to carry their own momentum (1976, p. 139). In spite of the fact that this aspect of the process has been neglected in the literature, it cannot be overemphasized. The relationships, the trust and openness of participants, and the expectations that are established are largely determined in the initiation phase.

Although each school district with which we work usually reserves the right to select the schools which will participate in the IDP, IMTEC sets down three conditions for participation: (1) the programme is not imposed on a school by central office personnel, (2) both the leadership and the staff of an institution express interest in participation and (3) the staff is not divided excessively in its interest to participate. Such conditions clearly limit the programme to schools that have *already* reached some consensus about seeking outside assistance.

After what usually becomes an extensive process of discussions, readings and conferences with selected people of an institution, the members of that institution eventually move into the contract phase (see next chapter).

2. Contract Phase

The commitment to engage in the IDP takes the form of a written contract with the school district. Informational aspects of the contract should include a very clear understanding on the part of the selected personnel as to what the IDP is designed to do and what it is not designed to do. School personnel must not go into the process with a misconception of what is to happen and what is to be accomplished. We shall see in the following chapters the importance of *clear contracts* between the school and the programme. Contracting includes financial arrangements, but more importantly, takes up agreements about time, psychological commitments, role of consultants, and procedures. Misconceptions can have destructive consequences on subsequent phases of the process (see Chapter Six). Lake and Callahan (1971, p. 144) report a particular project in which representatives of a large district had 'expected that the consultants were going to solve the various problems' which they had listed as critical and which they expected to be dealt with during an introductory meeting. These included items such as racial imbalance, poor public image and lack of materials. Even after the consultants had shifted the focus to 'problem-solving skills', the clients still assumed this was but an intervening activity which would help them understand how the consultants were going to solve the problems.

A psychological contract is just as crucial as an informational one (Bassin and Gross, 1980). The personnel of the school must understand that any renewal process involves expenditure of energy, frustration, and a good deal of time. Wyant (1974) claims that school-staff participation in the development of communication skills and problem-solving must last at least 25 hours or it can even have detrimental long-term effects. The Organizational Training Programme described earlier (Schmuck and Schmuck, 1971) required 70 hours.

Runkel and Schmuck (1976) have even found that approximately 160 hours of staff time in small organizations such as elementary schools have been necessary for major results to occur. These programmes are oriented heavily toward human relations and do not have a comprehensive survey-feedback component, which could well reduce time devoted to some phases of the process. In spite of the relative efficiency of survey-feedback, however, it also requires a major commitment. Experience from IDP schools indicates that a minimum of 20 staff working-hours is necessary for the assessment phases alone (steps one to six).

The formal contract involves a written statement of agreement between IMTEC and the school board or the policy body of the participating institution, indicating the agreement to participate and to transact agreed upon expense funds. The school district must provide administrative services, and select one or more consultant trainees from the district (see Chapter Seven). IMTEC is also obliged to spell out its formal commitments, including consultant training and supervision, provision of instruments and materials, and project management. Usually, even before the contract phase is completed, the institution has begun preparations for data collection.

3. Data Collection

From the beginning of the Institutional Development Programme, survey-feedback has played a prominent role. The Guide to Institutional Learning (GIL) is a unique survey-feedback instrument which measures a wide spectrum of organizational factors. Originally it was developed for teacher-training colleges and in this form it was subjected to extensive statistical treatments. The first version was extremely long because each organizational variable possessed multiple items. The data derived from early field tests led to a new revision which (1) retained most of the information which the first version was able to show, (2) refined the style and format of the instrument, (3) expanded the scope of inquiry into new aspects of institutions undergoing self-assessment, and (4) reduced the size of the instrument so that it was possible to fill it out in approximately one-and-a-half hours.

A third version took place when the GIL was adapted for primary and secondary schools. In the process, it underwent still further refinement of style, format, and content. The third revision eliminated the multiple-item-per-issue format, which necessitated developing a different statistical approach to establishing norms. Reliability testing was accomplished with this version by selecting a population of teachers and administrators who comprised approximately 10 per cent of the total population of 19 schools which were participating in the project. This group agreed to fill the instrument out a second time after a two-and-a-half week lapse of time.

Using Gamma coefficients, it was found that the test-retest correlations ranged from .40 to .90. Those few items which indicated low coefficients were either eliminated or revised so that a high degree of confidence in the reliability of the instrument can be assumed. We discuss the reliability and validity issue elsewhere in the book but we must point out the ongoing dilemma which we face. We wish to have a standardized instrument which meets all criteria of research colleagues, but we wish also to have an instrument which can be modified and tailored to individual schools.

There is no easy way out of this dilemma, but we feel we are making some progress toward both aims. It should be noted that a work party established by the school may reject certain questions or indeed propose additional areas for inquiry. It is crucial to the process that participants feel the instrument is valid *for them*.

At the time of this writing (Spring, 1983), the instrument has been tested in 100 teacher training colleges, secondary schools, and primary schools in five countries (Norway, Belgium, U.K., Canada, and the United States). The school version has a school staff, a parent, and a pupil form, each form having many items in common for comparative purposes, but many items are also unique to a particular form. The staff form is the most comprehensive and consists of approximately 200 questions which have been constructed to provide information concerning the five dimensions of the IMTEC organization model: environment, values, relations, structures, and strategies. Below you will find two examples of item clusters which appear in the school staff form. Note that, on scale E, respondents indicate the situation as they perceive it to exist (REAL) and how it would look in the ideal situation (IDEAL). On scale L, the ideal is assumed to be 5 on all items so no marking is required.

The actual administration of the GIL is accomplished by the consultant. We concur with the findings of Alderfer and Ferris (1972) that the administration of an instrument would best be accomplished if both an internal and an external consultant were present. For practical reasons, this is not always possible, but the consultant is trained to follow explicit and standard guidelines.

A faculty is usually seated together while filling out the GIL. A sample of students and parents is also drawn if the school wishes to do so. Among the points the consultant clarifies with the group prior to administration are the following:

a. this exercise is a part of a self-assessment process into which the institution has voluntarily entered;
b. there are no 'right' or 'wrong' answers in the GIL. Since we wish to obtain an accurate picture of the way different groups view this institution, it is crucial that you respond to the items as honestly as possible;
c. the instrument identification code numbers are confidential and your number will not be known to anyone in the institution except yourself. They exist because we wish to return the form to you so that you might compare your responses with the institutional profiles;
d. the data which we obtain from the questionnaire may or may not be important, but the *meaning you give to the data is what counts*.

It must be clear that the GIL is not the only data source for the school. The consultant is usually already close enough to the school to be aware of its situation. Other important data will have been gathered in the previous phases of the process.

Figure 12 Parts of Scale E and L of The Guide to Institutional Learning (GIL) (1978 Teacher Training version)

E.
Indicate
a) the ways in which your schools confront problems, and
b) how you think problems should be confronted

1	2	3	4	5
never				always

		REAL	IDEAL
1.	Staff deny there is a problem	1 2 3 4 5	1 2 3 4 5
2.	Staff debate without deciding	1 2 3 4 5	1 2 3 4 5
3.	Individuals or subgroups take the actions that suit them	1 2 3 4 5	1 2 3 4 5
4.	The administration may accept suggestions from staff but takes responsibility for decisions and action on their own	1 2 3 4 5	1 2 3 4 5
5.	Interest groups negotiate a decision	1 2 3 4 5	1 2 3 4 5
6.	Staff face the problem and work it through together	1 2 3 4 5	1 2 3 4 5
7.	Individual people and groups fight for their own interests	1 2 3 4 5	1 2 3 4 5

L.
These are items about persons in leadership positions in the school.
(If you are a leader, assess your own role.)
Most people in leadership positions that I interact with in my school

1	2	3	4	5
never				always

		Mark your responses here
1.	Give me the feeling that my work is important	1 2 3 4 5
2.	Act as if I am inferior to them	1 2 3 4 5
3.	Develop a real interest in my welfare	1 2 3 4 5
4.	Develop a "we feeling" in working with others	1 2 3 4 5
5.	Maximize utilization of the different capabilities	1 2 3 4 5
6.	Effectively communicate changes such as governmental regulations, and practices in other schools to keep our school up-to-date	1 2 3 4 5

4 Data Analysis

The GIL is designed so that every item is connected to a dimension, a subcategory or variable in the conceptual framework that was outlined in the first section of the previous chapter. The data are reported in the form of profiles which correspond generally to a variable of one of the organizational dimensions. These profiles change over time but in the existing version they are named and described as follows:

I. VALUES, BELIEFS, GOALS

The value discrepancies and similarities of staff, students and community are explored in this profile. Although some attention is given to fundamental beliefs (*Weltanschauung*), the major focus of the profile is devoted to values as they pertain to the organizational goals and tasks. We might stress here that it is important to explore values and beliefs, not because there should necessarily be consensus among members and between members of an organization, but because it is important for them to understand what these values and beliefs are and find ways in which institutional members can live with them and/or modify them.

Because institutional development is so crucial, certain items in this profile address, specifically, the issue of change and institutional member beliefs about change.

II. INSTRUCTIONAL GOALS

Teaching and learning are the dominant activities in schools and Profile II provides participants with an opportunity to assess the importance of various possible instructional aims. There is no end to the attempts of ministries and school boards to define such aims, but ultimately a school staff (sometimes also parents and students) must clarify its own instructional aims and the priorities various institutional members give to these aims if the aims are to become a functional part of the life of the school.

III. INSTRUCTIONAL PRACTICES

The instructional modes of teachers are of central concern. We do not assume that one teaching or learning style is better than another. In fact, evidence is clear-cut that differing styles have different effects, and their value can only be assessed contextually (McKeechie, 1967). This profile helps staff clarify what they do and what they feel is important to do. It is also critical to assess the gap between teacher and student perspectives and preferences.

IV. INSTITUTIONAL CLIMATE

This profile helps clarify the morale and general atmosphere of the institution. The level of satisfaction, support, trust, flexibility and competitiveness is assessed as well as the degree to which individual participants feel they are a vital part of the organizational process. This includes a measure of their own commitment to the institution as a humane, pleasant place to live and work.

V. NORMS AND EXPECTATIONS

Any institution possesses informal norms and expectations or a code of 'do's' and don'ts' which defines appropriate and inappropriate behaviour. They are not written and are therefore only learned by experience in the institution. This profile raises questions which should help institutional members clarify certain dimensions of this code and it also provides information which could be of potential help in altering the code in some productive manner, if they so choose.

VI. LEADERSHIP

There are two leadership variables assessed in this profile. The first looks at the managing capability of leaders, that is, the ability to maximize different capabilities and co-ordinate competing interests. The second looks at leadership style as reflected in dichotomous continua such as flexible-rigid, people-oriented and/or task-oriented, innovative-traditional, and enthusiastic-reserved.

VII. DECISION-MAKING STRATEGIES

Institutions establish certain styles for dealing with problem situations. An institution should be clear about how decisions are made and who makes them. Profile VII is intended to help institutional members reflect on the scope of data base they use in making decisions, the frequency with which they make important decisions, and the degree to which faculty confront or avoid problem situations.

VIII. INFLUENCE, POWER AND CONTROL

Human relations include the informal influence- and power-structure of groups and individuals in and outside the institution, such as parent groups, teacher unions, and central authorities. This profile allows institutional members to assess the perceived degree of influence of these groups on their own work, and it also allows them to assess the degree of influence they personally possess on their own work and on aspects of the institution as a whole.

IX. DEGREE OF INSTITUTIONAL CHANGE

It is crucial to obtain a measure of the perceived change which has taken place in the whole school, the work units, the individual realms in order to understand the judgements of individuals pertaining to other profiles. This profile allows participants to indicate the change which has taken place in these spheres during the recent past.

X. TASK AND TIME STRUCTURE

In this profile, we assess the workload, schedules, routines and relative time given to tasks and activities by school personnel. One of the major difficulties of a loosely-coupled organization like the school is that the same persons perform a multiple of different roles. The critical point of reference in this profile is the relative amount of time individuals devote and would like to devote to these tasks. We do not imply that one arrangement is better than another, but we do feel that because all personnel engage in so many activities, theoretically it is possible to establish a better fit between tasks and the individual preferences than typically exists.

XI. INCENTIVE AND REWARD STRUCTURE

An institution must balance forces for the *status quo* and change in such a manner that some stability is maintained during the renewal process. The reward structure can serve both as a stabilizer and as a force for change. There are two ways to look at incentives and rewards. The first is to assess the factors which the institution and broader school system deem important. The second is more personal in that each individual sets priorities and finds fulfilment in different

Figure 13 Profile II Instructional Goals

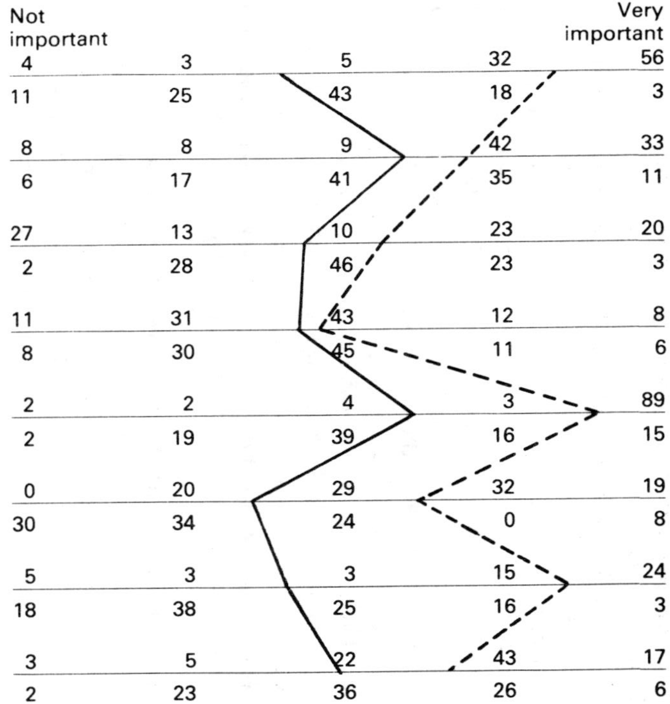

		Not important				Very important
1. To develop an integrated, balanced person	Ideal	4	3	5	32	56
	Real	11	25	43	18	3
2. To develop problem-solving skills	Ideal	8	8	9	42	33
	Real	6	17	41	35	11
3. To gain technical-vocational skills	Ideal	27	13	10	23	20
	Real	2	28	46	23	3
4. To understand ideas, concepts and theories	Ideal	11	31	43	12	8
	Real	8	30	45	11	6
5. To develop and improve social attitudes and skills	Ideal	2	2	4	3	89
	Real	2	19	39	16	15
6. To develop a sense of aesthetic qualities	Ideal	0	20	29	32	19
	Real	30	34	24	0	8
7. To develop an independent, critical, and tolerant person	Ideal	5	3	3	15	24
	Real	18	38	25	16	3
8. To develop the ability for creative work	Ideal	3	5	22	43	17
	Real	2	23	36	26	6

Numbers over line = Distribution in % of IDEAL
Numbers under line = Distribution in % of REAL

- - - - - = means of IDEAL
——— = means of REAL

ways. Both approaches are included in this profile. Each of the 11 profiles has a number of data forms, which are intended to facilitate data feedback and comparisons. Figure 13 gives and example of one of profile II listed above.

The profile shows the distribution of REAL and IDEAL responses (in percentages) and the mean responses of all members of the professional staff of a particular school. The numbers about each scale represent the distribution scores for the REAL scale and the numbers underneath each scale represent the IDEAL scale. The solid line connects the mean score for the REAL instructional goals which exist at the school. The broken line connects the mean scores for the IDEAL instructional goals as the staff would like them to be. We might draw attention to the fact that all items in this profile illustration are perceived as valuable in a collective sense because the staff would prefer that they all be given greater priority in the ideal case. The REAL scale suggests a somewhat balanced situation with all items except two (six and seven); these two appear to be of less importance than the other instructional goals.

If we look at the IDEAL scale, we can see great discrepancies between three items and their REAL counterparts. The staff appears to wish to emphasize more strongly (1) development of a balanced person, (2) social relations and skills, and (3) an independent, critical and tolerant person. The last item seems less important because it is one of the lesser-emphasized aspects of instruction in the present programme. It is also apparent that certain aspects of the programme are presently being emphasized as much as the staff would choose to do in the ideal situation.

In order to help the staff see the situation in even greater perspective, a second form of the profile is also plotted, this time giving the teacher and administrator REAL responses. (Mean scores and distributions on the IDEAL responses are available to the staff in computer printout form but they are not plotted). A third form is also available which gives the school an opportunity to compare its response with the combined means and distributions of all comparable schools participating in any given year.

To save space, in Figure 14 we shall show only the mean discrepancies for item number 1 of profile II in order to give some indication of the total information about means that are available on any one item.

We can see that the administrators of the school rate the present emphasis towards the development of a balanced person more highly

Figure 14 Discrepancy Information Available*

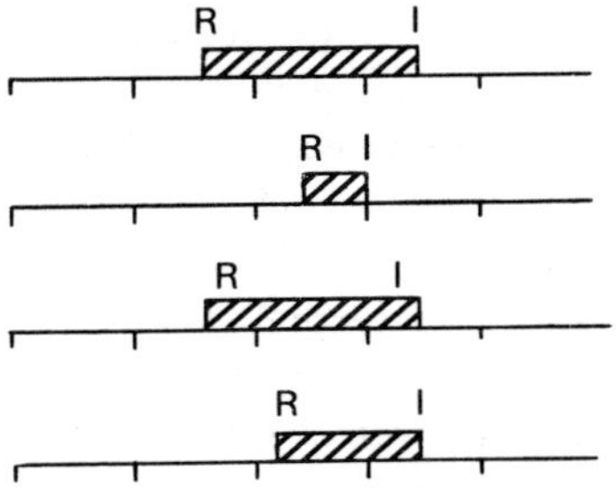

	Real	Ideal
Teachers	2.7	4.5
Administrators	3.5	4.0
Total Staff	2.8	4.5
All Schools	3.2	4.6
Students	not available	not available
Parents	not available	not available

R = Real I = Ideal

than do the faculty, and in the 'ideal' situation they do not think it should be emphasized as much as the faculty do. It is also apparent that the faculty of this particular school feel they emphasize this item less than do the other schools in general, but they indicate they would wish to do so, in the ideal case, at about the same level as the other schools generally wish to do.

The data which we have just reviewed gives us a quick overview of the situation. However, the distribution scores give us added insight about the response patterns. We shall draw on Figure 13 to illustrate how the distribution scores give us powerful knowledge beyond the simple mean scores.

Distribution figures are especially helpful in understanding the nature and degree of conflict and consensus of a school staff with regard to a specific item. For example, items three and four on the scale in Figure 13 indicate relatively little difference in the REAL and IDEAL means, which might lead one naively to conclude that there is little discrepancy with regard to these items. However, on item three, we note that there is a tendency for responses to flow toward the centre of the REAL scale; whereas the faculty is widely split in terms of the

* Footnote: parent-and-student data was not available in this school. So far, only 30 per cent of all schools have worked with parent/student data. Several schools, however, do choose to include parents and students at a later stage in the process.

IDEAL scale. More than a quarter of the faculty feel that technical/ vocational skills are of no importance at all, while about the same percentage feel they are very important indeed. In contrast to this outcome, on item four, the IDEAL distribution almost replicates the REAL distribution.

On items five and seven, we find a wide distribution of responses on the REAL scale while almost everyone feels these items are very important in the IDEAL. If we had referred only to the mean score we would have concluded that the staff sees the present picture as reflecting less importance than it should in the ideal situation. This is not the case; some of the staff perceive item seven as presently being stressed.

We find the opposite distribution picture on item six where there is a relatively clear consensus as to the REAL situation, but there is a wide spread in terms of its value as an IDEAL.

Where there is a large distribution consensus, caution must be used in concluding that no problems exist about interpreting the situation. We note on the scales just mentioned above that a very small minority of the staff is responding in a fashion opposite to that of the large majority. This may not be serious at all, but it might signal that a small faction, with radically different views from those of the rest of the staff exists in the school. This can only be confirmed by looking at other profiles and by raising the possibility of such a condition during the feedback period.

A variety of other information possibilities also exist. For example, we might discover that one group consistently responds in a similar manner to the administrators, or that another group is consistently in conflict with the administration's view.

We must emphasize, again, that the description given above is not prescriptive. It does not imply that the school should do anything. It does imply a good deal of discrepancy between several groups and between REAL and IDEAL responses. These are viewed as potential trouble spots which the school could do well to confront.

DISCREPANCY INFORMATION

In our discussion of profile II above, it was obvious that an important aspect of the Institutional Development Programme is the generation and use of discrepancy data. It is important to recognize that organizations are perceived and described differently by various people.

Recognition of these perceptual differences is important in defining the state of an institution and in determining where it ought to direct resources and energies. Therefore, it is important to define the differences or discrepancies among people and groups regarding the same issues.

In the IDP, discrepancy information is collected in the following areas:

1. Among individuals;
2. Among groups of individuals in various roles (such as student faculty, administration);
3. On what these individuals and groups perceive to exist at present (their reality) and what they would prefer to have (their ideal);
4. On the way(s) in which various factors of the organization 'fit' with one another;
5. Among various peer educational institutions in the region and internationally.

The presentation of such information can help to validate or invalidate assumptions which individuals and groups hold about one another. Also, by using the information they have a better understanding of the range of differences relating to the issues that should receive attention and the ways in which people are likely to be motivated to resolve these (their ideals). The understanding and appreciation of such differences in perceptions, values and commitments are important factors in defining the status and planning for improved institutional effectiveness.

5. Data Feedback and Dialogue

In accordance with the assumptions of the IDP, the data which is fed back to the institution by the consultant is treated by the consultant as being relatively value-free. The consultant joins the staff or representative groups of the institution before interpreting the data, which includes giving it a preliminary set of values. It is important to note that the GIL data is intended to serve as a springboard into analysis and exploration of genuine problem areas as well as strength of the institution. As the process proceeds, the GIL data itself drops further and further into the background.

As a starting point, however, there is no doubt about its value. Not only will the school be presented with the full range of opinions about the school, but also, any one person does not need to be blamed or 'stick out his neck'. So often self-assessment is not an open process because staff and students are afraid of hurting each other. The data base helps to get the process started without unnecessary personal conflicts.

However, the actual selection of strengths and weaknesses is not done in a vacuum, but evolves from the processes previously undertaken. The structure of the GIL is intentionally designed to give perspective as to ideals. Insights into items and variables where the REAL and IDEAL are generally similar are helpful in defining what is deemed positive about the institution.

Discrepancies are signs of potential weaknesses or at least potential problem areas. Awareness of these conditions in the data should help the staff funnel their energies toward appropriate items.

Because the GIL is comprehensive in nature, it becomes imperative to be somewhat selective in terms of strengths and weaknesses identified. This necessitates a dialogue arrangement that avoids biasing the itemized strengths and weaknesses toward safe issues or remaining at a superficial level. This can be accomplished by a meeting design such as breaking the staff into *ad hoc* parallel working groups which will undoubtedly arrive at different sets of items.

One should keep in mind that there are different levels of abstraction in problems and we make mention of the typical cycle that problem definition goes through when using the GIL. The items of the GIL are necessarily not explicit in nature. Therefore, problems which arise from it usually begin at an abstract level. However, it is necessary for staff members to become explicit in terms of the meaning of items as they pertain to a particular institutional setting. Therefore, by way of examples or specific incidents, staff members move from the abstract to the particular. These particular examples, however, are but symptoms of more basic organizational factors that must be handled eventually (Buchanen, 1972 pp. 10–12). It is necessary, after full understanding of specific examples, for the staff to move once again from the particular to more general organizational considerations which get at underlying causes of problems rather than mere symptoms.

Figure 15 gives a graphic picture of the process which usually occurs during the dialogue:

Figure 15 Dialogue Process in the IDP

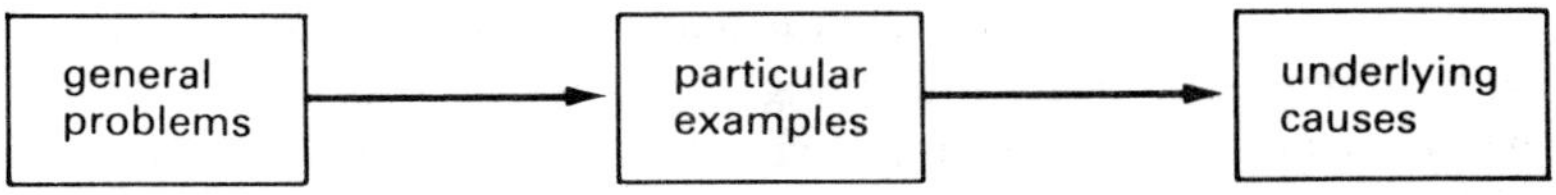

The process we are describing here has strong overtones of what Levin and Simon (1974) call a 'developmental dialectic' in that it not only helps members of an institution to clarify strengths and weaknesses, but the dialogue itself facilitates the development of common understandings, perceptions, and even vocabulary among institutions themselves. Until this happens, there is little likelihood that the staff of a school will be able to work productively in redefining their organizational functioning. Educators have a weak common institutional knowledge base. Each educator invents his or her own terminology and concepts of the organization and although many of these are fairly complex and sophisticated, they rarely lead to collaboration or synthesis of perception among staff members. One of the major functions of the IDP, and especially the dialogue phase, is to help the members of staff begin to develop a common vocabulary and frame of reference so that productive institutional development is better ensured. Once the staff of an institution are reasonably satisfied that they understand their situation sufficiently, they move to the next phase in the process.

6. Goal Setting

Goal setting can be divided into two components. First, a number of problem areas are identified which require immediate attention. They usually involve interpersonal conflicts or practices which are detrimental to the health and morale of the institution. Second, more fundamental problem areas are also identified which require extended attention and planning.

Before discussing goal-setting issues, we need to make a preliminary statement about the momentum of the IDP process. It can accelerate or falter during any phase but the goal-setting activity is crucial. Until this point in the process there have been natural points of stimulation and involvement. In the beginning, the novelty of the process was reason enough for active participation. The questionnaire was a specific and tangible activity, and the feedback and interpretation sessions also provided specific data and points of issue. The goal-setting stage can easily find the group stuck or resistant to definite work because the process itself may be stalled by underlying value and philosophical conflicts, some of which may only be partly perceived by staff members. There is no magic cure for this situation. A number of activities and exercises are suggested by Schmuck and Runkel (1977, Chapter Four) which might prove to be helpful. A series of exercises are developed through IDP to facilitate communication, problem-solving and decision-making.

The goal-setting process can be facilitated a great deal if the staff adopts two norms. These norms call for the goal phase to be looked at (1) in a positive perspective, and (2) in a problem-solving perspective. With regard to the first norm, Schmuck and Runkel (1974) argue soundly that goals should be seen more as 'rallying points and not fences'. These are the elements of the organization that can make the individuals in it feel they are living a more productive and satisfying professional life. If they are perceived as rallying points, it should be easier to generate suitable goals and maintain the momentum of the process.

With regard to the second norm, experience has demonstrated a common tendency of groups with differing values and philosophies to adopt a 'win-lose' pattern of work. That is, groups and individuals try to gain advantage over others in the institution, and sway the goal-setting process in such a manner that others are disadvantaged from the goals. If group members shift their thinking to a problem-solving position, a compatible solution is usually found. We do not wish to imply that we favour a consensus over a conflict-orientation. Conflicts are assumed to be a part of life and basic to all learning institutions. The crucial consideration about conflicts is to find how the institution lives with these conflicts and works out ways to satisfy divergent needs productively. In fact, there is growing evidence that it is possible for conflicting goals in an institution to be pursued simultaneously. One unit, for example, might wish to stress fundamentals and basics, while another might wish to stress social development (Perrew, 1973). This process may actually involve introducing intentional disparities into goal statements. Clark (1980) maintains that we might not only recognize disparate goal-orientations, contextual features, and programme and personal strengths, but that we try to take advantage of these differences in the goal-setting process.

Problem-solving involves still another dimension. It is tempting for staff members to rely on traditional practices in looking for solutions to problems. Successful problem-solving includes a willingness to look at alternatives and weigh the evidence for and against each alternative seriously. We are persuaded by the arguments of March and Simon (1958) that the best alternative among many is usually not possible to identify. The important part of goal-setting is that it actually improves the institution even though it does not attain any ideal state.

Logically, the specification of goals would follow from a sound tabulation of institutional strengths and weaknesses. To a degree, such is the case, but we must caution that any workable goal must account for at least four major levels of consideration. First, personal goals and individual needs of staff must be satisfied. They must help the individual gain a greater sense of personal achievement, a feeling of belonging, and a sense of personal power and influence in the affairs of the school. Second, sub-group goals must be addressed. We have mentioned that there is a considerable degree of autonomy in individual classrooms and subject areas. Individual goals may affect radically the sense of autonomy and control of specialized areas and any workable goal must strike a balance between individual and sub-group needs. Third, the entire institution has certain needs which must be satisfied. They may often be in conflict with individual and sub-group interests. Finally, the environment has expectations which must be addressed and any internal arrangements must be made within the frames allowed by the environment.

We must make one cautionary remark about all goals which are selected. They will have implications which are far wider than those initially perceived or intended. Therefore, even though they are designed to be solutions to problem areas, they must be somewhat tentative. They are best considered as hypotheses which may be substantiated or revised as more experience is gained, rather than as permanent choices for the future nature of the organization.

The goals at which a particular institution arrives may well be peculiar to that group. There is no hidden curriculum in the IDP that implies what the goals should be. However, we initially felt that they should conform to certain conventional standards. First, they must be explicit enough so that there is clear understanding by everyone about their meaning. Second, there should be general consensus that they are valued and important. Third, goals must not be so abstract that they have little operational utility. If they are to contribute to institutional growth, they must be stated in operational terms. Finally, the goals must be given a time-frame in which the institution works towards specific deadlines and review dates.

7. Planning for Action

In any plan of action, not only are goals and structures agreed upon, but agreements must be met in terms of methods of achieving these and the necessary resources to institute them. Renewal efforts are directed not only to organizational factors but might involve various types of in-service training activities, personal and group counselling, or human-relations designs, if it becomes apparent that the health of a school can thereby be improved. We may even note that it is not off limits to recognize that the formal leaders of the school might benefit from leadership training or other in-service experiences (Schmuck, Francisco, and Bell, 1981).

Although improvements in areas like communication, decision-making, inter-group effectiveness, and teacher/student relationships are important, most teachers will value any improvements in the instructional area highly. An action plan, therefore, usually also includes specific instructional goals and gives the staff (students and parents as well) a concrete task-orientation.

Planning takes place at two levels: at the institutional and at the classroom level. Although many activities involve all staff members (and sometimes students), IDP provides a number of choices. Individuals and groups (e.g. teachers and students in a class) might opt for certain activities (e.g. the improvement of communication, clarification of values or improvement of instruction).

A good deal of attention has been paid in the literature to the mechanisms that are crucial in order to effect action plans. Howes and

Quinn (1978) have recently attempted to synthesize this literature in such a manner as to create what they call a 'prescriptive framework' to guide action-plans. We have drawn on this framework in suggesting a checklist of considerations that should be taken into account as action planning takes place.

A. *Phase 1: Set up an Adequate Orientation Environment.*
   1. Set aside enough time for an adequate introduction to the change.
      a. Identify what will be changed.
      b. Plan workshops, meetings, and in-service seminars.
   2. Make the relative advantage of the change easily visible.
      a. Package it so that it is easily understood, easily referenced, and easily related to performance.
   3. Show organization members (users) that their efforts will be supported.
      a. Identify, obtain, and confirm availability of support services and resources.
   4. Show members it will be easy to institutionalize the change and that it will be relatively non-threatening afterward.
      a. Clarify the expectations of each member during and after implementation.
   5. Show that immediate superiors accept and support the change.
   6. Clearly identify the roles and relationships of all who will be involved in the change process.

B. *Phase 2: Set up Adequate Support Networks for the Implementation Effort.*
   1. Produce and make supportive services available.
   2. Set up formal training programmes to develop members' roles.
      a. Provide in-service training, continuing workshops, seminars, etc.
   3. Encourage and reward the use of horizontal and vertical communication channels.
   4. Relax standard operating procedures in affected (changing) units.
   5. Integrate change agents, managers, and members.
      a. Provide frequent and individual contact.
   6. Make sure members feel adequately involved.
      a. Establish problem-solving meetings and shared decision-making norms.

8. School Development

The task of implementing organizational change, even with clear goals and plans of action, is a very complex process (Gross, Giacquinta, and Bernstein, 1971). Those who are implementing an innovation will encounter a number of obstacles. Nadler (1981) indicates that there are three basic problems in implementing any change. First, there is the need to motivate individuals who are habituated to behave in ways not always consistent with that desired. Second, there is a power problem. The school is a political system (Tushman, 1977) made up of different individuals, groups, and coalitions competing for power, and when a school is in a state of transition the dynamics of political behaviour becomes intense. Third, the management system of the school becomes unstable. Most management systems are designed for somewhat stable states; in a period of transition it is often unclear how the school is actually being run. Nadler provides twelve action steps that can be taken to deal with these problems. They are listed below:

Implication	*Action Steps*
Need to motivate change	1. Identify and surface dissatisfaction with the present state
	2. Participation in change
	3. Rewards for behaviour in support of change
	4. Time and opportunity to disengage from the present state
Need to manage the transition	5. Develop and communicate a clear image of the future
	6. Use multiple and consistent leverage points
	7. Develop organizational arrangements for the transition
	8. Build in feedback mechanisms

Implication	*Action Steps*
Need to shape the political dynamics of change	9. Assure the support of key power groups
	10. Use leader behaviour to generate energy in support of change
	11. Use symbols and language
	12. Build in stability

Fortunately, the IDP schools are not left to their own resources in seeking to improve themselves. Most schools seek assistance from teachers' centres, other schools or R&D institutions which can offer advice on how to develop in a given area: knowing their real needs gives motivation, commitment and strength. The chances for a real dialogue with outside 'experts' are much higher than they are if a self-assessment process did take place.

Local teachers' centres traditionally have taken the initiative in relation to school renewal. It is now more common (in IDP schools) for the schools to define their needs.

At this point, the role of the IDP consultant changes. He or she might link the school to outside resources, but he or she is not part of any decision to contract any agency. The consultant may still however, participate in the renewal process if the school and the consultant agree. The school is in the process of institutionalizing new practices, a process that is difficult and which needs monitoring. The IDP consultant tries to assist in this process; gradually, however, he or she seeks to withdraw from the school to avoid any unhealthy dependencies (see Chapter 7).

9. Networking

Most institutions which undertake a self-assessment process benefit from experiences of other institutions. IMTEC facilitates the establishment of a communications and support system between institutions so that a more productive change process can be undertaken. Our rationale for encouraging networks is based on the very nature of IMTEC itself, which has avoided establishing a large, bureaucratic institution in lieu of a unique organizational structure; it relies almost exclusively on networks to accomplish its goals. All IMTEC networks have certain common features. First, the central organization is extremely small. While the total number of persons linked into all IMTEC networks reaches several thousand, the central staff consists of a small group which interacts in daily face-to-face relationships. Second, the networks are all of a horizontal nature. There are few lines of authority since individuals participate as peers in user-based and user-governed activities. Third, networks are built up to address widely different innovations and points of view. Fourth, the networks are not permanent, which gives them a flexibility and capability of expanding or contracting to meet direct, real needs.

The above principles also serve as guidelines for school-renewal networks. The superstructure of IDP, its formal organization, consists of a small core of people who work with the train school district-based consultants who serve as the main outside link to the school. Because the networks are not a part of the formal educational bureaucracy, the lines of authority which cut across them do not follow conventional lines. Typically, outside expert help is based on a 'parent' rather than a 'peer' relationship. Culver *et al.* (1973. p. 76) describe the conventional consultant role in the following manner: 'We were the 'haves' and the schools were the 'have nots' and our task was to share with them what we know so that they could benefit from it.' A network is by nature peer-oriented which reorients the support- and information-system away from one of doing something to an institution to one of genuine mutual assistance. Its function is to establish links outside the regular communication and authority channels. We do not wish to suggest that the conventional system is not vital and productive, but semi- and completely informal relationships do show potential for satisfying certain needs which are not being met in the format structure.

We must actually distinguish between two major types of networks. One focuses on individuals or small groups, the other on organizations. It is clear that the IDP can only initially formalize an organizational network. That is, at the very least, a network co-ordinator should be identified and a newsletter or some other communications organ scheduled. Individual schools should each select a network representative, and these representatives should meet at regular intervals in order to share progress and express needs that are becoming evident in the institutions. Ultimately, however, the major value of networking is lodged in individual contacts that are established.

Below are a few things which the formal network might do to foster these personal contacts:

1. Teachers and administrators can visit other IDP schools. These visits can be for the purpose of getting a general impression of activities or to visit specific subject areas;
2. The school can hold 'open houses' to which staff invite both educators and the general public to visit;
3. School groups can volunteer to hold workshops for other teachers in order to demonstrate how they have developed certain strengths in their school;
4. Particularly gifted teachers could be identified who would be willing to act as network 'experts' for the sphere of interest in which they happen to work;
5. Schools that feel a genuine need for outside help can collaborate by sharing resources and facilities to accomplish this aim;
6. IDP schools can hold a self-renewal 'flea market' where personnel from each school demonstrate its programmes and distribute information to interested visitors.

The study of networks is in its infancy in education. We are not exactly certain how they work, but of one thing we are certain: they are only as valuable as the members of the network decide to make them. If networks are to be a genuine information and support system for renewal schools, the school personnel must actively work to make them so.

10. Evaluation

One of the major assumptions of the IDP is that schools can learn. It is fatal to assume that the school is learning only if it is undergoing change. More crucial is its ability to monitor its own system constantly, and accept as well as reject new practices and new products as they are found to be appropriate and inappropriate (Nisbet, 1974, p. 32). Under these conditions, the learning school is responding continually to internal and external forces, confronting problems which arise and evaluating its organizational behaviour.

The major task of the IDP is to help schools learn how to learn. Schools which have engaged in the process are invited to join organizations such as IMTEC and school networks in recurring analysis and change. The GIL can be used for recurring self-assessment to give the school an indication of where it is moving: The situation of a school changes rapidly with new students and staff as well as with environmental changes. Self-assessment and renewal should become an integral part of the life of every school.

The conceptual framework provided for OD projects evaluated by Fullan, Miles and Taylor, already described in some detail in Chapter Two, is an important and helpful guide. It may be remembered that three types of outcomes are stressed: impact on the district as a system, positive attitudes towards OD, and the institutionalization of the OD process. At IMTEC we are presently experimenting with different approaches to evaluation, combining parts of the GIL instrument with group activities and observation. We face real dilemmas. Firstly, expectations regarding ongoing problem-solving and renewal are changing. It is simply not a reliable measure to compare 'real' data alone. In spite of the fact that the situation might have improved, expectations have also increased and therefore the understanding of accomplishments might not indicate progress. We find, however, that both REAL and IDEAL data prove to be more reliable because a smaller discrepancy score does represent an indication of improvement. Secondly, schools with an improved problem-solving capability and a more open climate have informal means of evaluation that seem to function well for them, although for research purposes they are inadequate. Finally, real data is difficult to gather, unless the schools are certain that the information belongs only to the school. Some schools, therefore, react negatively to any attempts of more 'formal' evaluation techniques.

CHAPTER FIVE

Institutional Development Programme: Practice

The purpose of this chapter is to look 'behind the school door' to see how the IDP has worked, so far, in five of the sixty-five elementary and secondary schools involved in the project*. In this chapter, we will restrict ourselves to descriptions of these five schools and the process in which they have been involved, and will leave a more detailed discussion of what has been learnt for our next chapters.

As we have noted earlier, schools are as different as people, and, therefore, only a case-description will enable us to see the IDP process in context. It is advisable to hold some variables constant, however, and we have chosen to simplify our task by drawing our cases from a single national context: Norway. The reader who requires some pertinent contextual information will find a brief statement about recent reform trends in that country in Appendix A. We will follow the case studies of the schools throughout the various phases of the IDP, and we believe our descriptions and analyses will show some common trends, although we do not seek to generalize at this point. In writing this chapter we do have one particular problem: we have agreed with all participating schools involved in the IDP that the data which we collect from these schools is confidential. It is a clear condition in our contract that every school will be protected from any public discussion of data. To us, it is crucial that a fundamental trust is established between IMTEC and the schools involved. We have no intention, therefore, of violating the rules of confidentiality. On the other hand, we all recognize the need for other people outside the 'IDP network' to learn about our experiences. The only way to deal with this problem, as far as we

*We have earlier reports from the first sample of 18 teacher-training institutions. Some of the new schools are not reported here.

can see, is to draw on real cases, but ensure that data is presented in such a way that individuals or individual schools can not be identified. We have chosen to describe single schools but to draw on our experiences from other schools in certain areas. This will only minimally weaken the authenticity of the descriptions while the anonymity of the schools is maintained.

Case Studies

We have attempted to select a variety of educational settings where schools experienced different levels of success with the IDP. The cases are as follows: Case 1: The New Innovative Elementary School; Case 2: The Rural School; Case 3: The Static School in an Innovative School District; and Case 5: The Traditional School.

CASE 1: THE NEW INNOVATIVE ELEMENTARY SCHOOL

A relatively new elementary school (grades 1–6) with a 'progressive' headmaster and a reputation of being somewhat innovative, joined the programme. Some of the teachers are newly graduated from the teachers' college; others have been teaching for only a few years. The school, in its short history, has been involved already in a number of innovative projects that include several subject areas, new methods of instruction, alternative education (extensive out-of-school activities), and school-community projects.

The headmaster is known as a very helpful person, who works 'day and night' for the school. He is very interested in everything that happens in the school and likes to participate at all levels and in every field. During his career, the headmaster has been active in innovative work; he has written textbooks, and he has been lecturing at seminars and working with graduate students. It is fair to say that he plays a dominant role in the school, but in a manner that seems quite acceptable to the staff. He wants to share his knowledge and experiences with his younger staff members, and this he does willingly. He is sensitive of his own role; he does not want to be a dominant headmaster who makes all the decisions. However, most of the ideas for innovation have come from him and he has played a major role in their implementation.

The IDP was introduced to the school by an IDP consultant who knew the headmaster and some of the staff members professionally. At a staff meeting, the process was outlined, step by step; examples of the questionnaire and the profiles were presented on an overhead projector and discussions took place about the relevance of the programme to the needs of this particular school. Following the presentation, the staff was allowed two weeks to discuss the proposal, informally, before a formal vote was taken in the teacher assembly. It was unanimously accepted.

During a two-hour session at a later meeting, the questionnaire to be filled out was administered by the consultant. IMTEC specialists analysed the data and drew up profiles. The consultant returned to the school with the feedback information within one month after the administration of the GIL instrument. The problems of the school can partly be illustrated by the combination of profiles in the figures below:

Figure 16

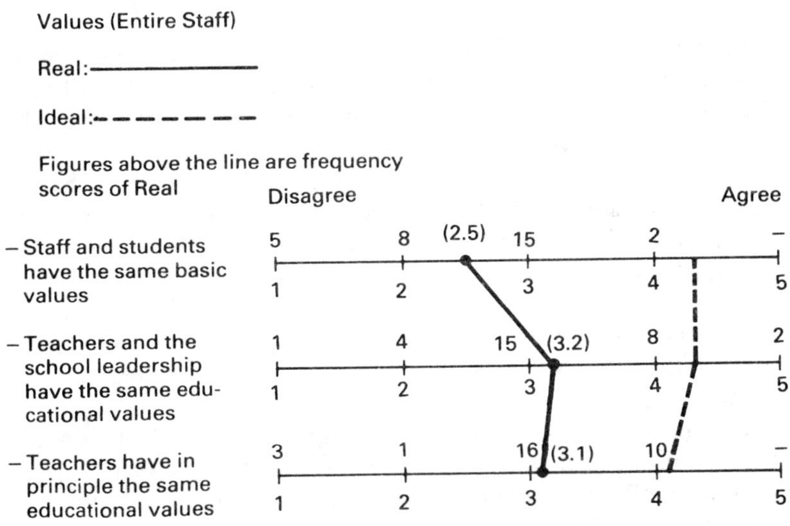

From Figure 16 it appears that the greatest discrepancy of values is clearly between the staff (teachers and school leadership) and the students. There is high consensus among the staff members that the situation at the school would improve if more uniform values existed between all parties involved in the school.

Figure 17

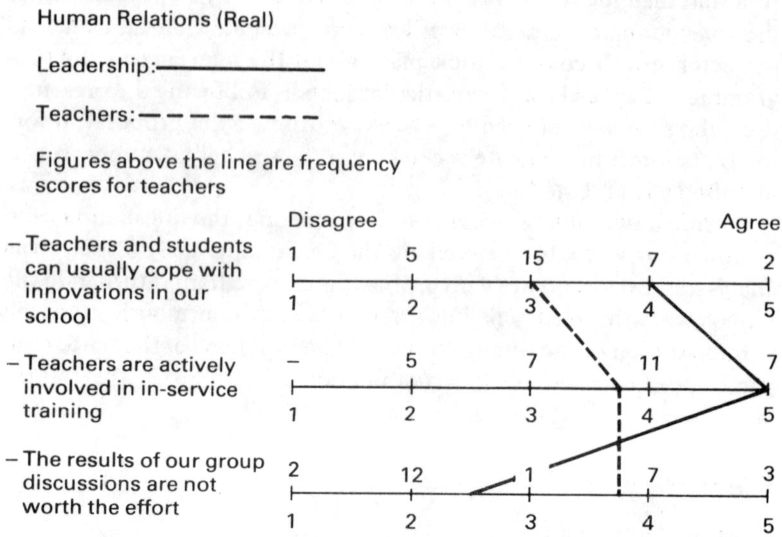

In Figure 17 we see that there is some difference in perception between most of the teachers and the leadership about the ability of the teachers and students to cope with innovations in the school, the degree of teacher involvement in in-service training, and the results of the group discussions. For example, the leadership seems to have a higher opinion of the capability of teachers than many of the teachers have of themselves. It is also noteworthy to point out that the spread of opinion among teachers about the human-relations issue in the figure is substantial. Fourteen teachers indicate that the results of group discussions are not worth the effort, while ten teachers respond positively to the issue. Significantly, none of the teachers is neutral about the subject.

In Figure 18 it is evident that there is rather substantial difference of perception about the relative roles of teachers and leadership in goal-setting, developing new procedures and practice, and even in developing materials. The leadership feel they are centrally involved in all of these areas while only a small group of teachers feel they are centrally involved. The school has the reputation of being innovative, but most of the teachers apparently feel they play little or no role in deciding what the school goals will be.

Figure 18

Roles and Responsibilities (Real)

Leadership: ————————

Teachers: - - - - - - - - - -

Figures above the line are frequency scores for teachers

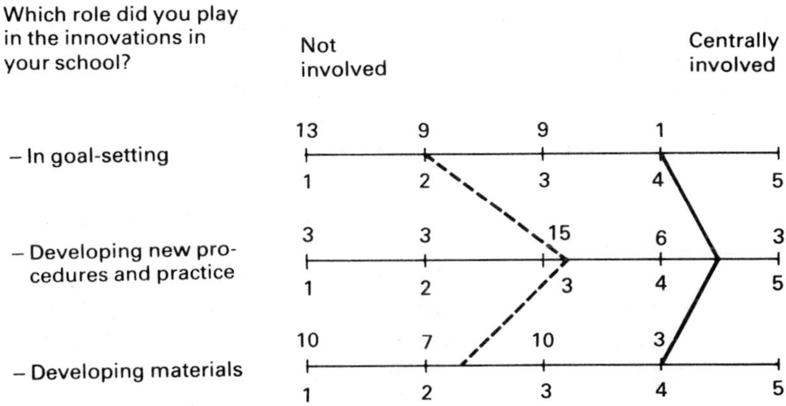

Figure 19

Conflict Resolution (Entire Staff)

Real: ————————

Ideal: - - - - - - - -

Figures above the line are frequency scores of Real

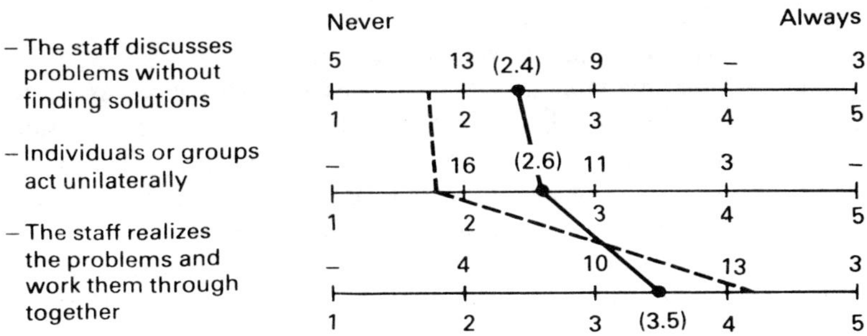

In Figure 19 we find some indication that the staff members respond positively about their ability, as an entire group, to resolve conflicts that arise, but they feel it would be to their advantage to work even more effectively in resolving conflicts.

The initial impressions of the consultant were outlined to the staff, but these impressions were held to be very tentative and were elaborated mainly to help the staff initiate its own extensive investigation and interpretation of all the data. A total of 15 hours was spent by staff members in diagnosing their situation and deciding on the following specific goals to improve their organization:

a. to reinforce a more supportive and open climate among staff;
b. to facilitate cooperation with teams and among teams;
c. to encourage individuals to take more responsible roles in the school;
d. to further develop the work environment in the open-plan section of the school.

The general reaction from the staff, after having gone through the data-feedback process, the dialogue, problem-solving, and goal-setting activities, was that they found that the degree of openness they had assumed to exist was not as high as they had believed. They felt now that their earlier feeling of openness reflected a superficial understanding of their relationships. The staff has begun to work more actively to integrate new teachers into the staff and to be more constructive and open about differences and conflicts.

School personnel made a conscious effort to encourage the expression of differences and to inquire into the reasons for these differences. The staff devoted considerable faculty-meeting-time, not only to differences with regard to issues being discussed, but to the exploration of why people felt as they did and the implications of these differences for related matters at the school.

After several months of focus on greater openness, the staff set about working on a more productive decision-making process. Some of the teachers, as the data indicates, felt that the decision-making process was somewhat problematic. The initial task the staff set was to determine why decisions were being made as they were. Clearly, one factor was the dynamic leadership style of the headmaster. He had assumed that it was his role to be the decision-maker and act as the authority figure when important decisions were at stake. Further, many of the staff members were relatively new to the profession and had initially relied heavily on the leadership of the headmaster to effect decisions. However, they were maturing as professionals and began to feel that the past decision-making process was no longer appropriate. They wanted to assume more responsibility and play a more active role in all phases of decision-making.

A final source of difficulty identified by the staff was the 'rapid speed of innovation,' that seemed to characterize the school. Reform project after reform project confronted them, and they barely had time to institute a project and see that it was effectively incorporated before another was under way.

After identifying the source of the problems, the staff set about rectifying some of them. The headmaster consciously began to loosen his grip on the school and slowly became less fearful of giving up some authority. The faculty members began to take a greater share of the initiative, and also began to experience the burden of responsibility for many aspects of the school programme.

The school, which is involved in several time-consuming projects, is now in its second year in the IDP, and continues to have a consultant on a regular basis. It may be difficult to find time for the staff to work with all four aims listed above. It may be that the staff, instead of working with one of these issues, will start working on other less dangerous projects and will do so successfully. After completing a successful project, they may feel strengthened and may want to start working on one of the more difficult tasks that were identified in the IDP process.

The consultant to the school identified several personal difficulties in his work. First, having only minimum training in the area of organization development, he feels that it was difficult to gain a clear picture of the programme and the work. He also feels that it was difficult to interpret the data and to contribute constructively as a process-facilitator in problem-solving. He believes he is accepted by the school, but knows that he needs to learn more skills in problem-solving, in conflict-resolution, and in direct interaction with the leadership. From the beginning of the programme, he has felt a need to acquire more skill and better techniques to cope with his daily work. The training given by IMTEC has been of value; in particular, the more practical 'how to do it' courses that have been organized are felt to be the most valuable of all.

CASE 2: THE RURAL SCHOOL

A small secondary school (150 pupils) situated in a remote rural area opted to participate in the programme. There are approximately 2,000 inhabitants in the district, and the students are brought into the school by buses, many students spending more than two hours a day in travel. The community consists mainly of unskilled labourers and small farmers. There is a small ethnic minority population and a few small religious sects also exist in the community.

The school is typical of most remote schools in that it has difficulty recruiting and retaining qualified teachers. Of a total of twenty teachers, almost half leave every year. In an attempt to rectify this situation, the community has provided above-standard housing for teachers, and they live in what they themselves call 'the teacher ghetto.'

The school had been identified as a 'problem-school' for a long time. First, the high turnover of staff is a problem shared with a number of schools in rural areas. Because nearly half of the staff is new every year, serious concerns are raised about continuity, cooperation among teachers, norms, and quality of instruction. Remote schools in rural areas are trying to moderate this problem in many ways by combining special incentives; housing for teachers, sabbatical arrangements, and in-service training. In spite of these remedies, many schools continue to face serious staffing problems.

One of the consequences of the staffing problem is difficult relationships with the community. Since the school is often identified with teachers who are recruited from outside the community, and who leave before they are really known to the community, the necessary trust-building process is hard to establish.

Our school was facing serious problems with the community. The 'teacher ghetto' area was looked upon as foreign to the community at large. Community members have only a minimum of formal education. Their norms are guided by strong religious beliefs, often not shared by the teachers, and some have special ethnic roots which are unknown to the teachers.

Teachers certainly felt not only the aloofness of the community but problems in day-to-day classroom situations: student motivation was low, some teachers were relatively inexperienced, and discipline was a serious problem. For a small rural school, such problems are rare and are more commonly associated with urban schools. The problems of the school had already become 'public' and something even the director of education in the region was concerned about. The most essential question was: how could a process of renewal even get started in this somewhat hostile situation?

The headmaster has tried often to get such a process started. He is well accepted by staff members, who feel he has good communication with them. The teachers had worked together to find ways in which they could improve their school situation but very often they had found themselves discussing the same problems, again and again, without finding solutions; they felt insecure about dealing with their problems and began to express the need for help from outside.

The idea of the IDP was introduced to the region by the County School Office. The headmaster knows the consultant well and only a short briefing was necessary before the headmaster and the teachers decided that they wanted to 'take the GIL instrument.' They hoped that the process would help them find new creative ways to deal with their situation. After filling out the instrument and getting the data back in three or four weeks, a single data-feedback session, lasting three hours, was held. At this session the teachers concluded that the data revealed a number of serious problems related to the school and its relations to the community. These problems were largely common knowledge to the staff and few new insights were gained. Owing to the school's geographical distance from the central office, and the unavailability of trained consultants living nearby, it was left alone with the data.

After some weeks, the staff started to discuss the data informally. They felt, however, that the information was so overwhelming that they could not go into a renewal process without help. The staff, therefore, left the data for some time and went back to their normal routine. After half a year, however, they started to discuss their practice again and also how they would like to develop the school. They went back to the data and found to their astonishment that what they were discussing coincided, to a large extent, with many of the discrepancies between REAL and IDEAL in the data. The following profiles illustrate some of the problems the school was facing:

Figure 20

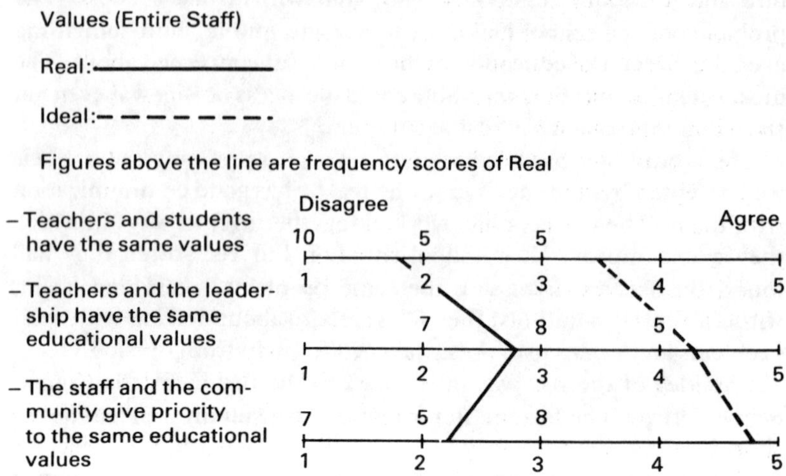

Figure 21

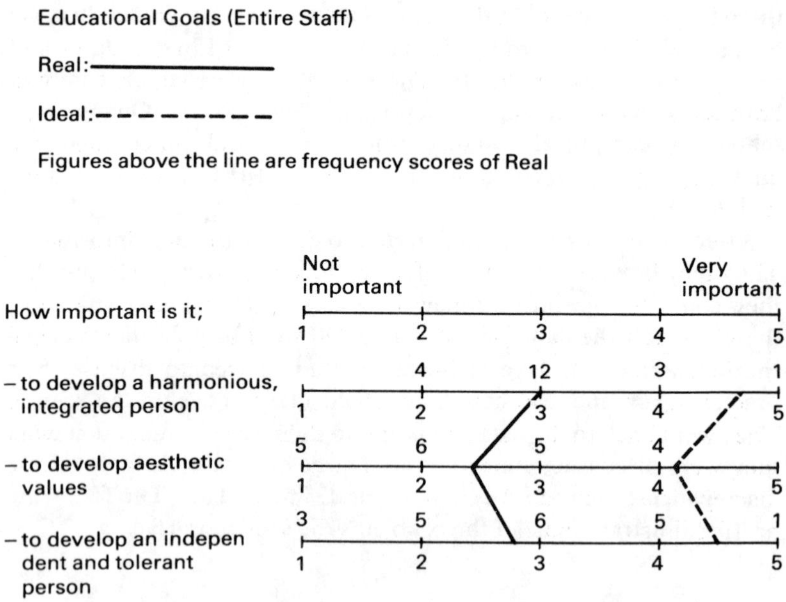

Figure 20 illustrates, dramatically, the discrepancy of values, perceived by the staff, between staff and the community (including the students). It also indicates an overwhelming sense that the school, in the ideal situation, would benefit from the existence of a more harmonious set of educational values than exists presently. There are also indications that the educational values represented by teachers, as opposed to the leadership of the school, are not as similar as they should be.

Several of the educational-goals items indicate potential trouble spots. In Figure 21, we note that staff-member priorities run from one end of the continuum to the other with regard to the emphasis they place on the development of an independent and tolerant person. The extremes are almost as great with regard to the emphasis they place on the development of a harmonious, integrated person, and the development of aesthetic values. Significantly, a fair consensus exists among almost all members that the staff, in the ideal situation, ought to place high priority on all of these items.

Figure 22

Tasks (Entire Staff)

Real: ————————

Ideal: – – – – – – – –

Figures above the line are frequency scores of Real

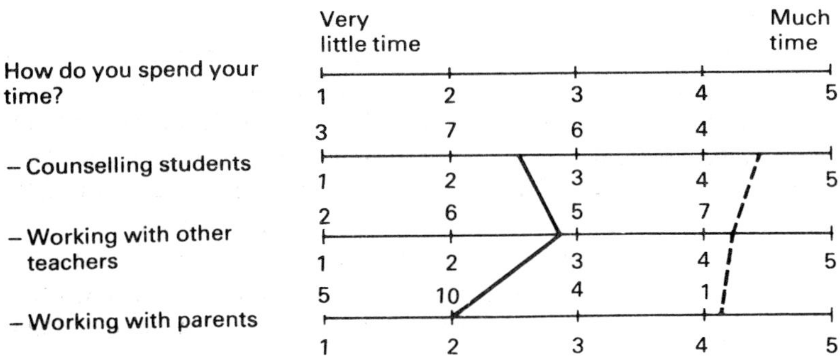

In Figure 22, we find great differences in terms of the time staff members devote to student-counselling and working with other teachers. A high consensus exists in terms of the time they feel they ought to spend. Few staff members spend much time working with parents, although most members feel this is important to do.

The staff members were surprised to discover how differently they perceived the REAL situation at the school. Informal discussions among them clearly illustrated the high degree of isolation most staff members felt in terms of professional, helpful discussions. The headmaster, who generally is regarded as a very able and supportive head, was surprised to find that so many teachers were not clear about their own educational values. Everyone discovered a need to talk more openly and to find processes to cope with their problems.

Another dimension of their own diagnosis was a revealing one; they found that there was considerable agreement among staff members about the desired state of affairs. In other words, there was consensus about what they wanted in their school. The main problem, however, was that probably the students and parents did not share their goals.

Eventually, the school was able to begin working productively with the IDP consultant. Although he felt insecure about the situation because he had not been able to live up to earlier promises and expectations, he found, that the staff was accepting and helpful. In theory, the role of the consultation is to help the school to create open and positive norms. However, he found the school personnel helping him to accept the realities enabling him to work openly with his own guilt feelings.

The consultant also experienced a school staff highly committed to the process, a staff that had become united possibly due to the trustworthy headmaster. They had created ownership in the process and the chances to build something new and better were already there. The GIL-data confirmed very clearly what many of the problems were. This had a clarifying effect on the staff on these issues, but the situation opened the way for exploration of problems only indirectly related to the data. Problems such as pupil-discipline had been avoided by the staff prior to the IDP. Discussions of this kind usually took place in the corridors and around the dinner tables, but these were not confronted openly and constructively in formal meetings. The data gave the staff an excuse to take these problems into an open forum, and it became clear that most teachers had problems with factors such as discipline. In fact, it was clear that the discipline issue had become more severe over the past two or three years. The relationships between students also were found to be problematic. There were small sub-groups in the schools, usually related to factions in the community, which were causing violence in the schools.

During discussions, teachers opened up and talked more freely about their concerns and how they dealt with discipline problems. Teachers then saw that they probably had different views about what students are and how to deal with them. Basic discussions about human values and approaches to upbringing led to the identification of another serious problem with the staff: a lack of common understanding and approaches to the educational tasks. Since teachers were dealing with particular students who have the same kinds of problems in quite different ways, the result was that students used such opportunities to polarize the staff.

The consultant had been relatively passive during the diagnosis phase of the process. Although he felt that the open discussion had helped a number of teachers, it had also given the teachers a feeling of togetherness that might only polarize the situation between staff and students even further. In this particular school, there was no GIL-data from the students themselves, nor from the community. The danger in the process at this stage was that the analysis would build on one-sided data and exclude student- and community-inputs necessary for problem-solving. The consultant felt a need to question some of the assumptions in the analysis: should all 'problem-students' be dealt with in the same way? What would be the effect of a 'united teacher front' on an already hostile community? What did the students and the community actually need? Could discipline be looked at in the light of a symptom of more serious problems?

The analysis of the situation turned to more basic problems of the school and the community. The relationship between the school and many of the homes was bad. There were communication problems and it was difficult to talk to the parents about the school. Many parents also felt that the 'teacher culture' was alien to them, and they were insecure about working with the school.

The staff soon realized that these basic problems could not be solved without the involvement of the community itself. The barriers that had been established between the school and the community had to be confronted. The teachers realized that this could not be a one-way process but a mutual-adaptation process by the school and the community.

The process, as the teachers experienced it at this stage, might have illustrated a more common problem in the change process: the consequences of negative history. How could a process of renewal be initiated that would overcome the feelings on both sides? Who would initiate the process and who should be involved? The discussions revealed basic uncertainties and also a lack of knowledge about what the 'community' really is. A much more complete and varied picture of the situation resulted from the discussion. Another aspect of the process can be given as an illustration: identification of the problems led to immediate problem-solving. The headmaster already knew some parents who, for some time, had asked if they could assist in some leisure-time activities. School-sponsored afternoon activities managed by willing parents and children, formed the basis of one strategy.

Another strategy that the school has been actively pursuing is that of alternative programmes involving students in practical socially responsible tasks in the community, activities that would include a systematic learning component. The community has a rich cultural heritage, including the traditions of the ethnic minority group. Several community projects have been planned that involve the students and the teachers in the community, using parents and other resource persons in the community as partners in the learning process.

The consultant did not participate in the meetings that led to the proposals mentioned above. In a 'consultation-meeting' with the staff, another problem was identified: namely, one of motivation and initiation. It was felt that even well-designed 'teacher proposals' would not be accepted easily by the students and the community and that the programmes would only be successful if shared ownership was developed. The need to involve students more directly in problem-solving and decision-making became a priority. As the first step, the teachers felt that constructive discussions, role-plays, and simulations where the students had full freedom to express their opinions, would be necessary, and that 'programme-proposals' would have to be the result of such a process, rather than the beginning. In other words, the process of self-assessment and renewal would have to be a part of the whole school culture involving the community if it should succeed.

Our case illustrates a school where the process has had fundamental consequences for the school. The IDP-process itself has many weaknesses, including the lack of available consultants. We have learned that the programme should not start in any school district without clear contracts with the districts and consultants that guarantee the school sufficient help.

The process has had consequences for the relationship between the school and the community, for the role of the teachers, and for the more fundamental, pedagogical situation. It may, in the long run, have some positive effects on staff stability as well.

The process illustrates the importance of data that allows difficult issues to be raised in a non-threatening way. Such a dialogue uncovers real issues and helps the staff to grow and mature. More important than the data is the concrete meaning the staff gives the data during the process, a meaning which often helps the school to define action.

This school was overwhelmingly in favour of the IDP and was not hindered by any factions in the staff; they all felt strongly that a new process was needed, and hoped for assistance through the IDP. They were often disappointed because they could not get help when they needed it. Although this produced some negative feelings, it also mobilized energies to 'work it out themselves'. With the help of a trustworthy headmaster, the staff developed confidence and ownership.

CASE 3: THE STATIC SCHOOL IN AN INNOVATIVE SCHOOL DISTRICT

This is an elementary school consisting of 450 pupils and 35 teachers, situated in a densely populated area. It asked to join the programme. The initiative came from a group of teachers, with some urging from the school administration. They argued that the project might improve cooperation among the staff, and it might help to renew educational practice and organizational structures in the school.

There were conflicts among groups of teachers in the school. One group wished to initiate some unconventional practices, but they felt that their suggestions were met with scepticism and negative attitudes both from other teachers and from the headmaster.

Some teachers were critical of the leadership in the school and felt that the lack of innovation was the responsibility of the leadership. The headmaster, on the other hand, has said several times that any teacher was free to innovate and that the teachers had as much responsibility as the headmaster. In spite of this progressive orientation, the leadership team also agreed that there was a lack of educational renewal, but they felt that this was the responsibility of the teachers.

In the teachers' council, such attitudes seldom surfaced. Rather, comments were made more informally among the teachers themselves. The problems of initiative and responsibility, increasingly, had become a concern, particularly because other schools in the neighbourhood had become known for their initiatives and successful innovations.

There was common agreement in the school, at the time the IDP was introduced, that the school ought somehow to be involved in educational renewal. So far, the teachers had worked more or less in isolation with their own projects in their own classrooms, and an effort at cooperation involving several teachers and the leadership had never been realized. Many teachers felt a need for a common, innovative programme.

Staff opinions about the type and extent of appropriate innovative efforts varied considerably. Some teachers felt a need for drastic changes; others felt that some smaller efforts within optional subjects might be a good start; others were quite satisfied with the non-threatening situation that existed. Therefore, the motivation to join the IDP varied, but all decided to support the IDP for different reasons. Some wanted to use the process to criticize the headmaster, others wanted to bring about fundamental change, and others thought they could use the process to demonstrate that they didn't need to change at all.

The IDP consultant had a meeting with the school leadership where the IDP process was explained. He outlined how participation in the project could influence decision-making. A three-hour meeting was organized with the whole staff. Following the meeting, a written vote was taken about participation in the project. The questions raised were the following: (1) Do you want the school to be involved in the IDP? (yes, no), and (2) If you feel that the school should *not* be involved, do you prefer to be an observer only, if the majority is in favour? About half a dozen teachers felt that the school should not be involved, but no one wanted to be only an observer when it became evident that a majority was for the project. The themes taken up at the orientation meeting were general in nature. The variations in motivation described above did not surface during the meeting. Comments of a more informal nature, however, revealed that some conflicts existed.

The GIL instrument was filled out by the staff in an afternoon meeting at a later date. It was processed by IMTEC and returned within three weeks. The reactions following the administration of the GIL were generally positive, indicating that the items were relevant or valid for their school. Some items, however, were considered too general and ambiguous.

In the early feedback discussions, the staff was mainly interested in the frequency scores. They were amazed to find that the staff look so differently at reality (the REAL) and what they wanted (IDEAL). The leadership, to begin with , expressed satisfaction with the aggregated scores from the 20 schools in comparison with their own school. After all, the problems identified in the school did not seem any more serious than usual. Several other schools had similar problems, and there did not appear to be any need to think the data represented serious problems.

The data-feedback meeting was three hours long. No attempts were made to discuss the meaning of the data. Two weeks later a second meeting was held, lasting six hours, where the data was given to the staff members and they were asked to prepare themselves for issues that they felt were of particular interest, and to try to associate the data with 'real-life' situations in the school. The staff was encouraged to study and to look for trends in the data. Also, they were asked to look for hypotheses that might be supported by data as well as contradictions in the data.

The staff experienced real learning through the study of the data itself. Most of the teachers felt that they were able to 'put the pieces together', to see some real meaning that was important to them. The consultant felt that he ought to give some help in data-analysis without making any form of interpretation. His technique was to mark some 15 out of 65 questions as particularly interesting for the school, but without any further comments. He suggested also that several other questions might be of particular interest and that each staff member in the reviewing time should try to identify his or her underlying assumptions about the school.

Several important dimensions are worth reporting from the dialogue phase. In general, the staff tried to link special incidents and practical examples to the data. Many teachers expressed satisfaction with the items since they tended to lead to central issues quickly. The dialogue was generally felt to be very rewarding.

Although one might have expected that the staff would be quite 'uptight' about confrontations that could have become difficult, the situation did not invite that kind of development. Instead of reactions like: 'This is difficult, dare I say something about this openly?', the issue was rather: 'What does the data mean in practice? Why, for example, do we see such a wide spread in the answers to this particular item' or 'Why do we see the situation so differently?' A situation like this seems to have two major advantages:

1. dominant persons, or persons in leadership positions, cannot, from the outset, define 'appropriate reactions' with statements like: 'In our school, as we all know, we work well together, but obviously it can be improved, right?' With this as a starting point, it becomes difficult to say that cooperation is difficult! With the GIL data on the table, however, the 'provocation' is already there – but not personalized. The discussion can then concentrate on the issues involved and not on the provocation or 'provocative' person;
2. considerable time is gained because it is possible to focus on priority issues right away since
   a. the data-review makes it simple;
   b. it is clear what views are represented.

The data was discussed in several working groups during the full-day dialogue. Several groups had chosen the same issues and it was not difficult to find common themes for the rest of the day. At the end of the day, a steering committee was elected, consisting of one person from the administration, the chairmen of the teachers' council, three teachers, and the consultant who would facilitate further developments. Specific issues for further discussion were identified for the group to deal with.

We might illustrate some other dimensions of the dialogue phase that developed in this school. For some, certain issues were difficult to face since they had not been confronted earlier. This, in fact, was perhaps the most positive experience for all since, with the help of the consultant, it was possible to discuss these issues without 'scapegoating'. Sometimes it was necessary to analyse certain incidents, but only to illustrate how given solutions did not function and to seek new and better strategies for the future. The discussion was constructive, aiming at improvements for the school rather than historical and personal judgements.

At a given stage, certain key issues were identified for further review and work. It was necessary to agree on norms for the discussion at this point. That is, it was important to legalize behaviour like openness, creativeness, and constructive criticism. At the same time, it was felt necessary to create 'shelter conditions' for the staff. For example, they agreed on norms for confidentiality. For some staff members, the norm-discussion was vital for their involvement in the process. They 'opened up' when they felt that this behaviour was welcomed, something not fully realized before a discussion of norms had been carried out.

The staff identified areas in which there was considerable agreement, such as:

a. too little time is spent on teacher cooperation;
b. there are a number of overlapping jobs;
c. teachers need in-service training in alternatives to traditional classroom teaching if they involve themselves in projects of this kind;
d. teachers are free to propose changes, but they have little influence on decision-making;
e. teachers use so much time in their school work that only a few would volunteer to use more time.

The staff also identified areas where there were considerable disagreements:

a. teachers look very differently at their own work situation in terms of job-satisfaction and job-security;
b. teachers disagree in terms of their understanding of appropriate behaviour in the school, in particular, in relation to norms like 'taking initiative', and 'being open';
c. teachers disagree about the usefulness and desirability of new teaching methods.

The IDP process created high expectations in the school. The staff hoped for a better school for the students as well as for the staff; a renewed trust and motivation in the future was evidenced. However, this created also a feeling of dissatisfaction with the *status quo*. Some routine procedures, that they had not even thought about earlier, were more difficult to live with. The level of aspiration and involvement had increased markedly. After some weeks, it was quite obvious that some teachers had begun to be impatient with what they considered to be slowness in developing new practices. All of this illustrates the responsibilities a school takes on itself in starting the IDP process. The school must have the capabilities to follow through; otherwise, the process may be detrimental.

The school has worked continuously with the priority tasks, and the process has been developed mainly due to two factors:

1. the administration has acted promptly, called the necessary meetings, and tried to facilitate the proposed changes;
2. the teachers have been motivated all along. In periods when the planning committee has been active, the teachers have been playing a low-key role. In periods when teachers have been dissatisfied with the work, or disagreed on certain decisions, they have gone 'back to the data', and renewed the dialogue.

Some teachers, who were previously hard-pressed and faced particularly difficult teaching tasks, have now received help from their colleagues. Many teachers feel that their work situation has improved, and the result of the programme has been real improvement of what they experienced as a difficult situation. The programme did not produce unresolved problems, nor did it open up difficult issues unnecessarily. It did, however, deal with problems that existed, that did hurt, but that no one had had the courage to confront. The staff learned that the process was helpful. The school situation improved, but the teachers also learned that it needs ongoing treatment. The staff has worked systematically to improve communication and has invested in 'laboratory training' as well as in more pedagogical seminars with topics such as alternative teaching-learning methods.

The school is now in the process of creating new administrative structures that will enable teachers, who would like to work together, to do so, while individuals, who prefer to work in more isolated environments, have the freedom to do so. However, the staff realize that there are limits to how differently they can operate, particularly in teacher-student relationships. Although teaching contrasts may not be more different from the traditions of two separate schools, the differences are now appearing the same day within the same building with the same students. The teachers are now working together so that these differences do not work negatively on the students. A series of IDP activities (called the classroom programme) is being implemented

– including exercises for students and teachers clarifying norms and values, improving problem-solving and communication, and the beginning of supervisory work.

Usually, the consultants have worked in the school simultaneously. They have always been available when the school has asked for assistance. In some cases, only one consultant has been working on a particular problem. In no way do the consultants feel that the school has become dependent on their help.

The school has several options for the future. Among these is another self-renewal phase. The school is interested in a renewed survey-feedback process concentrating on those profiles that were of most interest to the school. In addition it is necessary to develop items tailor-made to the concerns of the school, including more work at the classroom level.

CASE 4: THE WELL-ESTABLISHED SCHOOL

This is an elementary school with three classes at each grade level (450 students), 30 teachers, five of which are half-time. The building is fifty years old and is located in the centre of a small town . There is little mobility in the community; many parents have, themselves, been students in the school. Most parents are representative middle-class, white-collar workers while some are industrial workers.

The school building is kept up very well with few structural changes; it is still a typical, self-contained classroom school. Most teachers have worked together in the school for a number of years, although in recent years some teachers are beginning to reach retirement age. At the moment, there is a wide age-range in the staff. The headmaster is 60 years old. He was a teacher in the school for 15 years before he moved up six years ago. He is well known and respected in the community, participates actively in public debates, and is known to be in favour of a process of renewal that is solidly prepared and carefully implemented. The school is known to send well-educated students to the nearby secondary school.

The headmaster asked for the IDP, claiming that the teachers had asked him to get in touch with the school district's IDP consultant. Some younger teachers had participated in an inservice course in group dynamics, had been told about the IDP, and had suggested in the teachers' council the possibility of using the IDP as a starting point for renewal.

The consultant first presented the programme for the headmaster, the deputy, and the teachers' council chairperson. Later, during an evening meeting, the programme was presented to the whole staff. In the beginning, only younger teachers were active in the discussion, but slowly the older teachers also got involved. Most of the questions raised in that meeting dealt with the objectives and assumptions of the IDP, the validity of the instrument, the kinds of problems schools usually faced, and practical questions regarding the use of time.

The discussion revealed a generally positive attitude towards the IDP. Several persons made it clear that they felt the school was functioning very well, that cooperation in the staff was excellent, but that it might be of interest to initiate some small-scale, innovative work. No one disagreed when a couple of younger teachers suggested that the professional climate in the school had stagnated.

There were some concerns about confidentiality of the survey data. The headmaster felt that this was no problem. After all, since the data was to be returned to the staff, the headmaster pointed out that he felt that no one should be afraid of stating his opinions openly. In a later meeting, 75 per cent of the staff voted for the IDP, no one voted against, and 25 per cent abstained. It was decided to use the planning time already scheduled for the work.

All staff completed the questionnaire in a session administered by the consultant. The consultant reports that there was 'a quiet examination-like climate' when the survey was completed. Few questions were raised concerning the items.

Shortly afterwards, following data-processing by IMTEC, the data was fed back in a two-hour evening session. The dialogue meeting (a full-day meeting) had already been planned for a week later. During this day, there were activities everywhere, in plenary sessions and in a number of small groups. It was clear that the data uncovered a number of problems that were surprising to several school members. In particular, several teachers were astonished by the wide range of frequency scores on certain items.

In a plenary session at the end of the day, the following issues for further work were listed:

1. Further discussions of educational goals and underlying values must be held;
2. Decision-making must somehow be shared and made more efficient;

3. New teaching-learning methods, in particular, interdisciplinary project work and cooperation with colleagues within and across subjects, must be introduced;
4. Cooperation between school and home must be developed.

We shall now present some profile items to illustrate what the data revealed with regard to the issues listed above. We shall begin with the profile on educational goals.

Figure 23

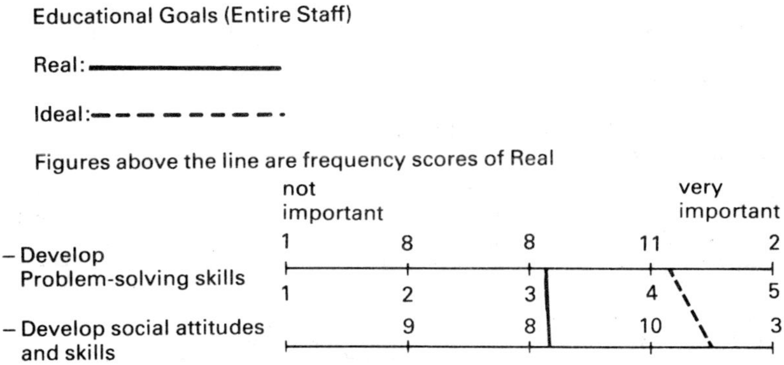

In plenary sessions as well as in smaller groups, difficult confrontations between different views were experienced. Some younger teachers felt that most teachers in the school did not give any priority to social attitudes and skills and were only concerned with subject-matter skills. The more experienced teachers stressed the view that the objectives of the school were, primarily, a question of transmitting basic knowledge and skills. Towards the end of a somewhat heated debate, a growing understanding of the positions of both sides began to develop – an understanding of the importance of both positions – and also a feeling that different goals do not necessarily contradict each other.

A second area of difficulty centred on the decision-making process at the school. This issue was initially considered in an elected planning group consisting of two teachers, the headmaster, and the consultant. The headmaster expressed surprise that some staff members felt that they were not involved, and pointed out that the same tendencies were apparent in the 'Leadership Profile.' He could not understand that he was viewed as an arrogant leader by some teachers (three staff members indicated on the items of this profile that he was *always* arrogant). The teachers in the planning group agreed that this was an accurate view of the headmaster, and they all agreed that it was healthy that the way teachers felt about the headmaster could be discussed openly. Some profiles are included below to illustrate the main issues that were considered.

Figure 24

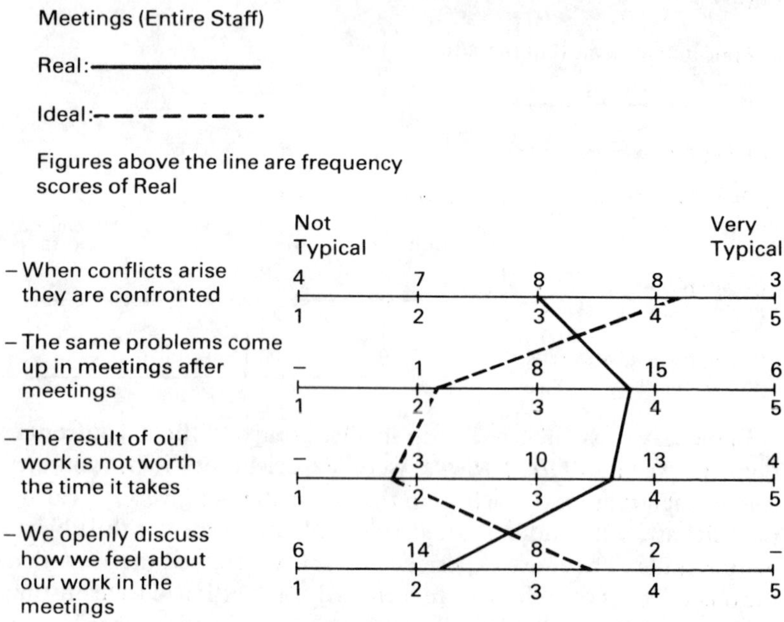

Figures 24 and 25 indicate a wide diversity of opinion about the way conflicts are handled, the productivity of meetings, the openness of discussions, and the manner in which problems are confronted and resolved. There was clear consensus that the situation was far from being ideal.

Figure 24 shows a wide divergence of opinion among staff members with regard to the value of innovations. Some indicated that traditional practice is as good as new methods, while others felt new methods were far superior. Some questioned getting involved in

Figure 25

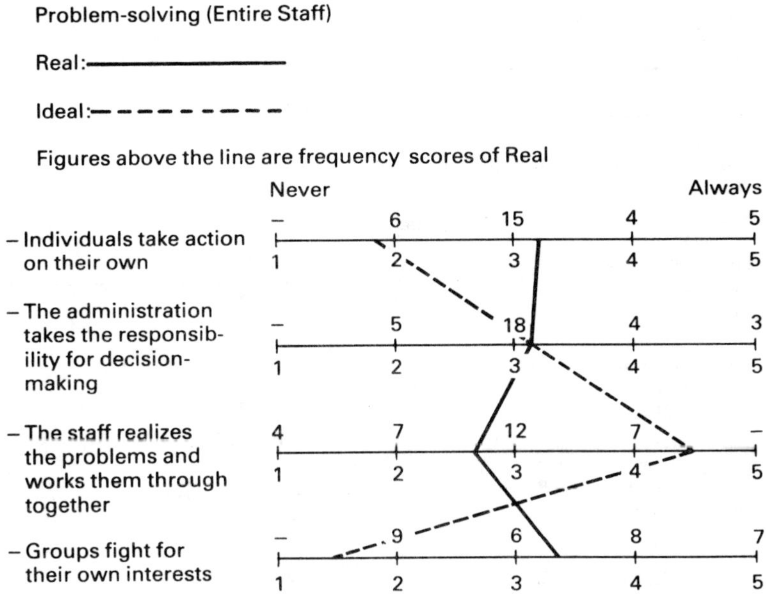

reform, because it only added to an already heavy burden of professional activities, while others disagreed with this attitude. Some were quite convinced that the school was doing so well that innovations were not necessary. Others indicated a necessity to revise the school programme. Significantly, the positions taken on the existing situation were quite similar to the positions taken for the ideal, hinting that the differences of perspective were probably based on fundamentally different philosophical- or value-opinions of staff members.

A full day was set aside to discuss the issues, and the staff experienced another active day in both plenary and group sessions. The task was to uncover what the data really meant. They concluded that the data reflected, in part, a conflict between 'younger' and 'older' staff members. The staff also realized that they lived in a school that was mainly consensus and compromise-oriented. The headmaster was seen as the great master at creating a feeling of harmony in spite of growing conflicts.

Two very different viewpoints developed during the day. Two active groups of teachers, each with four members, advocated quite

Figure 26

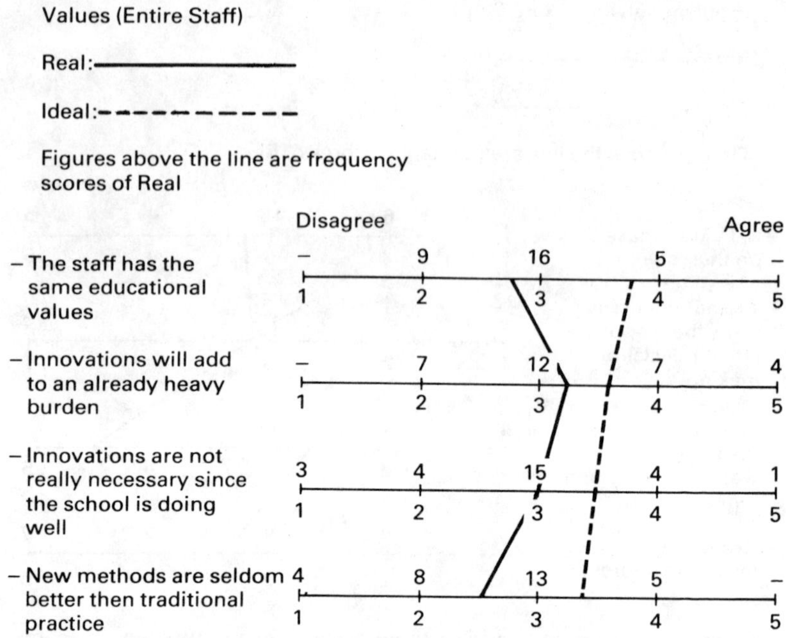

different positions, the first arguing that the harmony model was both necessary and good for the school, the other that the situation had to change and that the staff needed to learn to face conflicts more openly and use them constructively for developments.

The headmaster intervened several times, reminding the staff that, after all, he was the educational and administrative leader who had to make the final decisions. The climate in the meeting turned towards harder confrontations. Some episodes illustrating the dominance of the 'older' teachers were taken up. Several younger teachers claimed that the time-table was decided by the older people on the staff, and they claimed that resources in the school were not being equitably allocated. They demanded that a process be instituted that did not discriminate against them. The lunch break with sandwiches and coffee seemed to ease the tension somewhat! Everybody seemed to enjoy the informal conversations around the coffee tables.

Following lunch, the consultant suggested that smaller groups continue the discussion by taking up the concrete incidents and analysing what they meant in terms of decision-making. The day ended with concrete proposals for changes in the decision-making process, including a process for resource allocation, the development of the timetable, and the use of special rooms. For each proposal, a solid investigation of needs was built in. All proposals were accepted by the staff, including the headmaster.

The school had also identified problems in the way their meetings were organized and conducted. Another half day was allocated to this discussion. The day started with a discussion about the purpose of IDP, initiated by one of the 'older' teachers. He felt that so far the programme had created only disturbances and that the staff time, for example, the day they had in front of them, could be used more for subject-oriented discussions. This was met immediately by counter-arguments that the work was actually proceeding well and should be continued.

At this stage the consultant had developed a picture of the various groups within the faculty in relationship to the critical issue of educational renewal. These consisted of:

a. a small active group dissatisfied by what they saw as a stagnated school;
b. a small active '*status quo*' group, quite satisfied with the school, and appreciating its stability;
c. a large group of relatively passive staff members who would participate in discussions but would withdraw when actual demands were made on their time;
d. the administration, which was primarily interested in maintaining its control and 'law and order'.

The planning group had already listed several proposals for the renewal of staff meetings. The discussions dealt mainly with the content of meetings. Many teachers felt that the usual staff meetings took up routine questions only and seldom engaged the staff in more important discussions of principles. Towards the end of the discussion, another heated debate about the usefulness of on-going discussion was initiated.

The movement to renew the practices of the school is meeting considerable resistance from several staff members, and the school seems to be 'slipping back' to a social harmony model.

It is clear that the school needs an on-going input from an outside consultant to continue the process. Some fundamental problems are raised, however. The IDP process does *not* necessarily assume that changes are good; in fact, maintenance of the *status quo* might well be preferred. In this school, however, some staff members are seeing the IDP process as serving their interests for fundamental changes in the school and the consultant may be responsible (indirectly) for internal developments that would not have taken place without the programme, and that might be in conflict with a majority norm. The consultant needs to understand carefully the necessary balance and limits of the programme. Since the classroom programme provides a number of options for individuals and groups of teachers, one solution might be to initiate different kinds of developments with different groups, and at the same time encourage learning across groups.

CASE 5: THE TRADITIONAL SCHOOL

A small elementary school near a medium-sized city decided to join the IDP. For some time, the school had worked with the consultants from a nearby teachers' centre. The knowledge and trust already established between the consultants, who were from the teachers' centre, and the staff, in particular the new headmaster, proved to be important in their decision to join.

Many of the teachers as well as the consultants looked upon the school as being rather traditional. Also, many people were frustrated due to the lack of coherence and cooperation in carrying out educational tasks. In spite of the fact that there were a few attempts to 'bring the school together', teachers felt isolated and alone.

In this situation, a new headmaster had been appointed; that move provided the final and important motivation for joining the programme. The teachers looked up to him as an able and dynamic leader, a person who represented teacher interests. When he proposed joining the IDP, the staff agreed unanimously.

The survey feedback and subsequent discussions revealed a number of conflicts in the school. Some of these are illustrated in figures 25, 26, and 27.

In Figure 27, we see a relatively high degree of consensus with regard to the level of common values among the staff of the school. They also almost unanimously indicate a need for much greater degree of common values. There is wide divergence of opinion as to the commonality of staff and community priorities in educational values.

Figure 27

Values (Entire Staff)

Real: ————————

Ideal: - - - - - - - - -

Figure above the line are frequency scores of Real

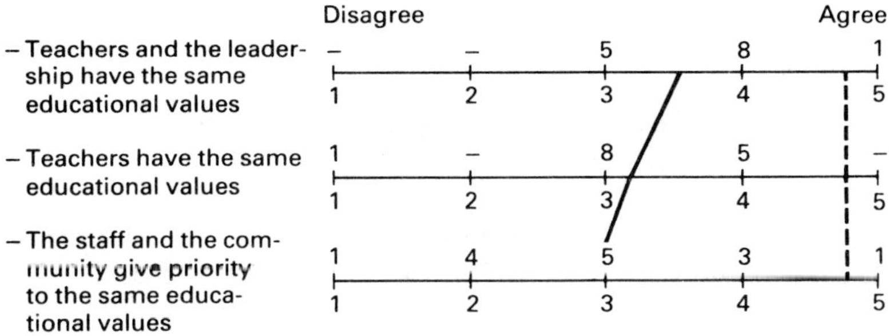

Figure 28

Educational Goals (Entire Staff)

Real: ————————

Ideal: - - - - - - - - - -

Figures above the line are frequency scores of Real

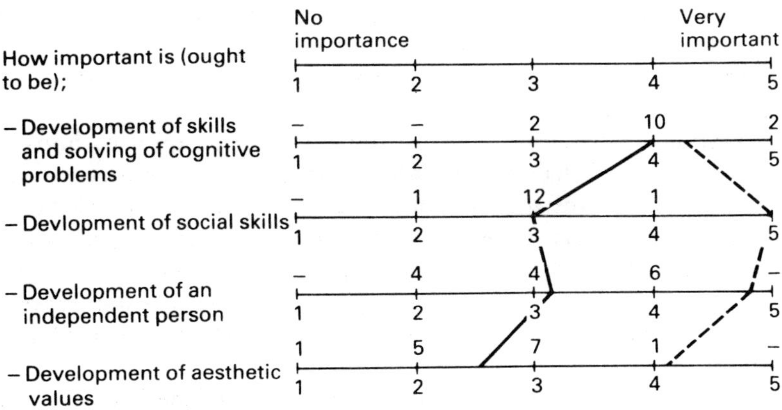

This consensus is also revealed with regard to the existence of educational goals. Curiously, almost everyone feels that many of the goals are not stressed enough, especially in the social, aesthetic sphere.

Figure 29

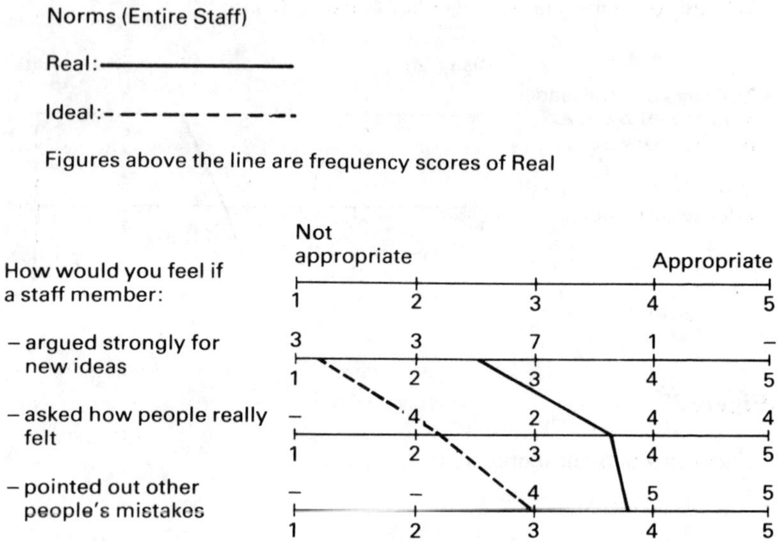

In Figure 29 we find some divergence of opinion with regard to certain norms of the school. Many people do not feel it is appropriate to ask people how they feel, or point out other people's mistakes. There was some feeling that it would be better if more openness existed.

During the feedback sessions, the headmaster expressed impatience and wanted changes as soon as possible. The staff, however, convinced him that the process would take time. The data revealed that there were conflicts at a personal level, but their main suggestion was that different value-systems had developed in various sub-groups over a long period of time. As the discussions proceeded, the staff experienced positive 'process-results' which further reinforced their willingness to spend considerable time.

The school is now in the middle of the process and the final outcome cannot be predicted. The staff, however, has given priorities to four areas of work, based on the following data:

1. To strive for more openness and support to individual teachers;
2. To develop a coherent educational profile for the school that all teachers can support;
3. To integrate new teachers;
4. To influence the teaching-learning process at the lower secondary level to reflect the norms established in the elementary school.

These are fundamental tasks for this school. The discussions of the staff members go deeply into values, instructional goals, communication, and problem-solving, and they raise fundamental questions of up-bringing and human relations.

The consultants observed several preliminary results in the second year. The IDP process has changed the atmosphere of the school; there is greater openness in the staff. Problems are taken up and confronted, there is more inter-group communication, and problems are solved more constructively. Also, it seems that there is less dominance by a few individuals and more shared decision-making.

Activities at the classroom level, like new forms of supervision, improved teacher-student communication, while clarification of instructional norms were initiated by several teachers. At the same time, on-going and more open staff discussions will hopefully develop a more coherent educational practice in the school.

The school is an example of a traditional school where a given practice has continued for years without fundamental analysis and renewal. Increasingly, pressure for change built up within the staff, and the IDP, along with a new headmaster, were the key factors necessary to get a renewal process started.

Lastly, a word concerning IDP in Britain. The National Foundation for Educational Research, in the UK, is currently testing out the GIL instrument in a number of schools, one of which is Thornbridge School in Sheffield. Because major differences exist between the British and Norwegian school systems, and the IDP approach has therefore been modified, it was felt most appropriate to include the Thornbridge School case study separately, as Appendix B. It is worth noting that the British programme seems likely to be launched without the help of external consultants.

CHAPTER SIX

Institutional Development Programme: Lessons Learnt

Initially the IDP was conceived in 1974. During 1975—76, 18 teacher-training colleges from the USA, Canada, the UK, Belgium, and Norway participated in the first pilot project. The results were brought together in several reports and presented at the IMTEC International Seminar for Teacher Training Institutions in 1976, whose theme was 'Training for Educational Change'.* Based on the experiences voiced at the pilot project, a 'new generation' of the IDP was institutionalized in 1977. At that time the programme itself underwent considerable changes in the following areas:

1. *Conceptualization*: Based on the organizational model developed in 1974 by Dalin (reported in 1978), a number of discussions took place to refine the GIL instrument. The refinements were based on a series of statistical analyses, such as factor analysis and reliability tests. The items on the original instrument were cut by about 30 per cent. In addition, a refined conceptual framework produced better categories. The end result was a shorter and clearer questionnaire.
2. *Adaptations to Elementary and Secondary Schools*: By 1976, it was clear that a number of elementary and secondary schools, particularly in Norway, were interested in the project. In cooperation with some major Norwegian school districts, especially in the city of Trondheim, the instrument was adapted to the Norwegian school situation.

---

*The proceedings will be sent from IMTEC on request.

3. *Process Clarification*: The original project was heavily oriented toward survey-feedback, did not stress sufficiently the change process itself, and lacked materials and resources for follow-through activities. In 1976, IMTEC developed a manual for the whole process, including stages from entry to institutionalization of renewal aims (see Chapter Four). A programme for consultancy training was started, and an attempt was made to clarify the contract conditions for the school districts involved in the project.
4. *Renewal of the Teacher Training Version of the GIL*: In 1978, the Canada Council gave a grant for further development of the IDP process in Canadian teacher training institutions. Currently, some twelve universities and colleges became involved in that programme, which has enabled researchers from the Ontario Institute for Studies in Education (OISE) in Toronto and Simon Frazer University, which lead this development project, to streamline further the questionnaire and refine the process.

Over the last 3—4 years the project has expanded in several directions. The most important developments are the following:

1. *Consultant training*: It became clear that the project was dependent on high quality OD consultants. In Norway – where the project had its main base – some 120 persons have been trained through a combination of intensive courses, practice under supervision, and a reading programme and 100 persons are undergoing a two-year consultant training programme. Most consultants have been recruited from teacher centres, R and D centres and teacher-training colleges. The training programme has extended over a two-year timespan for most of the consultants.
2. *Developments in different kinds of schools*: The primary and secondary versions have been tested in some 100 schools. The college version has also been tested in nurse-training colleges in addition to teacher-training colleges.
3. *Development of materials*: IMTEC, in cooperation with consultants and a large number of teachers, has developed materials in areas like communication, problem-solving, conflict resolution, goal-setting and value-clarification, supervision, leadership, and related areas. The materials can easily be adapted to an on-going programme in any school.
4. *Development of an international English version of the GIL instrument*: This project has been developed in cooperation with

NFER working with British schools. During 1986/87 a development project involving up to 100 Dutch schools is being initiated.

Our data-base for this chapter is composed of the profiles of the Norwegian primary and secondary schools, interviews with consultants, headmasters, and teachers involved in the process, and a questionnaire administered to the seventeen consultants who were working on the Norwegian project at the time this book was written. Since the IDP is not a completed but rather a continuously changing programme, we cannot discuss 'final outcomes'. We do believe, however, that the experiences and learnings to date are of interest to people involved in organization development in schools, and, consequently, that our information should be shared at this stage.

Nevertheless, we feel that some caution is necessary before we discuss our data. First, we have not conducted an independent evaluation of the project. This has not been possible, mainly because of economic constraints, but also due to the client-resistance we reported earlier. Also, the project is undergoing continuous change and renewal and only a process-oriented evaluation approach, where the researchers could follow the work in the institutions and in IMTEC, would help us to learn more about the IDP. This is, however, what the staff and the consultants have tried to do without external evaluation assistance. Our data, therefore, are biased towards the views of the consultants and IMTEC, who have personal interests in the project. To check the information from consultants, however, we have asked headmasters, teachers, and superintendents involved in the project to report independently their views about key concepts and problems. Therefore we do feel that we have a balance of views which we present in this chapter. On the other hand, it is quite clear that our findings are preliminary and that they will be modified over time as other aspects of the programme come into focus. We have chosen to use direct quotations from individual reports and will try to report a true representative sample of reactions.

We are concerned also that our data might be misused. It is very difficult, we believe, to generalize and transfer lessons learnt and work styles from one project of this kind to other projects of a similar kind in other cultures. We have a 'phenomenological' attitude to the understanding of organizations. We believe that the change process can only be understood fully in its context, i.e. in relationship to the characteristics of the setting itself, the individuals involved in the process, and the political-economic and educational conditions under which institutions operate. Let us assume, for example, that we find that one particular work approach is dominant in the Norwegian setting. This cannot be interpreted to mean that this particular approach is generally more important or relevant than other methods. It is only in the context we have studied that a given approach might be relevant. Only a diagnostic disposition towards organization development will, in our view, help us to develop a theory of organization development in schools and to avoid superficial generalizations.

Getting Started

We have tried to identify the motivation of school districts, the headmasters, the staff, and others in joining the IDP. The first general insight we have gained is that, regardless of national setting, an extensive preparatory period is usually necessary. We had expected that organization development was so familiar in some areas of the world, such as Canada, that the task of introducing a programme such as the IDP would be less complex than in areas such as Scandinavia where research and development efforts or politically mandated change are more common than organization development. Our experience has been that only school personnel at the highest levels are familiar with the literature. The task of educating the professional educators in the basic principles of institution-change programmes must be a part of any initiation effort.

A project of this kind, therefore, requires time to orient participants and 'unfreeze' them so that they are receptive to the proposal for change (Bennis, Benne, and Chin, 1961). We have found that it is highly unlikely that school personnel buy into any process unless they have felt a need for change in the first place. Such a conclusion is consistent with the findings elsewhere (Rogers and Shoemacher, 1971; Berman and McLaughlin, 1975; and Howes and Quinn, 1978). Even though people have a need to change, a further step is necessary for them to become receptive to a specific programme. We have found that two factors seem to have been important in motivating people to join the IDP. They are as follows:

1. *Personal Trust*: Most innovations, in our view, 'travel through people and not on paper'. In education, as in other fields, there

are several networks of people who maintain trusting relationships and who will take risks on new practices if these are recommended by trusted members of their network. This is also true for the way the IDP was introduced. On the one hand, individuals who themselves were educational leaders in their communities, had developed a trusting relationship with people central to IMTEC and the IDP. These individuals, on the other hand, maintained a basic trust in the school district sufficiently to 'introduce and convince the superintendent, the headmaster, or the staff that the programme could be useful'.

2. *Ownership and Involvement*: The IDP has been based on the principle that actors in the school should be involved themselves as much as possible in formulating the project, developing its components, and taking responsibility for its implementation and evaluation. We believe that some of the differences in the outcomes of the IDP are partly due to the relative degree of ownership that the various school districts have felt in the programme.

In one Norwegian city the teachers' centre (*pedagogisk senter*) director had known and worked with IMTEC personnel for several years. The superintendent describes the process of gaining credibility for the IDP, at the district level, in the following manner:

> The leader of the teachers' centre believed in the project. He is well known and respected in the school district, and he convinced the school administration that the school would benefit from the project.

In another community, the deputy superintendent had worked closely with IMTEC on a project resembling the I/D/E/A League of Cooperating Schools. This project had proved fruitful and he was aware that the 'community had a tradition in educational development and we wanted to join something that looked promising.' After investigating the possibilities of the IDP, he reported, 'since I expressed a commitment to the project, the school board followed.'

All levels of the educational hierarchy must support the project if it is to be successful. This includes central-office personnel and school boards at the district level. On the one hand, those at this hierarchical level may play a passive supporting role, allowing others actually to carry out the project; on the other hand, they may play an active and direct part in the process. For example, a deputy superintendent became the major force for the IDP in one district. He reported:

> Our community wants to develop better educational programmes. As a deputy superintendent, I felt that this project (the IDP) could be used, in particular in schools where I know teachers are restless and like to find better solutions, but do not know how to go about it.

Even when support is passive, it must be perceived by school personnel as being firm and clear (Beckerman, 1973, and Louis, 1977).

It is imperative that headmasters of individual schools find it in their own interest to support the IDP. Engeland (1979) found three major motives for headmasters to encourage participation in the IDP project. First, they were interested in innovations in schools in general. Second, they were interested in developing a good climate in their school. Third, they were interested in getting a picture of how the staff perceived their school. In one major city, IMTEC was asked to present the project for the headmasters in two day-long meetings. The headmasters themselves filled out the GIL questionnaire and became interested in a 'comprehensive approach to educational development that looks promising.' No doubt, some heads became afraid of the project, since they felt that their role might become more difficult. In the community just mentioned, it is likely that those schools which had the most secure headmasters were the ones which eventually elected to join the programme. One of the headmasters commented:

> I knew that I would be somewhat threatened by the process, but, on the other hand, the GIL instrument seemed to cope with a number of questions within my school on which I believed that we had started to work. So far we had no method of trying to cope with the complexities of the school as an organization. I believed that the process could help us to go through something that we had already started.

We have also found that expressed headmaster support was necessary before teachers in most schools would accept and support the project. Sound management theory would also support such an observation (Rothman, Erlich and Teresa, 1976).

Teachers must also find the IDP of value if it is to succeed. In fact, IMTEC stipulates, as a condition for participation, that a large majority of the staff support the project. In a few cases, the teachers themselves have initiated discussion about participation without the prior support of the headmaster. In most cases, however, it was the headmaster or the chairman of the faculty who asked the representatives of the superintendent in the school district to present the project for the school.

Some comments from consultants about teacher motivations are instructive:

> In particular, the school was motivated because a group of teachers wanted to get something started. Several new teachers had been hired for the new school year, and they were uncertain about their future. There was a limited degree of openness between the teachers and the leadership of the school but there was some tendency on the part of the headmaster to manipulate information. The need to develop a more healthy school and better communication and cooperation were central to the school's interest in joining the programme.

> Thinking in the IDP was in harmony with the development of the school district itself; in particular, this was true of the work on innovations in education that the district had developed. The teachers felt that they could join the programme on an equal basis with the headmaster of the school.

> The school is new, and the staff is very interested in educational developments. The teachers felt that the IDP would be an excellent start.

> The school is one of the oldest schools in the city, and many teachers felt that practice had stagnated and there was very little renewal going on. They saw the IDP as a possible opening for new practices.

> The teachers felt increasingly uncomfortable about the fact that they dealt with educational matters and discipline matters in such widely different ways. There was no coherent approach in the

school, and they felt a need for a fundamental discussion about values and practices.

The teachers had felt for several years that there was no response by the leadership to initiatives for change. The headmaster, as they saw it, was passive and had no ambitions. Many teachers, on the other hand, were quite interested in developments, but they felt that they had no problem-solving model or decision-making process that could help them to get the school moving.

We feel that any group can take initiative. Even students or parents can use the IDP as a vehicle to achieve a fundamental discussion about the values and practices of the school and to start a discussion about school renewal. However, our experience to date shows that schools are helped in institutionalizing practices by entering into the IDP only if the staff as a whole takes the process seriously. Positive results, in other words, will reinforce positive motivation by new schools to join the programme.

The way we start interaction with schools, the values we reflect in our own practices, and the approaches we take for information and communication are fundamental in achieving early identification with the project by the school people involved. We are also aware that the assumptions that participants make about the programme at an early stage have a tendency to survive even if quite contradictory information and experiences occur at a later stage. The *entry-process*, therefore, becomes crucial to project success.

Because all parties are important in gaining support for the IDP, consultants who represent the project must be fully conscious of the problems they may create when deciding how to approach a school, whom to talk to, and whom they become identified with. Usually, the project is first presented to the leadership of the school, which in turn takes the project to the staff.

Such a procedure is, formally, necessary and we encourage it. However, we have found that at times the project is then identified with the school leadership, and the consultants, in turn, are identified with the headmaster and his or her team. Although we believe that the school leadership must be fully aware of, and involved in, the project, it may be equally important to contact the teachers' association to clarify the project to its members and make sure of their support.

The manner in which the IDP is introduced to a school is crucial.

The few studies which have addressed this issue indicate that orientation workshops are important (Howes, 1974; Mann, 1977; Fullan, Miles, and Taylor, 1978). What this means is that the consultant should not be content with talking about the project. He must try to demonstrate the effects that aspects of the IDP will have, through reference to plenty of examples from his own experience, to situations already existing within the school and most importantly, through role-play situations. In other words he must make the consequences of the IDP process as real as he can during this initial, introductory, phase.

We have found that, so far, information sessions about the IDP have usually been too cognitive and traditional in nature. Information sessions that actually involve an abbreviated phase of the programme, a simulation exercise, or a role-play activity seem to give staff members a better feeling for the nature of the programme. It is more engaging and it has the potential of giving a clearer understanding of the activities that will follow.

Still another finding about the entry phase is a firmer belief in the need for a clear contract with participating schools regarding time, money and energies. One of the consultants says:

> I have only recently become fully aware of the use and value of a clear contract. Not only would this help the school to set priorities and set aside time, but it would also help me to clarify my own role. How much should I take the initiative? How much does the school expect me to give solutions to its problems? How much should I follow through and evaluate? It should be made clear in a contract what expectations the school has for the consultant and vice versa.

The time variable is taking on increasing importance. A school needs to understand clearly that at least 25 hours are necessary for all the staff to devote to the first phase of the project, including the dialogue following the survey-feedback component. Many consultants doubt that it is possible to go through any meaningful programme in less than a full school-year. In most cases the schools are involved for a second and third year, and it seems more likely that institutionalization of fundamental practices will take two or three years or more. Different consultants make the following comments:

> Most schools believe that the programme is over when the data is fed back. They become sceptical when they understand that they

> need to go through a number of meetings and exercises to learn new behaviour. They believe they don't have time to do it.
>
> It is increasingly clear that the IDP takes time, and it is almost impossible to get Norwegian teachers to work overtime.
>
> I sometimes feel it is difficult to inform them about the programme. Sometimes I look upon myself as a salesman and begin to defend the project. Maybe this is a problem in the introductory phase of the IDP in a school district. If, however, I am to be an effective consultant, I should not play a defensive role.

After several years of work we now know that the commitments to the schools and the school districts include responsibilities for the individual school over a long period of time, probably at least two to three years.

Survey Feedback Revisited

The main vehicle in self-assessment on which the IDP is based has been the Guide to Institutional Learning. We opted for a survey feedback approach rather than informal methods of data collection because the empirical evidence at the time supported its use. We have, however, attempted to remain open to further evidence as to its strengths and weaknesses as that evidence appears in the literature as well as in our own work. Below we note a number of survey feedback insights and issues arrived at.

To begin with, we feel survey feedback is an effective mechanism for assessing the general health of a school. If we were to use a medical analogy, we would describe survey feedback as analogous to a thorough medical examination. Our own instrument, the GIL, attempts to survey a wide spectrum of institutional variables and this general orientation is similar to that of other OD programmes using survey feedback. In 1979, Porras reviewed the literature and reported that previous survey feedback projects in his review all tended to collect and feed data back which were relevant to the organization as a whole, rather than to narrower concerns.

In spite of our enthusiasm for survey feedback, we have concluded that there is no single best method. It has been our experience that there are times when survey feedback is inappropriate as a school improvement design. For example, we began an IDP process in California, but before we could proceed far enough to engage in the actual survey, a crisis emerged which eventually resulted in the principal's resignation. It was absolutely imperative that the school energies focus on that specific, central and in many ways disruptive issue before it could proceed with a more orderly and general self-assessment process.

Still another insight leads us to the conclusion that survey feedback is not always appropriate. According to Dowling (1975), no one change-approach can be said to be inherently superior than others. One of the key contingencies influencing choice of approach is the focus of the institutional improvement process. Hellriegel and Slocum (1980), for example, maintain that the potential of survey feedback is high with regard to people-issues, low with regard to technology-issues, and low to moderate with regard to structure-issues. In other words, they feel a different approach would be more valuable if the central issues in the change process were technological or structural. This is a conceptual projection, but there is some supporting evidence. After two and a half years in one project which looked at the differential impacts of three different interventions, Pasmore and King (1978) found that survey feedback was effective in improving exployee attitudes but was not impressive in improving the productivity of a food processing facility.

An example of a process involving structural issues would be that of Adams and Sherwood (1979), who evaluated the success of survey feedback activity in a military setting. They found that the general process resulted in no significant change in work-satisfaction related to specific tasks as well as inter-group relations. One of their conclusions was that the isolated units were not touched by the process and a different process than that which they had developed was needed for sub-units of the institution. This suggests that a process which deals with the general organization may not always be appropriate if problems relate to sub-units of the organization.

In our own work, we have found that the IDP focuses on general institutional interests and does not address classroom and instructional issues, including work and climate issues in the classrooms. Our own response has been to develop a Classroom Development Programme (CDP), which addresses the specific needs of these loosely coupled sub-units of the school.

Probably the most serious recent challenge to survey feedback has been from school development consultants who have worked in urban areas. Basin and Gross (1980), for example, who have worked in Buffalo, New York, suggest that the only OD approaches that will work in a complex urban school setting are those which are short, focused on practical results, and inexpensive. Scheinfeld's (1979) experience in Chicago also supports the position that only issue-oriented approaches are appropriate.

The above point of view brings us full circle to the fact that survey feedback is mainly appropriate as a general diagnostic approach. Everyone would probably agree that it would be good to have a thorough examination from time to time. Strong voices are being raised which suggest that in this period of limited resources and negative attitudes about education, the school only has the time and energy to deal with specifically defined illness and problems rather than devote considerable time to diagnosis and improvement of general health. This is probably one of the major reasons Noel Tichy found that the use of survey techniques declined relative to other diagnostic techniques between 1972 and 1977 (1978, p. 474).

In our own experience, we have found that schools do tend to maintain high involvement, and that the IDP leads to concrete, even instructional-oriented solutions to institutional problems. We respect those responsible consultants and welcome recent evidence of productive alternative approaches to institutional development; we also reject the broad tendency which McDermott (1982) observes: experts and other change-agents are apt to jump on the 'productivity bandwagon' with its bag of 'quick-fix', 'off-the-shelf' packages of tricks that promise institutional health at minimal expense and little commitment on the part of participants. As we have increasingly worked with classroom teachers we have developed a series of instruments for specific purposes as well. They include instruments dealing with climate-issues, leadership-issues, norms (e.g. 'what is a good teacher?'), as well as instruments of a more evaluative design relating to specific classroom activities (e.g. evaluating a particular seminar). Used as instruments in a survey-guided development sequence they have proved very effective.

The Guide To Institutional Learning

Turning now to the GIL itself, we remain committed to it as the main diagnostic vehicle in the programme and we have found it, generally, to be well accepted by participants. There are, however, many concerns about the instrument that have been expressed by school personnel and consultants.

The first concern pertains to the length of the GIL. While we have found it difficult to abbreviate the instrument so that no one would complain about its length, we have devoted considerable time to streamlining and reducing its size. Recent versions of the GIL have been reduced greatly, but the instrument still requires one and a half hours to fill out. We believe it is difficult to arrive at a shorter version without sacrificing the comprehensive nature of the diagnostic tool as a starting point in the process.

The second concern expressed about the GIL instrument has centred around its *validity*. The GIL has *face-validity* since it has been tried out by several small samples of individuals in participating schools in development stages of the project. These individuals then suggested ways in which the GIL could be modified to suit their particular needs and interests. The initiation and contract phases of the IDP also draw participants into a discussion of the instrument. As they work through it and find that it is of potential value for their situation, it takes on *face-validity*. It also has *construct-validity* in that each item is intended to help explain some aspects of the organization. Because the IDP is an outgrowth of the IMTEC theoretical framework of schools as organizations, it probably has as high a construct-validity as is possible.

The third concern expressed about the GIL is its *reliability*. This clearly is an important issue particularly if we wish to make generalizations and predictions. Ultimately, we wish to use the GIL data in helping to understand schools as organizations and the process of educational change. We are improving the reliability of the GIL instrument continuously and feel that eventually we will have an instrument that can be used for these purposes. Our concern now, however, is to generate data which is useful in helping a given school diagnose its situation more adequately. Ideally, it would be good to have an instrument which meets all the criteria of reliability. Since, however, the programme and the instrument are in a constant state of change and redevelopment, it is premature to establish fixed reliability criteria. We believe, with Bowers and Franklin (1978), that the main issue at this stage in using the instrument in a survey-feedback process is that the items should be internally consistent (rather then stable). Do the items hang together in a consistent fashion? More importantly, reliability can be situational. The professionals in the schools participate with us in modifying the GIL so that it suits local needs. The meanings of the items may be coloured by local interpretation, but they are assumed to be reliable because they have special and known contextual meanings. In fact, one of the important aspects of the IDP project is ownership (including ownership of the instrument) by the participants involved. We are, therefore, faced with a problem, namely one of creating an instrument capable of general application which is reliable and also adapted to local needs. We believe that these problems can be solved, but that it is too early to do more than produce a reliable instrument in the context in which it is used, namely within the single institution.

In the first phase of the project, the GIL instrument was a major component of the project, and many participants understood the project as a data-feedback project. We agree with Bowers that data feedback alone has very limited value for an institution. It is necessary to integrate data-feedback as one component of a more comprehensive concept of survey-guided developments (Bowers 1974). The whole development of the IDP programme indicates that the GIL instrument is a necessary, but not sufficient, component of educational or institutional self-assessment and renewal. Some of the comments from consultants might be useful to understand the role of the GIL instrument:

> I used to think about the IDP as a relatively heavily data-based project. This is still true, maybe because we are not good enough in leaving the data from the GIL instrument and building the process on *the meanings* that the participants give the data. It is always useful to 'get back to data' to prove a given point. I believe that, as we are trained as consultants, we will become more independent of the data and we can use it for what its purpose is: namely, as a starting point for dialogue.

> In the first phase probably we were too concerned about the instrument. On the other hand, we probably needed the instrument for diagnosis and to start a process that was clearly understood in the school. The GIL instrument in the project was the starting point. It gave us the right direction. Being a ski-jumper, I know how important it is to make the right initial spring into the air!

During the feedback process, the school personnel begin to identify the strengths and weaknesses in the school. We mention several problems which are possible in this critical phase:

1. Sometimes the school's problems are so overwhelming that it is hard to find a strategy for further work. It often becomes necessary at this stage for the consultant to take much initiative and become more directive than at other stages in the process. Such a finding reinforces findings elsewhere that consultation requires differing degrees of directiveness depending on the context of the situation. There is, therefore, no ideal role for the consultant in terms of directive-nondirective behaviour, even though the typical consultant-orientation is to avoid intervening too forcefully in the process.
2. Although many schools are interested in developing the climate, the decision-making process, problem-solving process and communication of the organization, most schools are interested mainly in concrete, educational outcomes. Often, the staff looks to the consultant for practical guidance on educational development issues. This may shift the role of the consultant to being a 'change agent' rather than a 'process helper'. There is a norm in the IDP project that the consultants should avoid being a salesman for given organizational or educational solutions. The norm is to present alternatives and help the school look at the costs and benefits involved. Sometimes, however, schools and personnel feel that this over-intellectualizes the problem, and they expect concrete answers.
3. Some consultants are too isolated from the resource base in the school districts. They must be familiar with the resources available at teachers' centres, R&D centres, and other institutions which may provide the types of educational experts and materials necessary for further developments.

Planning and Implementation Insights

Our concern in this section is with certain insights we have gained regarding the actual planning and implementation of practical changes in IDP schools. We tend to agree with Basin and Gross (1980, p. 130) that the bottom line for school improvement must be the successful implementation of planned changes. The programme has been successful in many schools, but we also have sobering insights about the process.

You can't save them all: A major understanding we have gained is that failure must be expected in at least some cases. Of the 100 and more schools that have participated in the Norwegian project, eight simply chose to withdraw following the feedback process. Of course, some of the schools found that they were living in such a healthy environment that no further work was necessary; however, certain of these institutions manifested severe problems but were unable to proceed to the point where they were resolved.

Tempered rationality: In our original programme design, we placed what we now recognize as undue trust in the rationality of the change process and even the rationality of school systems. This became especially apparent as we encountered the goal-setting, planning and implementation stages of the process.

It is much tidier to assume that goals would conform to conventional standards, for example being explicit enough to ensure that there is clear understanding of their meaning by everyone, or that there is consensus as to the goals. Our experience has been that some schools get locked into the goal-setting process and become so engrossed in their explicit definition and meanings that they are unable to move on.

Likewise, conventional wisdom dictates that in plans of action complete agreement should be reached in terms of methods of achieving those explicitly-stated goals. We also adhere to this design because it is cleaner and rational, but we have come to recognize the importance of working from a reality base rather than from a strictly rational framework.

In recent years important new insights have been gained into the way planning actually takes place, and we shall describe this process to illustrate our own tempered rationality. The work of the Institute for Research on Teaching, at Michigan State University, has focused to a large extent on planning. Through studying extensive teacher self-reports, Clark and Yinger (1980) have found that teacher-planning is plural, important and invisible or private. Teachers who are just doing their routine work devote on the average 12 hours per week to planning.

The type of planning that goes on does not follow the so-called linear model of planning, where the plans begin from a set of specific objectives that generate alternative ways of meeting them. Planning follows what Simon (1969) argues is the principal mark of professional activity: the process of design. That is, design is the process of devising courses of action aimed at changing existing situations into preferred ones. Even lesson-planning does not follow the linear model. Teachers typically begin with an idea for an activity, then elaborate and adapt it to fit the time available, student- and teacher-interests, resources at hand, and so forth. It is rare that the linear model is followed where teachers begin with a specific objective, generate alternatives, and then select the best one (Ibid., p. 16).

In our own work with schools, we have sensed a process in planning that is not dissimilar to that of instructional planning. The school usually focuses on design issues and changes that do not reflect long-range school aims, but which satisfy immediate and personal interests. These become agenda-items even for long-range organizational reorientation.

The work being done at the Far West Laboratory supports our experience with organizational planning (Clark, McKibben, and Malkes, 1980). The view that educational organizations are goal-driven, rational systems is being called into question. If we devote too much time to goal-setting, we are likely to be constrained to behave as if we know exactly what to do to accomplish these goals. In actuality, it is just as difficult to obtain consensus on means as it is on goals. If we are clear that there are diverse resources and unclear technology, we might decide that we will use what is available and move with the strengths already available rather than allowing goals, as such, to dicatate too exclusively what our plans will be.

Participation and Collaboration: Most of the change literature stresses that certain participative modes must be maintained if the change effort is to be successful. Writers typically stress the importance of maintaining an open, supportive, productive environment if implementation is to be successful (Tye, 1969; Berman and McLaughlin, 1975; Havelock and Benne, 1969; Miles, 1964). Further, it is usually considered fundamental that interaction of individuals and groups takes place in an on-going steady series (Hameyer, 1981).

We have learned that much more needs to be done regarding the degree and type of collaboration that is most facilitative. We have come to feel that the collaborative process takes different forms in this phase of the improvement process. Swierczek's recent work has been helpful to us. After surveying 67 cases of organization change, he draws the following conclusion:

> Collaboration is clearly present in the phases of problem determination, goal setting, and solution in the intervention, but its character changes. In problem determination, negotiation is the most important factor; mutuality is most important in goal setting; and consensus is most important in the solution phase (1980, p. 438).

In our own work we have found that the planning and implementation stages often demand strong leadership and even unilateral decision-making, though with full awareness of these actions on the part of faculty. These activities are not part of routine teacher-behaviour and may require special administrative skills or may be too time-consuming to carry out in a participative manner. We have found, for example, that at this stage the consultant role often necessitates his becoming more a leader than an adviser, a finding which supports others pointing to the flexibility necessary in consultant roles. These seem never to be static. It is not possible to describe them in 'ideal' terms. One constant generality, however, is that forceful intervention is normally to be avoided.

Zaltman and his colleagues (1977) support our experience when they suggest that the implementation phase may be accomplished more efficiently by consciously 'switching' to the authority structure in order to tap both managerial expertise and the advantageous organizational location of administrators.

We do not imply that the school reverts to 'business as usual', but that the administration simply carries out the collective mandate, the 'consensus' mode which Swierczek has identified.

Maintaining Commitments: We have already given a rather extensive account of the need for initial commitments on the part of IDP school participants. We have come to realize more fully that commitment is not something which is present at the beginning of the process and then propels an institution to some distant conclusion. In fact, certain schools have begun with high perceived commitment only to drop out at some stage because they lacked the energy to carry the process through. Because the programme requires commitment over a long provide time normally channelled to staff development and planning subjective quality is maintained.

Our first observation is that the programme is very inexpensive in terms of cash, but that it is expensive in terms of time. This is one of the precious commodities in education and must be considered at least as valuable as money itself. Districts must commit themselves to provide time normally channelled to staff development and planning purposes if time is not to be taken entirely from the participants' own free hours.

A second observation is that we feel a dialectic positive/negative process is at work with regard to any change-commitment. Support for the process becomes translated into support for actual innovations, but at the same time shifting negative dispositions emerge. Connor and Patterson (1982) describe at least one sequence of negative commitments that are interacting with the positive commitments. Initially, unawareness of the programme and the change-notions may exist. This then shifts to a state of confusion, followed by negative perceptions of the change, which is followed by a decision not to support its installation which leads to a decision to abort the change either after initial utilization or even after extensive utilization. Each of the shifts just mentioned requires its own positive intervention measure, which must counteract the negative input if the innovation is to be successful.

Outcomes

It may be remembered from Chapter Two that Fullan, Miles and Taylor, in their evaluation of OD in North American schools, stress the importance of distinguishing between, and examining carefully, the impact of an OD project, attitudes towards it, and the extent to which it is institutionalized or made durable. We find these distinctions quite useful for discussion of outcomes and will try to be consistent with their definitions in our discussion.

One of the problems of discussing outcomes, institutionalization in particular, stems from the early stage of our project development. The pilot institutions (teacher-training institutions) which started the project in 1975—6 were not evaluated systematically and therefore we cannot report systematically about the consequences of the programme. The Norwegian schools have been involved for a period of one to six years, and it is now possible to identify some outcomes.

Impact

We find a positive impact on areas like communication, decision-making processes, problem-solving and general climate in the schools. Some of the comments from consultants and headmasters might be illustrative:

> They found that the openness maybe was not as high as they had believed. However, following the data survey the school has worked hard to include the new teachers in the work and both young and old teachers now say that they feel much more involved. Now they are more open about their real problems, and there is much more enthusiasm about the daily work.

> There is more openness, change of practices in decision-making and more effective group work.

In Engeland's* survey of headmasters, he found three major personal learnings which they had often experienced. First, they feel they have learned ways of working together with the staff. Second they feel they have learned the value of putting themselves in the teacher's position. Third, they feel they have learned to avoid the pitfall of seeing their school more positively than the teachers do (1979).

Two-thirds of all IDP schools in Norway report progress in the areas just mentioned. Such a finding suggests that the programme is resulting in greater power equalization in participating schools. What this means is that teachers tend to become more involved in the school's decision-making process. Although our data is highly subjective, we tend to concur with the predictions of Tannenbaum (1968) that the increase in teacher participation and, thus, power, has not lessened the perceived power of the headmaster. We are aware of data from Bartunek and Keys (1982) which suggest that the head actually does

---

*The data cited from Engeland (1979) in Chapters Six and Seven come from a survey of schools where the IDP has been instituted.

lose power, but we remain optimistic that power-sharing can be a positive outcome for both the heads and the teachers.

Some schools had expected more rapid developments in educational issues. A negative consequence, therefore, is that a few schools became frustrated by the amount of time involved and the lack of 'concrete results' in terms of educational outcomes. Several other schools, however, are seeing educational outcomes as one or two of several that will mature at a later stage.

The impact on the school districts themselves may also be interesting to look at. In one of the cities involved, the superintendent's office has taken a considerable interest in the project, and the educational leadership has participated in IDP-related activities. The co-ordinator of the programme in the city has worked with the superintendent on the implications of the IDP on the behaviour of the school district office. A number of positive actions have been taken to give the schools more autonomy and freedom to innovate.

In other districts, the district office is more neutral towards the project, but is happy that 'something' is happening and that 'teachers are involved.' In two of the smaller districts, there is concern about the costs of the programme both in terms of cash and time used by the staff. In one of the districts, there is some political resistance because there is some general scepticism about whose interests are served by the IDP project.

Our conclusion is that the more a school district invests in the project, the more consultants that are trained, and the more comprehensive the process is, the more positive the attitude of the school administration becomes. The danger for the small district is that they have very limited resources available for consultants. When the 'results' take more time than expected, some scepticism is unavoidable. More information about the programme, further clarification of expectations, and more interaction among school districts will be necessary to develop the project further in the smaller communities.

Attitudes

The attitudes towards the project in the schools themselves are quite positive in most cases. There are 'ups and downs' in all schools, partly because the project is difficult and therefore complete success is not easy to achieve. One of the great difficulties in Norwegian schools is to get teachers to involve themselves in activities outside the regular school hours. A sign of positive attitudes, therefore is always that teachers are using their free time to work actively to improve the work climate and programme of the school. This is taking place in a number of IDP schools. In a few schools, interest in concrete educational development projects has increased considerably since the IDP programme started.

Some comments from participants might prove helpful:

> I feel that the IDP is essential for real renewal in schools. In my view, other projects that have tried to improve cooperation among teachers and students are superficial compated with the IDP. We must base renewal on a respect for, and understanding of, the individual school, its culture, and its potential. Solutions must be found in relationship to what the school is and what it likes to be.

> For me, the IDP forms an ideology of renewal that fits my own value system. It is important that the project itself reflects the values of ownership, self-reflection and renewal. I have seldom felt a closer relationship to people and more ownership in any project in which I have been involved. There are many problems in the IDP, problems that we and the schools face together, but they are all problems that can be overcome.

What is a successful IDP school? When, for example, does the programme end and why? We have had schools in the project that have gone through self-analysis and opted *not* to have any major changes at present. Is this programme a failure? Other schools work actively over several years using processes and techniques learned in the IDP, but they do not consciously relate this to the IDP. Has the programme ended in these schools?

We do not assume that all schools should change their practice. In fact, self-analysis might result in a renewed trust in the existing structures and practices. Most often, however, schools will decide to alter some aspects of the organization. We believe that the most successful IDP schools are those which continue to use a systematic, problem-solving mode, are able to renew themselves, and call it their own.

We have asked one of the headmasters in the programme, Mr. Eiliv Olsen, to reflect on his experiences as a headmaster of a school in the IDP.

A Headmaster's View of School Renewal*

What is it that starts a process of school renewal? It certainly is not those well-thought-through and detailed projects that are set in motion by some group outside the school milieu. It is more likely to be some apparently trifling event, a chance occurence happening once, or even many times, at a school, which suddenly leads either to self-assessment or to a critical self-appraisal where minds open up to possibilities presenting themselves in the environment. These possibilities for the school to begin to develop working arrangements become the substance through which individuals, working with others, can critically appraise and again reassess their situation.

From my personal vantage point, I have experienced such occurrences at both of the schools I have worked in. These have 'set in motion' a group of us who have been working in the school. In my last school, which consisted of six parallel groups in each grade-level and possessed a relatively high degree of openness, I can say, perhaps, that one thing which set school renewal in motion was not simply an accidental occurrence. There was a new physical environment which more or less forced us continually to weigh and change our working methods.

I have considered myself to be a relatively open headmaster who has the wisdom to chat regularly with individual teachers in the teachers' room, and the wisdom to keep social company with teachers in our free time. I thought I had the ability to listen and grasp the opportunities which presented themselves in this milieu, and the skills to define and put the thoughts and ideas of the personnel into action. Because my office is situated between the teachers' room and the front office, used as a passageway by at least six persons an hour, I assumed that all fear of authority on the part of my staff had been eliminated.

Even though I was willing to admit (in theory at least), that in a living milieu, at the very minimum, contradictory interests must be recognized, all of my actions were guided to a great degree by attempts to reduce conflicts by finding compromise solutions quickly; consequently, I formed a teachers' council. In teachers' council, I often said, 'I believe that we are, in essence, all one.' When presented with

*by Eilif Olsen, Huseby Middle School, Trondheim, Norway. Translated from the Norwegian by Val D. Rust.

the possibility of involving myself in the IDP, I recall feeling, as the head-master, a touch of uneasiness, first and foremost because it would require interacting with a person outside our milieu. Also, I knew that this person would have some overview of the milieux of other schools. That implied, in itself, the possibility of my control becoming reduced both within my own milieu and in the broader context. At the same time, I was uneasy with thoughts that the consultants were not in a position to see the consequences of the different points of view in our milieu and that they would create unfortunate conditions where contrary, and even destructive, latent tendencies would surface. I was, therefore, very concerned about getting a consultant in whom I could have full confidence. (Retrospectively, I have become even more convinced that the quality of the consultant is an important factor when evaluating the results of the IDP.)

The personnel at our school can be divided into two general groups. The one group consists of more experienced teachers who have come by conscious choice to an open school. The other group consists of young teachers without special experience in other schools. The thing all have in common is that they have initiative and a relatively firm belief in their own abilities in assessing and extending the various elements of the school.

Because staff members of the school discussed whether they should use their time on the IDP, it was imperative that they understood that a survey instrument which must satisfy certain criteria was to be used. First, school personnel must feel a sense of control over the structure and items of the instrument. Second, the instrument must promote or alter processes that were already under way. Third, the instrument must set in motion only new activities which the school genuinely wished or needed. If these criteria had not been satisfied, our faculty would have rejected the new instrument.

In turning now to an assessment of the results of the IDP in my school, here are the salient points.

Even though the instrument brought out the existence of conflicts between teachers and between the faculty and leadership which I had not anticipated, at the time none of these appeared very serious. Now, in retrospect, it is clear that they were there and that they could not be laughed away; it was a fact which had to be admitted. During the dialogue phase, the image which I had constructed of myself as a dynamic, democratic headmaster came to an abrupt halt. The process led me to the point that it was necessary to think through my role anew.

Differences were debated in the general teachers' council. We began to inquire about the types of differences which existed and why they existed. Did these differences have a negative influence on our milieu? The results of these deliberations led, at least in my case, to a new and, I think, a deeper understanding of the dynamics of a cooperative work situation. I believe, now, that conflicts can be of a positive type. The closer people live together, the more involvement they have with each other. This openness gave us the courage to work ourselves beyond our existing interests, our narrow perspectives; also we accepted greater responsibilities for our professional roles. We continue to have conflicts. The important thing is to value being open and to recognize differences. I never say any more in the teachers' council that 'we are basically united'; I say, 'Here is a clear conflict situation. Should we do something with it? What can we do, etc?'

The other surprising observation I made about myself, as a consequence of the IDP process, was that the consultant's presence changed my role. I felt that I must begin to argue for the points of view which I held in a way very different from my usual one. Regardless of how adjustable a headmater is, I believe that, without even wishing it, he is changed by the role-expectations which exist in the milieu. Even weak positions and weak arguments for things begin to carry great weight in the milieu where one is the designated and formal leader, and such a situation leads to a degree of apathy on the part of the leader.

Because a leader becomes so used to being listened to, he tends to become irritated when he encounters contary arguments. This he discovers only when he encounters a situation within his own milieu where he must argue well in order to be heard. This occurs when an external person, such as the IDP consultant, who has an insight into and understanding of the school, leads a discussion about the school.

Further, I would note that the consultants who worked in my school tend to act as a support for many teachers in debate situations. I believe that the reason teachers have felt secure in debates has been that those who led the debates have been willing to support their comments and have refused to move on before the staff has been able to see all the consequences of these arguments. Teachers have received help in formulating their ideas even when they themselves have been unclear about their positions. Given this situation, it is no longer easy for their ideas to be brushed aside by a Head who, all too often, has been so taken up with his own ideas that he has not been in a position objectively to assess the ideas which have arisen during debates.

I feel that consultants have been able, in this manner, to engage in fundamental discussions. As a headmaster, I am relieved of the responsibility to interpret and place items of discussion in context. I have also begun to consider more seriously positive dimensions and possibilities in the teacher's arguments. I have been able to argue more freely and pick at weaknesses in others' arguments while, at the same time, I have been able to be cautious about using arguments of my own which I knew were not 100 per cent valid. There are now fewer arguments of the type: 'Unfortunately, it is not going according to our scheduled time plan.'

The third area in which I can say I have seen consequences of the IDP is in the distribution of responsibility at the school. I think that the teachers now feel themselves to be more involved in that which happens; now they feel more responsible for it. Fortunately for me, they are caught, in some ways, in their own line of argument. That is, today the description of the school situation and their perception of the ideal school situation stand plainly in everyone's view. The basic question is: How shall we get to where we want to go? Let me illustrate with an example involving a clear statement of interest on the part of particular teachers about becoming more centrally involved in the changes that the school is undergoing. The teachers' council that debated how the teachers were to attain that objective, passed a motion, recommended by several groups, that all should meet at least two days prior to the beginning of school to debate the projected course for the coming school year. This time would be in addition to the five study-days (the so-called 38th week) required throughout Norway.

In general, the IDP has led to the point where leaders, in all discussions, are a bit more concerned with the consequences of their points of view. I believe this is related to the working procedures which were used in the programme, especially in the dialogue sessions which serve as Guidelines and have led to the point that essentially all notions now come from, and are understood by, all.

For my own part, I feel somewhat freed from the necessity of always feeling compelled to take initiative and follow up on things. There is now a growing norm that it is legal to sit on the sidelines and to see to it that others in the school milieu take initiative for some things. I no longer feel that to do this is a sign of being a poor headmaster. It is not necessary for everything to be channelled through leaders; a teacher has the right to say, 'this relationship in the school must be corrected' without the headmaster having to feel that such a statement represents an attack against him. Teachers are beginning to feel that responsibility for initiating things at the school is as much theirs as it is the headmaster's.

The weaknesses, problems, and wishes which the IDP disclosed must still be met in different ways. It is not always sufficient to rely only on the resources that exist in the milieu. One must also go beyond the milieu in order to obtain information. We have already taken a nine-hour course on co-operative working practices. The positive thing that was experienced in this course was that we were not fed information from some external source, but had discovered a need in our milieu and went out ourselves and requested the information which we felt was necessary to solve directly the responsibilities we were confronted with. Following a very brief introduction on some general points of veiw about co-operative working practices, we were able to work very concretely with the ways in which we could incorporate these into our own situation. I experienced thereby a motivation that is seldom observed among our teachers.

Now to return to the question I raised in my introduction: 'What is it that sets a renewal process in motion at a school?' I believe it is an event which is basic to persons at a school and which moves them to assess their role and their practice at the school. There are special circumstances where some externally designed process facilitates this; however, it is only effective when it links with some critical circumstance in the school itself.

We have also asked two consultants to make a more detailed listing of the learnings which they have formulated while working with the IDP schools. Their statement follows:

Consultants' View of the IDP *

We maintain that concepts and practice based on the IDP are able to provide a systematic foundation and a structure sufficient to lead to an understanding of the organization and development both of teachers' colleges and basic schools.

*by Bjørn Sigmund Nilson and Fridtjof Lande (Lecturers at Trondheim Teachers' College, Trondheim, Norway)

As far as the teachers' colleges are concerned, this can happen, in part, if the IDP strategy is used by the colleges on themselves, and, in part, if the students are able to follow simultaneously and observe a renewal process taking place at a basic school.

Preferably, these activities would occur in such a coordinated fashion that they would help increase the student's ability for self-understanding, both with regard to the school's organization and the various individual and group roles in the system. Further, the IDP should be able to inculcate an ability as well as a will to act. Needless to say, in the process, the teachers at the basic school and the teachers' college would thereby increase their own understanding and action skills. For the students, this type of process pertains both to prevailing theoretical studies and to external clinical activities.

From our experience up to this point in working with IDP, we are able to identify some positive aspects:

A. General observations about what the IDP represents: the GIL possesses the diagnostic ability to identify specific problem areas of the individual school as well as generally valid problem areas which condition and define present-day schools.
The multiple-problem structure and its parts are so interrelated that one segment of the development work (i.e., an individual part or individual problem area) can only proceed in conjunction with the content of a general overview and interconnectedness with the other segments.
The democratic practice in the IDP's survey feedback strategy stipulates that all participants have the possibility to contribute and take responsibility. This is a powerful orientation especially as it becomes apparent that the GIL data and feedback process sanctions the taking up of problems which, for interpersonal reasons, may be difficult to raise.

B. The structure of the schools (in combination with the work time set apart for self-assessment and self-renewal) and the wishes for decentralization of power laid down by the law and ministerial directives, provide conditions for the right of a school to engage in the IDP.
We are certain that if contracting parties (school leaders, teachers, parents, pupils) work seriously with the IDP, they will exercise a genuine influence in school renewal outcomes.
The IDP has difficulty providing conventional learning which can

be gained in courses on such things as school development ('Now we have learned this'), although it provides understanding of a continual renewal process. However, during the renewal process, participants, at specific points, define the needs for future special courses which do provide more conventional learning.

C. We, the external consultants, are jointly responsible with the internal IDP consultants of individual schools both for the technical procedures and to act as catalysts. That is to say, we are jointly responsible for keeping the process going, calling attention to problem situations, and suggesting alternatives for their resolution.

Consultant activities give the consultants themselves a systematic and broad perspective with regard to the inner life of the school. This contributes much to their professional practice, especially to those engaged in basic-school teacher-preparation.

The experiences gained from the consultant process provides consultants with transferable models for the way they can work as teachers at the teachers' college, especially the establishment of qualities necessary for teachers who act as dialogue-pedagogical partners.

Unexpected effects

It is sometimes of more interest to understand what the system does to the innovation, than to see what the innovation does to the system. That is certainly true for IDP in Norway. To understand what we would call 'unexpected effects' we need to look briefly at the Norwegian system and IMTEC's role in this system.

Innovations in Norwegian schools are of two kinds: those initiated from the individual school, and those planned and implemented by central authorities. Up to now the school-based developments have only in very rare cases been supported financially. Although a number of interesting initiatives have been tested, they have seldom survived that one-trial stage by the enthusiastic teacher or head. Little has been spread or learned by these activities.

At the central level one body – the National Council for Innovation in Education (NCIE) has played a dominant role in educational innovations. This body has had nearly all resources ear-marked for innovative projects. NCIE has been responsible for large-scale reforms like the planning and implementation of the nine-year Comprehensive School, the introduction of the Comprehensive Upper Secondary School, and a large number of associated projects.

Two other central bodies, also reporting directly to the Minister of Education, the Advisory Council for the Comprehensive School (ACCS), and the Advisory Council for the Secondary School (ACSS) have become powerful as the NCIE has been terminated (1985), as a move towards more decentralized control of innovations in Norwegian schools.

IMTEC, basically an *international* body, became operational in Norway in 1973. It had no formal role within the Norwegian Educational system. Its financial structure, Governing Board structure, and staffing was quite different from the bodies mentioned above. Also, there was no tradition in Norway to have an *independent* body initiating innovations in the system – a system that has had very little room for independent schools or any other independent initiatives.

In 1974—5 the Director of IMTEC proposed that an OD project for Norwegian schools should be launched in cooperation with NCIE. The reaction was neutral to negative. At that stage the OD strategy was unknown, and, we would guess, partly threatening to NCIE itself. Therefore, IDP began without central support in Norway, albeit with considerable enthusiasm from local school districts.

Over the next few years several attempts were made to interest NCIE and the other two central bodies to engage themselves in a cooperative venture. Specifically such a design – now with full involvement of the largest Norwegian school districts – was proposed in 1978—9. At that stage interest in the design was evident; interest in practical cooperation from central bodies was very small.

In fact, in 1979—80 NCIE launched its own OD project with a design very close to that of the IDP – and heavily financed by NCIE. The project was staffed with people with no former OD experience or training. (NCIE also financed an OD project in one of the counties on the West Coast). In 1980 the ACCE launched a large scale project called 'Climate and leadership' (the so-called MOLIS project), an OD project based originally on leadership training. However, increasingly it became a comprehensive OD project.

The ACCE had no money for the project. Instead, with the understanding of the National Teacher Association, 10 per cent of the resources that are normally provided for innovations at the school district level was centrally withdrawn, to be paid back again given that the district would be involved in the MOLIS project. MOLIS soon became the largest innovation project in the Comprehensive School system. ACSS also started its own programme. No coordination or cooperation was developed among the three central bodies; in fact the competition between NCIE and ACCE became particularly strong.

What consequences did this have for IDP? Firstly, it had consequences for the consultants trained under IMTEC's supervision. Since the State projects had few people with experience, they needed help from IMTEC consultants, if not from IMTEC. Many consultants experienced a sense of difficult conflict, mainly of loyalty to IMTEC, but also because they considered much of the work to be below acceptable standards. Secondly, it had consequences for the school districts' abilities to pay IMTEC for its services. It was hard to convince politicians in the local School Boards that IMTEC should be paid for what looked (on paper) like the same services provided by central authorities – services they had already paid for anyway.

From 1981—2 the dissemination of IDP in Norway almost stopped. Although several districts continued in spite of difficulties, and new districts came into the project, the large scale dissemination we had reason to expect did not occur. In spite of these developments, however, the consultant group (about 60 persons) continued professional development through regular IMTEC training seminars, and IMTEC OD materials were heavily used. In fact all central bodies bought training places for their staff and consultants at IMTEC training seminars. As from 1985 a number of school districts are requesting assistance from IMTEC – and IDP is very much alive again!

The positive effects, in our view, are obvious: IMTEC as a pioneer organization was able to initiate an OD movement in Norwegian schools. (Many in central bodies will not accept this). Secondly, our key consultant group has played an important role in making Norwegian OD projects better. Thirdly, our publications and materials have been of importance in the process of building OD competence in Norwegian schools. Finally our international Fellows have brought in perspectives and contacts in other countries now being used by a number of Norwegians.

From a change process point of view, a number of conclusions can be drawn.

1. It is not the 'quality of the innovation' itself that determines successful implementation, but rather organizational issues like power structures, conflicts of interest, institutional structures, and personnel questions. This is a conclusion which is congruent with the findings of the RAND-studies.
(Berman and McLaughlin, 1979)
2. The ability of an organization to adapt to its environment (in this case IMTEC's ability to find an acceptable role within the Norwegian system) is vital for its ability to manage innovations within the system.
3. Schools are vulnerable to their environments and cannot choose freely among alternatives. Money is the main power-vehicle that in the final analysis will determine the fate of a project. Since the school is not organized *horizontally* – that is, as a powerful force at the grass-roots level – but is rather dependent on a *hierarchy*, independent initiatives will have to meet with the approval of that same hierarchy.
4. Since schools are 'protected', it is hard to measure their quality. It is possible, even for a school displaying bad practice, to receive new students each year and thereby money for its operations. An innovation strategy that is based on *quality development* alone is not likely to have any particular appeal. Decisions are *not* based on *rationality*. Schools in a hierarchical system do not necessarily choose an innovation because it is *better* than an alternative; they may well choose an alternative that is clearly professionally inferior, so long as it is *acceptable*. In any case, the school will adopt a project which fits its own purposes anyway.
5. As long as the individual school is not dependent on an independent assessment by its clients (students, parents, and local environment) for its survival, but rather is guaranteed continuation by central authorities, an OD strategy with the purpose of building a problem-solving capacity within the school is an innovation strategy that will be chosen only by a few schools, and not necessarily by those schools that one would think need it most.

CHAPTER SEVEN

The Institutional Development Programme Consultant

We have learned that the IDP consultant plays a key role in the project, and in this chapter we attempt to deal in some detail with the role-issues, the question of methods and techniques, and the training of consultants. In doing so, we realize that it is very hard, indeed, to separate the consultants from the particular school settings and the specific problems they face. This raises the question of 'generalizability' which, as we have noted before, is a complex issue. There are no general answers to the questions of consultant-roles, role-relationships, and techniques. The individual characteristics of the consultants, the schools they are working in, the people they encounter, and the problems under discussion, will influence the strategies they choose and the degree of success they will have. We have to realize that it is the attitudes and the behaviour of the consultants and their diagnostic skills that will enable them to succeed in the difficult task of being an IDP consultant.

We would like to begin by defining what we mean by an IDP consultant. The term 'consultant' does not have universal meaning, and usually serious questions are raised in discussions of the IDP about the consultant role. Margules reminds us that organizational consulting has two primary traditions. The first tradition has been to provide technical and expert service to a client. The second tradition has been 'to facilitate an organizational diagnosis of the internal and sometimes the external process that affect the organization's behaviour and subsequent performance' (Margules, 1978, p. 61). Most school systems have been accustomed to consultants who assume the role of expert or advice-giver. Usually the consultant has knowledge and skills in a relatively narrowly-defined area, such as language methods, curriculum design or school management. The typical expectation of the consultants is that they will come up with some concrete advice that will enable the school to solve its problems. Quite often, but by no means in all cases, consultants express a particular point of view. For example, in dealing with methods of language teaching, they see their task as one of 'installing' a new practice in the school which conforms to their methodological orientation.

The IDP consultant is conceived in a way quite different from this; two major factors distinguish the IDP consultant. They are process- rather than content-oriented, and they avoid translating their personal value systems into the goals of the schools.

1. *Process Versus Content*: IDP consultants are not advice givers. They refuse to play the role of expert on certain specific curriculum questions, or in any other content-area. They have a knowledge-base in the area of organizational theory and management, but their role is not even to give specific advice in this area either. Their task is to facilitate the process of school self-assessment and self-renewal, to help the school itself solve its problem. They have expertise in the *process* of educational change. That is, they are able to diagnose the school as an organization, help the individuals and groups in the school understand the strengths and weaknesses of the school, and institutionalize a process of development.
2. *Values and Goals*: As we have discussed earlier, the IDP consultants and the programme itself are not value-free. A number of assumptions are built into the IDP about schools as organizations, and about the process of development, but neither the programme itself nor the consultant represents specific educational goals, programmes, methods of instruction, or even general views about school organization and management. Even so, we realize that no person can work in an ideological vacuum. What is important is to deal openly with the values of the consultants when the need arises.

Such a role definition causes some discomfort both with consultants and the school personnel that in they often feel the need to impose the conventional consultant role on the situation. One consultant, who was just beginning to work with a school felt pressure to revert to this role:

> So far I have not really had any very difficult problems in the schools, but I think that problems might come up in the problem-solving phase. The teachers feel uncertain about the way to go and would like much more concrete action from my side. It will be a difficult balance between process-oriented work and involvement in the decision-making process about alternatives.

The consultant is also faced with the dilemma of withholding what might be valuable insights in an attempt to allow the staff to chart its own course. Another consultant comment illustrates this problem:

> The difficulties start when the data is given back, discussed and understood. When the problems are clear and presented on the flip chart we all feel a great need for more time, more help and methods to go further. Although I think I do have some answers, I am reluctant to impose any of these on the school. I know that we could move further quickly, but the purpose of this project is to help the school in self-renewal and not to impose one innovation or the other from the outside.

Consultant Selection and Placement

There are few universally agreed on guidelines for selecting consultants. We have drawn from a quarter-century of experience in evaluating consultants by Ronald Lippitt (1979) in constructing a check-list to which we refer during the consultant selection process:

1. How well might the consultant form sound relationships at the IDP school?
2. Would the consultant create a relationship that does not make the school personnel dependent?
3. Is the consultant able to focus on problems and conflicts and not gloss over them?
4. To what extent is the consultant non-judgemental and tolerant toward other consultants and fields of study?
5. To what extent would the consultant respect the confidence of school staff members?
6. Is the consultant able to be clear about his or her financial arrangements?

7. To what extent would the school staff respect the consultant?
8. Is the consultant clear about the skills he or she is able to bring to the relationship?
9. Would the consultant be able to inform the school about the programme and his role in it?
10. Would the consultant be willing to have his or her service evaluated?
11. Is the consultant a part of an association or network that can serve as a source of professional growth?

Consultants for the IDP program are actually selected through a joint process involving (1) the school districts (2) the participating schools, and (3) IMTEC. The roles of these three groups in the selection process are as follows.

The district role: Typically, the consultant is formally selected by the school district which has entered into a contract with IMTEC. A number of factors account for this policy. First, the consultant must have a working knowledge of the community and the educational system where the IDP school exists. Second, the consultant must already be professionally trusted by school people in the district. Third, the district assumes responsibility for any consultant costs which might occur. This usually means it will draw personnel from its own pool, if at all possible. We encourage local-consultant selection because the consultant training will provide communities with a valuable future school-development resource; that is, we want the district to build its own capacity for school renewal. According to Øystein Engeland (1979), school-district administrators find they are not in a position to conduct training programmes for organization-development consultants. At this point in time the task must be handled by a division or group such as IMTEC with that type of professional capacity. Øystein Engeland maintains that superintendents often see it as very useful for local consultants to take part in a programme like the IDP, because, during training courses etc, they learn techniques and ways of working with schools, headmasters, and teachers in ways that improve other aspects of professional performance. The consultant training activity is still – after eight years – an important IMTEC activity in Norway.

The school role: The school has a right to approve or reject the appointment of a consultant to that school. The consultant is usually already known to certain members of the school staff, and it is crucial that his or her reputation and background be acceptable to everyone. Engeland (1979) finds that school headmasters attribute the success of the relationship between the schools and the consultants to the fact that they have been very well-known in the particular school beforehand. The typical school staff was found to be a 'bit suspicious of outsiders, experts, coming into the school'.

IMTEC role: IMTEC assists school districts and consultants to clarify the types of individuals who would be most suitable for work with the IDP.

Consultant Background

The consultants are typically psychologists or individuals with a background in teaching counselling or organizational theory. They are drawn from four major sources: the school district office, the local teachers' centre, the child-guidance clinic, or the local teachers' college.

Consultant Pairing

We have found that often it is important that two consultants work in the same school simultaneously. This is clearly useful in the training of consultants, but it also has other advantages, namely, that two consultants can share the demands, often difficult, put on a consultant, particularly when he or she is expected to become involved in the process and at the same time observe it. It is now quite common for two consultants to share these responsibilities, prepare the sessions together, share roles, and debrief as part of further development and training.

Internal–external Pairing

In Chapter Two we discussed the issue of internal consultants versus external consultants. We are committed to the concept of having some balance in terms of the contribution insiders and outsiders can make in the renewal process. So far, however, we have not used personnel of IDP schools as consultants, although we arrange to have the school select a liaison individual or committee that acts as the link with consultants. Usually, at least one of the two consultants working with a school is associated directly with the school district involved; this ensures a measure of inside perspective. Often, one of the consultants is external to the system, providing the desired balance. If this is not the case, the consultant network and the recurring IMTEC sessions provide a positive source of external input and support. It becomes increasingly obvious, however, that one staff member of the IDP school needs to receive training and act as an internal consultant. There are several reasons: first, he/she would be in a better situation to assess ongoing needs; secondly, scheduling of events is easier when the person works in the institution; and thirdly, it is one way of reducing dependence on outside-consultant help. A training programme for internal consultants, therefore, has become a priority in the IDP.

Consultant Support System

A consultant-support system has evolved consisting of the consultant partner, consultant network, local sponsoring-school system, and IMTEC. Evaluations carried out over the last year of this support system indicate varied levels of support: cooperation with the consultant partner has, for the most part, been perceived by the consultant as being the most valued, followed by interaction with IMTEC staff and resource persons. Few consultants have felt that they have received much help from the school in which they serve. It is likely that most consultants find it difficult to raise their own problems in the school.

Consultant Challenges

There are many difficulties in the role of an IDP consultant. Because the IDP is an international programme, some of these are related to cultural factors. For example, in the Norwegian context, the schools themselves are not oriented towards a 'process orientation'. Usually, they expect an outside consultant to be an 'expert' in his or her area and to help the school find solutions to its problems. Also, the schools very often tend to be dependent on a consultant, which again means that a consultant needs to constantly review his or her own practice. The consultants are faced simply with a dilemma of conflicting expectations: those of the programme goals, and those of the schools and the community.

Some consultant comments might be useful:

> The most difficult problem I had as a consultant was with what I would call 'the personal/professional problem' of a new role. Who am I in the school? What did I do and why didn't I do something else? How was I seen by the participants involved? Quite often, I looked upon myself as a foreign element put into the school. After a while, open discussions about my role with the teachers and the headmaster helped us over some of these problems. Also, during the last consultant seminar, I was helped to see my role more clearly and I think now I am better equipped to go into my role.

> I am uncertain how I shall tackle the problem of expectations in the school. They look upon me as 'an expert' and want solutions. I need a great deal of help, including supervision, and I need to talk openly with the school about my dilemma.

The need for 'concrete action' in the schools is quite clear. In some schools, the participants themselves take very little initiative and the process may stagnate. Should the consultant take initiative and get involved as a 'process stimulator'? We believe that this is sometimes necessary.

One consultant gave the following comment:

> The difficulty is to get the school to keep working on the problems already identified. I thought that the headmaster would take the necessary initiative and help the school to continue the process that was started through the GIL instrument. I was frustrated, however, to find that he did not take such an initiative, and without my intervention the process stagnated. I know there is a need in the faculty, but, so far, we have not been able to develop a problem solving model that helps the school to continue on its own.

In the situation just recounted, it may be helpful to remind ourselves that in the consultation process, as in most activities, it is wise to avoid polarities and recognize that there are virtues in the technical-consultation model and virtues in the process model. The existential dilemmas faced by the consultant merit continual consideration and use of available approaches (Margules, 1978, p. 67).

There are also other problems, such as the question of confidentiality. The consultant receives highly sensitive information from the participants. It is a necessary condition of participation in the IDP for a consultant to be trusted with confidential information. This is particularly important when he or she works with other consultants in the community who would be able to help, but the consultant is not in a position to share confidential information if the disclosure has not been agreed to by the school. The consultant has no problem respecting the confidentiality norm in formal meetings and in relationship to decision-making bodies; the problematic role is to protect information in informal settings where the question of confidentiality is tested most often.

Related to confidentiality and the process of openness is the question of setting limits. If a school, for example, decides to develop more openness and communication in the staff, it needs to be dealt with very carefully and developed in a systematic manner. For example, even openness, at a too early stage might backfire in some schools and stop the process. Careful consideration of sensitive issues involved is necessary on the part of the consultant; the question of openness is an example of an issue that has to be dealt with case by case. First, it raises questions of norms. How are the discussions in the school normally conducted? How would the staff react to a new norm of openness? How could such a norm, which is critical to self-renewal, be introduced and internalized without creating withdrawal? In certain cases, the staff and students will easily agree to strive for more openness but the consultant realizes that there are a number of hidden agendas. In other cases, it is very hard to get the acceptance of openness but the dialogue is both real and honest, although clearly many issues are not taken up.

It might be necessary for all participants to go through a training period. Exercises, games, and simulations in communication and interaction analysis might prove helpful. In some cases, the staff decided to go to a resort for three or four days simply to go through 'laboratory training'. In other cases, some shorter exercises might be developed in the situation itself; and more often, it is agreed that the consultant will help in the process of identifying problems of communication and openness as part of ongoing activities.

A further difficulty pertains to community resources. Some consultants are so unfamiliar with the resource base of the school districts where they are working that they are unable to provide sound and constructive assistance. It is imperative that they become familiar with the resources available at teachers' centres, R&D centres, and other institutions which may provide the type of educational experts and materials necessary for further developments to take place.

When we asked the consultants about their most difficult problems in working with the school, some of the issues mentioned above did surface. However, some other comments from consultants might also be instructive. A new consultant said the following:

> I felt myself quite helpless when the data were presented, the problems identified and when we all felt the need for some action. How should we develop the process further? Since we needed to renew the decision-making process, how did we do it? I felt myself sometimes as a foreign element in the group, and I did not often feel that I could be of much help. The group, however, still decided to work with me and still feels that an outside 'process helper' is of use to them.

More experienced consultants are confronted also with difficult role problems. These are reflected in the following comments:

> My most difficult situation was a particular incident: the headmaster of the school realized that the perceptions he had about himself and the school were wrong and this was emotionally very difficult to bear. I knew that more openness would create a very difficult personal crisis for the headmaster. I felt a great pressure on me in the situation where we discussed the role of the headmaster in the decision-making process.

> It is difficult to understand the processes that take place in the staff. Also, I feel that when a problem is identified, it is hard to know where to go with it. Again, I think that I am used to the notion that I am an expert and, therefore, need to know the answer. I am beginning to understand that my job is to help the staff themselves find a way out.

Consultant Training

The consultants continually express a need for further training and supervision. Their training consists of a mixture of theory and practice, using the actual IDP cases as a basis for training. The consultants are rarely OD specialists and the training therefore has evolved out of an immediate 'need-to-know' format. The consultants undergo several days of formal orientation training before they begin working and, as each phase of the programme is entered into, further training is given. The programme, then, follows a scheme somewhat as follows:

Figure 30 IDP and Consultant Training Phases

IDP Phases *A* ---► *B* ---► *C* ---► *D* ---► *E* ---►

Consultant Training *A* ---► *B* ---► *C* ---► *D* ---► *E* ---►

In the programme, consultant training has averaged approximately 10 days a year. These are broken up into formal training sessions lasting from two to four days each.

A second training dimension is related directly to the ongoing school situation. Wherever possible, as noted above, two external consultants are assigned to each IDP school. The consultants act as sounding boards for one another and also give direct immediate feedback about the processes they are engaged in. One consultant generally takes a relatively passive role in the sessions, acting more as a participant observer, and thereby is more easily able to assess their tone, possibilities and limitations.

A third training dimension involves IMTEC specialist assistance. On request, programme personnel visit individual consultants and work with them on special programme difficulties and process barriers. The entire process leads to a network of consultants who continually help and monitor each other's progress, and it builds a system based on trust and cooperation. Some consultant comments are instructive:

> I had no experience with organizational development and very little theoretical background, although I had been teaching and counselling in schools for several years. What I have been missing for a long time have been practical techniques and models for my work in the schools. Increasingly, I am now getting a better theoretical understanding as well as tools to work with. I have a great need, however, to continue my training and find it exciting that I am learning.

> Although I have considerable training in the area of organizational development, I still feel a need for courses in conflict management, group dynamics and strategies for educational development.

> The exciting thing about the project is that I am learning on a continuous basis. I discover that there are many more areas where I need further training and I hope that we can all learn more about the theoretical basis of organizational development as a basis for further reflection and refinement of the project.

Evaluation data collected over the last year from the IDP consultants indicate that they have experienced the most difficult problems in phases of problem-solving and conflict-resolutions. The programme seems to face only minor problems in the diagnostic phases. It is in the continuing process of development, when different interests need to be confronted, that most consultants have found the need for further training.

Training Processes and Techniques

Because the IDP is comprehensive in nature, it is probable that a consultant will use a large array of processes and techniques during the course of the programme. We have relied on the categories described by Schmuck and Miles (1971, p. 9) which we described in Chapter Two to assess the types of process and technique which are most common. These are as follows:

1. training or education;
2. process-consultation;
3. confrontation;
4. data-feedback;

5. problem-solving;
6. plan-making;
7. OD task force establishment;
8. techno-structural activities.

We have asked the consultants to indicate to what extent they actually are using these methods and which they would like to use more. The general conclusion we can draw from this is that it is very difficult to generalize. The various processes involved are related directly to the problems and the setting itself. Whereas, for example, data-feedback is used in all projects (because it is an integral part of IDP), it does not mean that it is a necessary component in all OD programmes. Also, we realize that the use of one technique in one place might have a different rationale than in another setting.

We can conclude also that all consultants have used a variety of techniques in different phases of the programme; an integrated project like IDP is not dependent on one particular technique. The need, as the consultants express it, is to be able to diagnose any given situation to use the appropriate method of work for the purpose of the programme.

Programme Alternatives

In those communities where several schools have been involved and a group of consultants have been trained and gained practical experience, several new needs are emerging. Schools not involved in IDP, would like to learn about methods and techniques in the project. Headmasters sceptical about a school-assessment process would like to be involved in the headmaster-training component. Most schools are involved in educational-development projects and have discovered that IDP provides a number of exercises that might be of use in their work.

IDP is built on certain concepts that so far have resulted in a school assessment–school development cycle. This programme might be conceived as too rigid for some schools. Increasingly, as a local school district gets experienced consultants it can tailor-make programmes for individual schools, by using the many components of the programme. Ideally speaking, any OD programme should be designed to meet the needs of each school. This is true for the entry phase as well as all other phases in the programme.

CHAPTER EIGHT
Can Schools Learn?

The purpose of this chapter is to raise a number of issues that confront anyone who is interested in engaging in a project like IDP. We shall review the meaning of organization development from the framework of the IDP; we shall discuss a wide array of dilemmas which could limit the use of OD in schools; and we shall review issues related to schools as organizations. We wish to conclude by discussing several trends that have emerged out of the IDP programme.

What is Organization Development?

In our earlier discussion about organization development in schools, we referred to the definition presented by Fullan, Miles and Taylor (1978):

> Organization development in school districts is a coherent, systematically-planned, sustained effort at system self-study and improvement, focusing explicitly on change in formal and informal procedures, processes, norms or structures, using behavioral science concepts. The goals of OD include *both* the quality of life of individuals as well as improving organizational functioning and performance.

At this stage, we would like to make some comments on this definition as interpreted by the actors in the IDP. The first reaction is that it is hard to 'disagree' with a statement like this because it is of such a general nature! However, the definition is vague in certain respects. For example, a consultant pointed out the following:

> I agree with the definition because it includes the school as a total organization, but, to me, it is unclear what the school means. Do we mean the whole school system? Do we mean elementary schools in a district or one particular school?

The IDP has focused, so far, on the individual school. We believe the individual school is the most important unit for educational change, but this does not exclude in any way using organization-development as a change strategy at the district or even at the national level, and the definition should be stated so as to allow for such extensions.

A second example of vagueness comes from the following comment by a consultant:

> I am somewhat sceptical to the notion of 'quality of life' as a goal. I can accept this as a general goal and as an ideal or desired consequence of the programme. But it is more difficult to use this as a criterion for programme success. To me, 'quality of life' is a very difficult concept to define; what is good for the whole organization may be looked upon as a problem for the individual actor.

A third example of vagueness in the definition has to do with the term 'behavioral science concepts'. One consultant points out the importance of these concepts, but questions stressing them as having priority over more philosophical issues. He states this in the following way:

> I would use operational categories and statistical methods as a starting point, but the phenomenological dimension of organizations is to me most important in organization development. It is not, I believe, the 'objective' description of the organization that is important, but the experiences of individuals in their organizational situation.

Most participants agree that organization development, as they work with it in the IDP, includes both the individual and the organization, although the IDP seems to be mostly concerned with the whole organization. Some consultants' comments illustrate their concern:

> I have felt it difficult to practice the norms reflected in the definition. I have felt it increasingly important to have the individual actor in focus but I have seldom succeeded. I do think, however, that I have somewhat succeeded in assisting the school in getting the system to function better.

> The feeling of the individual will be dependent on a number of factors. Individuals will react differently to any interaction. Some might be threatened by the notion of change itself, maybe because their own positions might be weakened. Some might feel threatened by openness in the school. Conflicts for some are difficult, something they wish to avoid. This is particularly important if there is not sufficient support and follow-up to make such changes productive and meaningful.

There may be a cultural bias or context to the definition in that it relates mainly to activities which Fullan, Miles, and Taylor have observed in North America. We find, at least in the Norwegian context, two other issues have been discussed in relationship to the definition. First, the definition does not seem to include changes in educational processes. For most Norwegian schools, practical educational outcomes, in terms of achievement-increases or student-retention rates, are important for IDP motivation and success.

Another issue is the implied notion that the individual schools or school districts themselves are responsible for educational renewal. In most European countries, the State plays an important role in educational change, determining the contextual factors more rigidly than in North America. The extent to which an individual school or school district is autonomous in relation to the State is a crucial issue in using organizational development as a strategy for educational renewal.

The IDP is built on the assumption that the individual school may develop its practice in relation to the general objectives stated by the State. We find that, at present, at least in Scandinavia and the UK, schools have the freedom to renew their own practice under relatively generous State conditions. It is not so much a question of 'being allowed to change' as of using the opportunities that exist in the structure that have not yet been explored by the schools themselves.

Dilemmas in Organization Development

Organization development is a strategy for educational renewal.

What is not clearly understood are the limitations of organization development. We will, in this context, look at some of the dilemmas that we believe could limit the use of OD in schools:

CONSENSUS VS. CONFLICTS

Several authors have discussed the underlying assumption of organization development as reflected in its practice in industry. Since OD originally was a technology adopted by management for organizational renewal, it very often assumed consensus as an implied value. We feel also that consensus is clearly an important outcome if it does reflect the real feelings and goals of the actors involved. We do not, however, see consensus as a necessary goal of organization development. In fact, we do believe that in most schools conflicts over values and practices are natural phenomena, partly related to the multiple missions of schools in our societies. We have learned through IDP that conflicts can be important and valuable starting points for renewal processes. In some cases, schools will have to live with conflicts and tensions. Sometimes, these conflicts change over time, take other forms and might be resolved. The important dimension is that a consensus-making process is not necessarily the goal in all instances.

RE-STABILIZATION VS. RENEWAL

In many OD efforts, the schools strive for a new *status quo* based on the uncomfortable feeling that 'something is wrong' and needs to be changed. The goal of OD activities in this case is to analyse the existing situation and modify it so that the school is stabilized through changes in practice. This might well be one of the alternatives. We like to think, however, that in most IDP schools a process of self-analysis and renewal is a continuous process. By this, we do not assume that all schools need to change! In fact, a school might find through self-analysis that it is quite satisfied with its current practices. The important dimension here is that schools have the energy to go through searches for better practices and have learned how to use the techniques necessary for changes to take place.

An unintended, negative consequence of OD interventions might be an unwillingness to engage in an activity that one feels is threatening. This could happen, in particular, if the first intervention has left 'scars', that is to say, if the activity has been a one-shot affair with no commitment to follow through. IDP has clearly indicated the comprehensive nature and consequences of OD intervention. It takes considerable time – a minimum of two to three years; it takes psychological energy – the programme must have a follow-through capability; and individuals need not only to be protected but also assisted if necessary. Without these kinds of guarantees, it is likely that the maximum impact will be a revealing discussion and a return to the *status quo*.

THE INDIVIDUAL VERSUS THE ORGANIZATION

We have already discussed the difficulties of keeping attention both on individual needs and organizational needs. We do not believe that these concepts are necessarily incompatible. We have learned from practice, however, that they are hard to combine. This might be a simple question of resources, but, also, perhaps many organization-development programmes tend to materialize into organizational training (often human-relations training) which we believe to have limited value, in isolation, for the school in general.

The ethical issues involved, however, are potentially difficult. The first is the voluntary issue. IDP has stressed voluntary participation. All staff should be able to vote for or against the programme. To some extent, even with the careful entry procedures in IDP, group-conformity effects are hard to avoid (Walton and Warwick, 1973).

The most difficult issues are those of confidentiality and individual privacy (Miles, 1979). The GIL instrument protects the individuals from being unnecessarily exposed, at least in theory. There are a number of cases, however, when the consultant will be faced with problems of choice between the protection of individuals versus the organization. Basically, IDP consultants have chosen to go no further in revealing information than the degree of openness acceptable to the individuals involved. The danger is always that necessary organizational issues might not be resolved.

LEADERSHIP VS. THE STAFF

As mentioned above, one of the dilemmas of organization development is the identification of consultants with top management. We have learned, however, from several evaluations of OD projects in schools, that the support of top management is essential for programme success (e.g. Fullan, Miles and Taylor, 1978). We believe also that management needs to be informed and supportive of the programme. Equally important, however, is the support of the staff and their unions. It is crucial that a programme is not identified with any subgroup of the school, but establishes itself as a vehicle for serving the whole organization.

The GIL instrument provides a comprehensive picture of potential strengths and weaknesses while giving a picture of various views through frequency scores. Too many OD interventions take management views of 'the problems' for granted.

The issue, of whose interests a consultant is serving is, in our view, an essential one in the whole process. The starting point becomes vital. We even suggest that any diagnostic instrument ought to have high validity as well as reliability. It does not guarantee results but it tends to launch diagnostic process that ensures full participation and trust in the ability to take all views equally into account.

PROCESS VS. CONTENT

The 'neutral' consultant, we believe, is a myth. We have learned that all consultants and all programmes represent values. On the other hand, we strive for a *goal-free* consultancy-process because consultants should not take a stand on given solutions, but present alternatives, as well as their costs and benefit, for the staff itself to make the choice. In practice, however, even this distinction may be artificial and difficult to live with.

The *ideal* of OD practitioners is to *facilitate* a process of renewal. IDP, however, has told us that it is very hard indeed to avoid questions of values. Whose goal is the process serving? Our view is that *openness* about intended and unintended (negative) consequences is important. To avoid a discussion of values – indeed a discussion of whose values the process is serving – is dangerous. The ethical issues here are hard to resolve. Ambiguity and lack of openness will make it even worse.

In the forseeable future, most of the consultants in schools may be recruited from the school establishment. At this stage, we do not know if consultants from staff positions (e.g. research and development centres, teachers' colleges, etc.) will function in a different way from people recruited from line positions (e.g. superintendents' offices). The data from Fullan, Miles and Taylor indicates that some 35 per cent of the internal consultants are based in school districts and 26 per cent work from university settings. Some 11 per cent are based in state or provincial departments and nine per cent are freelance (Miles, Fullan and Taylor: volume III, 1978). It is not clear what impact the roles of the actors had on the outcomes of the programmes. The better-trained consultant had a higher success-rate, but outcomes did not correlate with staff or line roles. The study concludes, however, that 'developing the skills and operating power of regular school personnel who will be doing OD anyway seem to make the most sense.'

What is important to note is that most personnel from school districts will be identified with educational development tasks. They will face a considerable challenge in shifting from an educational adviser role towards a 'process role' in OD work. Most likely, if consultants are recruited from regular district staff, it will be hard to distinguish between process- and content-roles. One of the consultants makes the following observation:

> I believe the consultant should be attached to the school more or less regularly for the first two years and that his role should move from a process orientation to more concrete advice-giving in matters of the structure and organization of the school as well as instructional programme.

We find this solution difficult because the consultants may find themselves taking a stand on issues and become identified with certain interests. More appropriate, we believe, is a situation where the consultants can draw upon several pedagogical resource persons from other schools, a teachers' centre or other support organizations.

As noted earlier, the IDP is moving towards a clearer distinction between internal and external consultants. In the long run, we believe that a staff member (e.g. a teacher) within the school ought to receive the necessary training for follow-through activities within the school. This does not eliminate the process/content dilemma, but it might enable the external consultant to stay away more and possibly assist in an observer role.

OWNERSHIP VS. SELF-INTEREST

Organization development assumes that school personnel should have a maximum degree of ownership in the renewal process. Research on change indicates that successful implementation is highly correlated with a sense of ownership of the ideas, the process and solutions found (Dalin, 1978).

This seems to exclude OD as a strategy when a participant's self-interests are at stake exclusively. If the work conditions or the decision-making power of participants through a change process will be altered in a negative or threatening direction, it is unlikely that OD will succeed. If, for example, teachers will have to stay longer in school in order to move from a self-contained classroom practice to a team-teaching structure, it is unlikely that the teachers themselves will opt for such a solution. If one group does not see a need to share its power, it is unlikely that this group *alone* will move in such a direction.

To us, this issue depends largely on how 'the school' is defined. If we mean the staff only, we can hardly expect changes that are looked upon as unfavourable to the staff. If by the school we mean all actors, including students and parents, it is more likely that a co-operative process will help everybody to re-define tasks. We realize, however, that sometimes the common interest of the school and community is at stake (e.g. closure due to declining enrolment). Although the interests of the school are vital, we believe the issue is one in which the whole district should be involved. The general principle is that the OD process needs to involve all principal-interest groups to facilitate a realistic self-assessment and renewal process.

The IDP stresses the voluntary nature of the programme which has so far been introduced to the staff. Although students and parents have often been involved, they have been concluded through the initiative of the staff. Clearly, this procedure has limitations both in terms of what kind of changes can be expected and what kind of process is conceivable.

We have pointed to some basic dilemmas in organization development. Earlier, we have described the process of change as 'mutual adaptation and development'. We see organization-development as a vehicle to assist the school in its continuous effort to balance environmental demands to internal needs. Sometimes, these forces are in conflict, sometimes not. The purpose of the programme is to enable the school to be conscious of itself and the environment, and to function as a mirror showing the practices and ideals reflected by the actors. What is important to us is that a school that is willing and able to learn about itself also reflects a learning culture. Organizational learning, in turn, becomes an important part of the school curriculum.

THE CASE FOR RATIONAL DECISION-MAKING

At the bottom line, OD as a change strategy is based upon the assumption that 'schools' – i.e. those who take decisions about what schools should do – will base their decisions on some form of rationality. *Rationality* is here defined broadly as taking into account any evidence, feelings, values, and aspirations that are considered important for a given decision.

This does not mean that schools behave *logically* in the traditional narrow sense of that word: i.e., that only empirical evidence counts. But it *does* mean that schools are likely to be *goal-seeking* organizations. Again, a distinction is necessary. It does *not* mean that schools necessarily strive to achieve the official goals stated by the authorities. The assumption is rather that those constituting the decision-making group in a school will try to achieve those goals that are important to them (among which official goals may be included).

The question, then, is to what extent there is evidence in IDP that schools are goal-seeking institutions. Some researchers who have studied universities and other schools of higher education have compared these institutions to 'organized anarchies' (Cohen, March, Olsen, 1972). Others have compared schools to 'loosely coupled systems' (Weick, 1976). Others again have noted that schools generally have vague and unclear goals (Miles, 1967) and that low internal interdependence is a characteristic of schools (Derr, 1967). People don't need to find *common* solutions, therefore they will not have the energy to try. Finally, if you combine the fact that school goals are often vague and in conflict with each other (Elboim-Dror, 1970), that the same goals are very hard to measure (Miles, 1965), that the 'core-technology' (the instructional process) is not based on generalizable empirical knowledge (Averch, 1972), and that schools have close to a guaranteed life in that they do not need to compete (Sieber, 1980), why should schools try to improve their practices?

We have tried to find out why some schools are interested in IDP in the first place. First, how many have showed an interest? We cannot answer this question with much precision, simply because we don't know how many know about IDP, how they know about it, and what kind of information they have. During 1980 IMTEC mailed an IDP brochure to be placed on the bulletin-boards of all Norwegian schools. This 'campaign' resulted in 200 requests from a total sample of 4000 schools. We do know, however, that a very large percentage of the teachers never saw the brochure since the headmaster (or the person receiving it) chose not to spread the information. Almost without exception new schools have been recruited, as stated above, by teachers and heads who have heard about the process from colleagues they trust. It is fairly safe to say that our sample of IDP schools is not a representative one. The majority of schools would not voluntarily undergo self-assessment as a basis for self-renewal.

It is our experience that most schools deal with their day-to-day problems in a rather piecemeal fashion. Systematic, long-range, rational planning is not typical of schools. More serious problems would normally be dealt with, often in an indirect way, which means that they are, however, seldom clarified, analysed thoroughly or openly confronted. It is seldom that a cause of action from among *real* alternatives would be chosen, as recommended by the ideal problem-solving approach.

Another issue is openness. The OD process as we have practised it depends on some degree of openness. Participants should be increasingly willing to look at problems openly, share their feelings about the problems, and strive towards more open communication. Again, we find that to a large extent the ideal is foreign to the school culture. In fact, the adult community within schools too often withdraws to independent classroom activities where they are 'in control'. Clearly this varies considerably from school to school.

And this, of course, is the most fascinating aspect of our experiences. Schools are different. There are schools with staff members as well as students who are deeply committed to a systematic improvement process. We have, as we have discussed several times in this book, several hypotheses about why schools are different. We shall not repeat those arguments here, except to say that we are lacking in systematic empirical knowledge about schools as organizations. In this area, an international *comparative* study would probably give more insight than any other approach.

Finally, we are still committed to OD as a change strategy in schools. We know it can work. At the same time, we are also convinced that the OD process is a major innovation in its own right, difficult to implement, and hard to evaluate. We know that the more we gain insights into schools as organizations, the more we shall be able to master the complex process of school renewal.

In Dalin's last publication (1983; 1986) (so far only in Norwegian and German) OD as a strategy is assessed as it relates to various *School Development Stages*. OD, as any change strategy, has costs and benefits, and this last study illustrates some of the implications for school improvement.

APPENDIX A

Trends in Norwegian Basic Schooling and Teacher Education*

Introductory Perspectives

In recent years, Norwegian education has been in the process of experiencing fundamental change, a good deal of which has to do with the change from something we can describe as a hierarchical, 'bureaucratic' organization toward a more open and democratic organization (Ebeltoff, 1974, pp. 14–15). Burns and Stalker (1968) describe the earlier organizational system as being mechanical while the newer ones are organic. The Norwegian system is presently involved in a period of planned and desired decentralization of power away from central authority toward the individual school, which, by virtue of its unique perspective, is gaining the right to have a stronger influence on the decisions which pertain to it.

As a part of this process, legislative laws and regulations are now written in broad rather than detailed terms. Those in the educational sphere have recently received only general and advisory guidelines rather than specific and detailed directives.

Such a deliberate power transfer from central to local organs creates the necessity for establishing working relations and open communications between particular participants and groups in the school. In contrast to earlier times when participants were expected simply to carry out the mandates of the central authorities, now they must come to terms with an expanded array of responsibilities having to do with broad areas of concern as well as those touching on individual spheres.

* by Bjørn Sigmund Nilsen and Fridtjof Lande (Lecturers at Trondheim Teachers College, Trondheim, Norway). Translated from the Norwegian by Val D. Rust.

For some, the nature of a decentralized system is unclear and difficult to grasp or perceive. It does, indeed, carry with it a certain level of psychological insecurity for individual participants. Consequently, one often hears demands for a return to central guidance and definition in terms of how the school is structured and what it does; however, we maintain that an open and democratic system is crucial in today's world, and that anything beyond centralized guidance is undesirable. Participants themselves must build up their own organizational structure within the boundaries of political constraints, including the definition of their value-priorities, specification of work-forms, and descriptions of responsibility which are required to reach institutional goals. Decisions must always emanate from the contextual situation in the school, and not from abstract rules which are applied to specific cases.

Therefore, individual participants must themselves, in conjunction with other individuals and groups in the school community, reflect about, and develop a notion as to, their own and others' roles in the organization. Further, they must learn to be responsible for the consequences of their actions.

In the light of this orientation, we wish to outline some of its implications within the Norwegian basic school (nine-year compulsory education) and the teacher training college, which prepares teachers for the basic school, followed by comments about our own personal experiences with regard to the Institutional Development Programme.

The Basic School (Ages 7–16 years, first to ninth grades)

Since 1945, Norwegian basic schools have attempted to extend opportunity and greater justice, based on equality and cooperation. The central authorities have guided this development. Before the last half of the 1960s, priority was given to external structural change of the school organization. Political interests focused on the creation of a unified basic school and it was necessary to rely on central decisions as the means of school development. As part of this process, the central powers tended to involve themselves in schooling to the point where they were engaged in many small details of school life. Teachers, parents, and pupils were expected to adjust themselves to central requirements, and it is not surprising that they were also largely passive and uninvolved.

In the mid-1960s, proposals reflecting a desire for genuine decentralization began to appear in legislative plans; these were a part of a general tendency toward democratization. The value of exercising greater influence on one's own situation began to find increasing expression in the schools. The result of these activities was a new basic-school law (1969) and a new master-plan for schools (1971). These spelled out external structural requirements but also provided for the possibility of local influence within the framework of the skeletal law and the skeletal plan.

We shall mention but a few examples of the provisions of this plan:

— It provides for local influence with regard to courses of study and time arrangements;
— Teachers and their students can determine the content and the working arrangements which flow from the structural plan, and the pedagogical plan lays stress on such items as local subject matter and the continual use of the local milieu as a resource in instruction ('local school' v. 'national school').

— It allows for the introduction of a structural timetable, which gives schools the possibility of managing their teacher-resources.

Accompanying the government programme to extend the areas of decision-making authority into locally-developed county, community, and individual school plans, it anticipates an increasing interchange and involvement among parents, pupils, and teachers with regard to their particular situation.

In order that teachers might increase their effectiveness and renew themselves in terms of subject matter and methodology, they were given one full week of their work to engage in in-service training (the so-called 38th week). Even though the work-challenges were clearly outlined in the plan, it was still very difficult for educators to make productive use of the 38th week. This can be explained by a number of factors:

Tradition: 'Twenty years ago the criterion for defining a conscientious teacher was individualism; cooperation was seen as representing a cry for help – you are unable to get on top of your job.' This was said by a primary school teacher in a course on cooperation.

> The formal hierarchical organization of primary schooling: The headmaster takes responsibility, and teachers dutifully, but without enthusiasm, accept it. The experience of parents, pupils, and teachers has been that power does not extend to the grass-roots level. That is to say, it rests with the school director, school board, superintendent, and headmaster. Those at the grass-roots level feel that they are only small fragments of the power structure affecting them and that there is really no reason to get involved.

The crucial and central working task in the Norwegian basic school at the present time is to create a healthy inner-life in the school. That is, to make the school organization internally functional.

One conclusion which must be drawn is that the individual school needs help in coming to an understanding so that its skeletal structure is made clear. At the same time, the school need help in learning how to change its own organization. Further, help is needed in setting in motion a self-renewal process which is based on self-determined goals.

In our current school debate, we recognize persistent forces which wish for control and central direction. One purpose of pre-service teacher education, therefore, has been to place students in a position to participate actively in a sound school renewal process based on the principle of decentralized local control.

Teachers' College (Three-year basic education for instructional competence in the basic school)

Teacher-education is experiencing a running battle between two distinct orientations. The first, voiced by advocates of general education, proposes an academic professional preparation in the instructional subject-areas of the basic school. The second lays stress on practical matters which basic-school teachers must face. In other words, it advocates clearly defined and deliberate vocational training. For all practical purposes, the general education trend is probably emphasized today, although a set of precisely formulated goals which attempts to prescribe a more comprehensive framework in teacher education has been laid out.

On the one hand, instructors must resist placing so much stress on narrow, practical problems that a student becomes a teaching technician, excluding a broader, more humanistic approach to upbringing.

But, on the other hand, instructors must not become so oriented toward general subject-matter goals that teacher-preparation becomes irrelevant to the future teaching profession. In the conflict between these two views, students often experience a lack of continuity and integration in their work. It would be a good thing to establish a teacher-education programme which would provide a more comprehensive preparation for students. If this long-overdue goal had been met, teacher education could have played a more forceful role in the general development of education than is the case today.

It is clear that there is no easy way to move inductively from specific school problems toward an understanding of some central concept or issue. But certain grounds for optimism can be found in the development process in which we are engaged at the teachers' college. We find clear parallels, in the teachers' college, with the tendency outlined for the basic school discussed earlier regarding a breakdown of the power-hierarchical-organizational system. In fact, we are working toward a co-operative effort between the basic school and the teachers' college with regard to this development process.

Although we agree with the emphasis of democratic participation, we are also mindful that most organization systems, including the schools, are in need of clearly defined leadership. These leaders must be both task- and process-oriented, rather than the types of leaders we see so often today: leaders relying so heavily on their formal role-status.

Our teacher preparation programmes have been controlled by central state regulations with regard to the more important issues, which has resulted in the domination of a traditional power-hierarchical, organizational, 'mechanical' system. However, in 1975, the teachers' colleges felt the effects of a new law which, in conjunction with new directives, gave the individual college a large measure of self-determination. For example, colleges function now according to skeletal guidelines which give the individual school relative autonomy with regard to content, instructional approach, and evaluation matters.

If this autonomy is to be retained as something positive, the individual participants must exercise a measure of commitment and dedication and help their institutions engage in a constant renewal process. Participants in the school community must develop a sufficient overview of their situation, including a collective understanding with their colleagues, so that creative thinking and cooperation become possible.

Autonomy must be experienced as something positive where one places oneself in a position to shape one's future. When autonomy is experienced as chaos, without any form of leadership, demands will be made for 'strong men' and this type of leadership will be likely to take over.

Because of their different views of teacher-education, accompanied by a lack of a complete picture of the situation, a cleft in understanding between the individual subject-specialists and between teachers and students appears to have developed. It is our hope that a common understanding of the purposes of education will come about such that goals can act as guides to content, instructional methods and evaluation. It is also clear that there are deficiencies in understanding the mechanisms of a democratic (organic) organization system. This is our central problem in this essay as well as the issue about how individual and collective efforts can put such a system into genuine practice.

The inner life of the teachers' college should begin to model the basic concepts of local democratic management to a high level, thereby reflecting the kind of inner life which they want the basic schools to develop; only in this manner can the teachers' college hope to contribute to the inner development of the basic school.

From this, we see that those who are at the teachers' colleges are faced with two challenges:

a. that they practice an open and democratic (organic) community with their students. This requires that they do not allow their instructional leadership to be connected with their formal teaching status, but allow it to be problem-related and coupled with co-operative participation.
b. that they strive to make the teachers' college, as an organization, function openly and democratically.

These two aspects are, of course, interrelated and mutually dependent.

We maintain, in conclusion, that the existing law, plan, and directives, both for the basic school and the teachers' colleges, provide the foundation for development of a constructive, organizational system. However, the participants within the systems must become adept enough to guide its development. It is important, on the one hand, to acquire insight and practical capability, and, on the other, to exercise genuine influence over the distribution of resources so that both external and internal structures and processes of the organization can be improved.

A working model of these things can be developed and clarified from different perspectives:

a. An individual plan–based on individual psychology
b. A group plan–based on social psychology
c. An organization plan–based on organization theory

Organizations provide the boundaries for individual behaviour and therefore determine much of the action. It becomes imperative to develop an understanding of the school's organization if one is to understand, describe, and defend one's own and others' roles in the system. If we assume that the school's organization is in constant flux, and that the changes of the past 10 years have gone in the direction of decentralization of power and toward local influence, it becomes important that an education student, during the course of studies, is given the opportunity to develop a reflective notion about the following:

> An organization is a social unit which is constructed with purposes and is reconstructed to attain special goals. (Etzioni, 1977, p. 9)
>
> A school's organization consists of different dimensions, such as values, structures, strategies, interpersonal relations, and the social environmental milieu.
>
> The teacher's role takes definition in the context of a school's organization.
>
> Teachers, in conjunction with other parties in the school community and within politically defined boundaries, can affect the school's organization.
>
> A democratic working style can influence the structure of the school.

APPENDIX B
A Case Study in an English School

Thornbridge School, Sheffield. Headmaster: Mr W Goddard

The purpose behind IMTEC was first introduced to the Headmaster of a comprehensive school in the North of England by the Senior Adviser of the Local Education Authority. It had already been introduced to two other schools, one Primary and one Secondary in the Authority. Since taking over the headship two years before, the Headmaster had introduced a number of changes both curricular and pastoral into the school but found the concept of IMTEC an exciting proposition, particularly as GIL offered a comprehensive opportunity of self-assessment to make all the staff contribute to change and to identify particular problem areas which might hitherto have been either ignored or not felt of sufficient importance to be considered.

A staff meeting was called by the Headmaster early in December 1980 and the issues presented by the Senior Adviser were discussed. It was clearly seen that the idea of participating in self-assessment was acceptable but the question of confidentiality was of utmost significance. It was stated that if a questionnaire was completed by the staff they, and they only, would be the arbiters of its use. However it was agreed that when a questionnaire was presented this would be completed as the first stage in the process and then a review as to procedure would take place. A vote was taken early in January 1981 and the staff on the whole agreed to accept the questionnaire and complete it.

In the meantime the GIL instrument had been reviewed and amended with some of the questions rephrased to meet specific English conditions at a meeting held for this purpose at Schools Council in London.

The amended GIL arrived in the school and was completed by the staff in February 1981. It was noted that there was still some difficulty expressed in interpreting some of the ideas. Other positive criticisms were voiced during informal contacts made by the Headmaster. These can be listed in no rank order of importance as:

1. Positive identification of more key staff was needed;
2. The lumping of management together did not allow as individual a response as many would have liked;
3. Personal-type questions, for example on staff issues, were felt necessary;
4. Lunch hour activities vary from year to year;
5. A number of staff teach more than one subject;
6. A question for the management team should have been 'Do you feel someone in the team can listen to your problems?'

However, application of the instrument produced the following benefits:

1. It gave an indication to staff that all aspects of work in school can be evaluated;
2. It showed that a thinking reasoned approach to all work in school has value especially in attempting to review attitudes to specific issues;
3. It indicated that if all staff are involved in self assessment including the Headmaster then the technique has substance;
4. It demonstrated that if all staff are expected to make a contribution then their worth as individuals is not ignored;
5. It illustrated that if all staff are given an opportunity to voice their opinions before the instrument is used then a collective team approach to problems is fostered. Collective responsibility also emerges. Unity in the staff of a school is vital to its development.

It became clear also that before GIL is used a careful preparation of the staff is vital for acceptance. Some aspects of the instrument, it was felt, could have been used for the production of smaller units for departmental use and that the more complex issues, e.g. school climate, required a more detailed response than a simple 'yes' or 'no'. Obviously the instrument had prompted a positive response from the staff who had to wait until the end of June 1981 before further consideration.

When the returns were sent to the school the Headmaster distributed the profile analysis to all the staff. A checklist was made of the areas for discussion and a meeting of the school's management team was arranged with a similar group from the other Comprehensive School in the Education Authority who had conducted a similar exercise. It became clear at that meeting that the returns from the one school presented a mirror image of the other. Yet these were schools of a different size, staff, pupil population but not necessarily ethos.

At a staff meeting in July 1981 it was agreed that a working party should be established to consider the analysis and a cross section of the staff volunteered to consider the next step. The Working Party consisted of the Headmaster, two members of the senior Management Team, two Heads of Departments, and three other members of the staff. The Headmaster was asked to chair the meeting and a member of staff acted as Secretary. The areas identified for discussion were:

1. Aims and objectives;
2. Teaching objectives;
3. Teaching method;
4. Staff relationships and co-operation;
5. School climate;
6. Leadership.

The main reason for taking these areas for discussion was that the analysis revealed a considerable disparity between the ideal and the real on the profile analysis. This disparity was especially noticable in the area of 'School Climate'.

With the establishment of the Working Party four meetings were held in the Autumn Term to discuss the areas of study. Much detailed discussion led to an interim report being published for all the staff. This was followed in January 1982 with a final report. This report considered the areas identified by the Working Party and made specific recommendations for staff to consider. A follow-up session of the final report was undertaken on 1st March, 1982 when the majority of the staff (others were absent or did not wish to participate) divided into four working groups under the leadership of the members of the Working Party. Verbal reports were prepared for a plenary session and written reports followed.

Thus stage two of the IMTEC programme has been completed. The next stage is the detailed preparation of key matters and practical implementation of the positive solutions offered. Much has been achieved but the snowball effect has been for staff to press for more time to be made available for discussion and in-service training, matters which amongst others have been highlighted by the developments so far. The practical benefits gained so far are:

1. A recognition by the majority of staff that change is essential especially to meet the needs of the 1980s;
2. A realisation that all school work, not just the curriculum, can be evaluated and assessed;
3. A willingness to participate in change if the aims and objectives are clearly identifiable and possible to achieve;
4. A reaffirmation of the staff's role as teachers and a belief in the school with a preparedness to look at any development, scheme or project as long as it is beneficial to the school;
5. A recognition that communication is one of the key features in any change and that communication between the headmaster and his staff and amongst the staff themselves must be clear and unambiguous;
6. Practical solutions of problems, e.g. information for staff on issues to be debated in staff meetings, has been agreed by the Headmaster and is being displayed on staff notice boards.

APPENDIX C
Survey Feedback

by Birger Bertheussen: an IDP consultant

After having gone through this process of filling out the instrument and getting survey-feedback, one must admit that some interesting things were revealed, matters which had not been clarified through earlier discussions with the staff, in spite of the fact that these discussions had seemed to take place in a very open atmosphere. Among other things, it was quite clear that a small number of teachers felt themselves to be part of an out-group, and that this characterized their attitude concerning several conditions in the school.

It was obvious that the discrepancies between the staff and the administration were larger than had previously been believed. Before the survey, the administration had considered themselves to be sociable, not very solemn, and they believed that they had good contact with the teachers. They thought the atmosphere at staff meetings was easy-going, open and accepting. However, it turned out that this openness had not been sufficient to make all the staff members feel part of what happened at school. Several teachers pointed to the fact that they felt important decisions were made over their heads.

The material also clearly showed where the major discrepancies lay between the agreed-upon targets and the results that had been achieved so far.

These are some of the issues that were revealed during the survey-feedback. It was important to continue the work, and to try to solve problems that the material had brought to light.

DISCUSSION

The mere fact that this material existed – showing that there were expectations, contrasts and discontent among the staff members –

made it difficult for either the headmaster or the leading members of staff to try to explain away or to conceal this fact. The fact that the feeling of discontent had been stated and accepted made the individual teacher feel that he was not alone in his point of view. Because of this, he felt safe enough to advocate his opinions and to discuss solutions, instead of reacting in a sour, negative way.

Throughout these discussions, the aim was not always to compromise, or come to an agreement. There was an attempt to find causes and to accept contrasts, whether they were due to differing values or to different roles, as a positive factor in the development of an environment. Doing this, it was no longer a strain to put forward points of view deviating from the norm.

Another reason why the discussions were so successful was that an external consultant was present.

It can often be tempting for a headmaster to reject suggestions or points of view from teachers if he dislikes them, or cannot bear the unrest which always follows when innovations are to be implemented. In these cases headmasters may tend to use superficial arguments, even when these are untenable. Often we heard this way of arguing: 'This is impossible, because it means altering the timetable, and that cannot be done at the moment.'

Reactions like this are often due to the fact that teachers do not have time to look into all the possible solutions implied by their suggestions, and thereby expose the headmaster's arguments. If a consultant is present during the discussions, he can help to clarify all the consequences of the suggestions and also help to find out if it is possible to carry them through.

In having a consultant present, the administration felt more inclined to see the possibilities in the teachers' propositions, even if these propositions were not always clearly put. It goes without saying that it is always the headmaster's duty to help clarify any possibilities in connection with suggestions coming from staff members; however, this task is almost impossible if external conditions are not set favourably.

On the other hand, the headmaster felt that the consultant relieved him of a heavy burden: namely, trying to draw out other people's points of view at the same time as arguing for his own. This responsibility was now the consultant's. The headmaster was able to express his own arguments more vigorously, without feeling that he was subduing the others simply by being the headmaster. Because of this, the discussions covered a broader range and became more invigorating.

The consultant also took responsibility for seeing that the assumed working methods were being used – for example, small group work, and the putting up of newsletters on the wall. These methods were adopted to ensure that all viewpoints were being brought forward. However, the staff needs time to get used to these methods before they become convinced it is worth the time it takes to split into small groups and put news-sheets up on walls, and some staff members easily fall back into the old habit of working in plenary sessions. The reason for this is partly that the most eloquent of the staff often prefer plenary sessions, where they may be able to gain greater influence.

We think we could say that the school staff members, through participating in this IDP programme, have learned many working methods which give the individual teacher, or groups, greater possibilities for presenting their points of view openly. In addition, the programme ensures that their ideas will be thoroughly discussed. We now have many ideas regarding methods for problem-solving. The school administration has been forced into a situation where every proposal or action taken has to be seen in connection with decisions previously made by the staff. We also believe that the working methods we have learned through participation in the IDP programme are very useful in dealing with the pupils or students: it is possible to find many parallels between teacher/administration relationships and those between teacher and students. By engaging in a problem-solving process within the staff, one is better able to go through a similar process with students.

We must point out that not all aspects of our experience with the IDP have been positive. We encountered many negative reactions concerning the effectiveness of working methods. Some were of the opinion that discussing problems from an administrative point of view could well make the problems more foggy than clear. We also experienced frustration with the fact that some members wanted more involvement in school work (and planning) but at the same time felt that they spent more than enough time on their work at the school already. Some said that the administration used the programme to split the teachers up, and to manipulate them. Remarks such as that seem to have become rarer as the programme proceeded, however. Some of the reasons for such negative reactions could lie in the fact that in the beginning we made a clear differentiation between IDP-programme meetings, and other staff meetings. We now consider a distinction of this nature to be unfruitful, and think that all staff meetings should be seen as a whole, and that the same working methods should be used at all of them.

PROFESSIONAL HELP FROM OUTSIDE

It seems self-evident that a systematic attempt to disclose needs and expectations in staff members implies a follow-up. As will be seen from the remarks above, we have set several proposals into action, partly with help from outside the school and partly through the use of resources within, from among the staff.

Out of these we could mention introductions to new techniques, using a broader perspective in our school work, reallocating resources, sorting out new priorities for goals and objectives, helping staff members to see what implications new priorities and goals will have for practical work, and so on. The important thing for us is an understanding that proposals will not be set into operation until the teachers ask for them. We feel that if a school does not have the opportunity to give the teachers support in this way it would be wiser not to set the process in motion within that school.

The head also will often have the need for support from outside. It may be a considerable psychological burden for him or her to participate in a process such as the one described above.

In the introductory phase, during the survey-feedback process, we were often tempted to look back to find scapegoats for the discontent that was revealed. It is therefore important that, as soon as possible, the staff enters into a dialogue phase, that it is forward-directed to the goals that are defined; and that the discussions first and foremost be concerned with the proposals the staff wants to set in operation.

QUALITIES NECESSARY IN A CONSULTANT

Great demands are placed on the consultant concerning insight into organizing, problem-solving and the general understanding of human behaviour. The school would not have much use for poorly-trained consultants travelling about, not knowing the school district or school environment. We feel that when the consultant does not live in the area it is difficult for him to maintain running contact with the school, or the school with him – and it is often necessary to draw the consultant in at short notice in connection with staff discussion meetings, etc.

Another insight we gained is that one ought to avoid using a person who holds authority directly over the school, such as the office of superintendent, regional director and the like, as a consultant. Such a person can be perceived as an instrument of the administration, and this can disturb the school's feeling of the IDP programme being its own.

IMTEC was established by the OECD Centre for Educational Research and Innocation as a management training and development project. Since January, 1977, it has been a totally independent, non-profit-making educational foundation under Norwegian law, operating from its current base in Oslo. Inquiries and further contact should be directed to the Oslo address as follows:

IMTEC
Rosenhof Skole
Dynekil Gata 10
0569 Oslo 5
Norway
(Tel. (2) 373420)

Bibliography

ADAMS, J. and SHERWOOD, J. J. (1979) 'An Evaluation of Organizational Effectiveness: An Appraisal of How Army Internal Consultants Use Survey in a Military Setting', *Group and Organization Studies*. **4**, 2, 170–82.

ALDERFER, C. P. and FERRIS, R. (1972) 'Understanding the Impact of Survey Feedback'. In: W. W. BURKE and H. A. HORNSTEIN (eds.) *The Social Technology of Organizational Development*. Fairfax, Va.: National Training Laboratories.

ARENDS, J. H., SCHMUCH, R. A. and ARENDS, R. I. (1980). 'Students as organizational participants'. In: MILESTEIN, M. M. (Ed) *Schools, Conflict and Change*. New York: Teachers' College Press.

ARFWEDSON, G., GOLDSTEIN, M. and LUNDMAN, L. (1979) *Skolan och lärarna. Om skolan, närsamhälle och lärares arbetsvillkor.* Stockholm: Högskolan for lararutbildning.

ARGYRIS, C. (1970) *Intervention theory and method*. Reading, Mass.: Addison-Wesley.

AVERCH, H. A.., *et al*. (1972) *How Effective is Schooling? A Critical Review and Syntheses of Research Findings*. Santa Monica, Ca: Rand Corporation.

BARTUNEK, J. M. (1980) 'Participation Training, Agreement, and Teacher Participation in Decision Making', *Group and Organization Studies*, 5, 4, 481–504.

BARTUNEK, J. M. and KEYS, C. B. (1982) 'Power Equalization in Schools Through Organization Development,' *The Journal of Applied Behaviorial Science*, **18**, 2, 171–83.

BASSIN, M. and GROSS, T. (1980) 'Turning on Big City Schools: Pragmatic, Participatory, Problem Solving'. In: M. M. MILSTEIN (ed.) *Schools, Conflict, and Change*. New York: Teachers College, Columbia University, 114–31.

BECKERMAN, M. (1973) 'Educational Change Agents: An Inside-Outside team', *Educational Leadership*, **30**, 6, 530–2.

BENNIS, W. G. *Changing organizations*. (1966) New York: McGraw-Hill.

BENNIS, W. G., BENNE, K. D., and CHIN, R. (1969) *The planning of change*. London: Holt, Rinehart, and Winston.

BENTZEN, M. (1974) *Changing the schools: The magic feather principle*. An I/D/E/A report. New York: McGraw-Hill.

BERG, G. (1981). *Skolan som organisation. Slutrapport fran SÖ-prosjektet: Modeller för lokal utvecklingsplanering och utvärdering (prosjekt 6041)*. Uppsala.

BERG, G. (1981). *LGR 80 i ett organisationsperspektiv*. A report from the SIAU project, no. 35. Uppsala: The Pedagogic Institute.

BERMAN, P., and McLAUGHLIN, M. W. (1975) *Federal programs supporting educational change: A model of educational change*. Santa Monica: RAND Corporation, R-1589/1-HEW, Vol. I.

BERMAN, P. and PAULY, E. W. (1975) *Federal programs supporting educational change: Factors affecting change agent projects*. Santa Monica: RAND Corporation, R-1589/2-HEW, Vol. II.

BERMAN, P., and McLAUGHLIN, M. W. (1975) *Federal programs supporting educational change: The findings in review*. Santa Monica: RAND Corporation, R-1589/4-HEW, Vol. IV.

BERMAN, P., GREENWOOD, P. W., McLAUGHLIN, M. W., and PINCUS, J. (1975) *Federal programs supporting educational change: Executive summary*. Santa Monica: RAND Corporation, R-1589/5-HEW, Vol. V.

BERMAN, P., and McLAUGHLIN, M. W. (1977) *Federal programs supporting educational change: Factors affecting implementation and continuation*. Santa Monica: RAND Corporation, R-1589/7-HEW, Vol. VII.

BERMAN, P. and McLAUGHLIN, M. W. (1979) *Federal programs supporting educational change: An exploratory study of school district adaptation*. Santa Monica, Ca, RAND Corporation, R-2010-NIE.

BERMAN, P. (1980). Toward an Implementation paradigm. For the Program on Research and Practice. National Institute of Education.

BERMAN, P. (1981). 'Educational Change: an implementation paradigm?' In: LEHMING, R. and KANE, M. (Ed) *Improving Schools*. London: Sage.

BLAKE, R. L., and MOUTON, J. A. (1976) *Consultation*. Reading, Mass.: Addison-Wesley.

BLUMBERG, A. (1972) 'The school organization as the target of change', *Educational Technology*, October, 9–14.

BOLAM, R. (1974) *Teachers as innovators*. Paris: OECD.

BOSS, R. W. (1979) 'Essentials for Successful Organization Development Efforts'. *Group and Organization Studies*, **4**, 4, 496–504.

BOWEN, D. (1977) 'Value dilemmas in organization development', *Journal of Applied Behavioral Science*, **13**, 4, 543–56.

BOWERS, D. G. (1973) 'OD techniques and their results in 23 organizations', *Michigan ICL Study*, January/February, **9**, 1, 21–43.

BOWERS, D. G., and FRANKLIN, J. L. (1974) 'Basic concepts of survey feedback', *The 1974 annual handbook for group facilitators*. La Jolla, Calif.: University Associates.

BOWERS, D. G., and FRANKLIN, J. L. (1972) 'Survey guided development using human resources measurement in organizational change', *Journal of Contemporary Business*, Summer, **1**, 3, 43–55.

BOYD, W. L. (1979) 'The Politics of Curriculum Change and Stability', *Educational Researcher*, **8**, 2, 12–18.

BROWN, L. D. (1972) 'Research action: Organizational feedback, understanding and change', *Journal of Applied Behavioral Science*, November/December, **8**, 6, 697–711.

BROWNE, P. J., COTTON, C. C., and GOLEMBIEWSKI, R. T. (1977) 'Marginality and the OD practitioner', *Journal of Applied Behavioral Science*, **13**, 1, 493–506.

BUCHANAN, P. C. (1972) 'Organizational development as a process strategy for change', *Educational Technology*, October, 10–14.

BURNS, T., and STALKER, G. M. (1968) *The management of innovations*. London: Tavistock.

CAMPBELL, J. P., and DANNETTI, M. D. (1968) 'Effectiveness of T-group experiences in managerial training and development', *Psychological Bulletin*, August, **70**, 2, 73–104.

CARLSON, R. O. *et al. Change processes in the public schools*. Eugene, Oregon: Centre for the Advanced Study of Educational Administration.

CLARK, C. M. and YINGER, R. J. (1980) 'The hidden world of teaching: implications of research on teacher planning'. Paper presented to AERA, April 1980, Boston.

CLARK, D. L. (1980) 'In Consideration of Goal-Free Planning: The Failure Traditional Planning Systems in Education'. In: CLARK, D. L., McKIBBIN, S. and MALKAS, M. (eds.). *New Perspectives on Planning in Educational Organizations*. San Francisco: Far West Laboratory, 1–16.

CLARK, D. L. (1962) The function of the United States Office of Education and the State Department of Education in the dissemination and implementation of educational research (Chapter IV). *Phi Delta Kappa Symposium on Educational Research: Dissemination and Implementation*. Bloomington: Phi Delta Kappa.

CLARK, D. L. (1981) 'An Inventory of Alternatives to the Bureaucratic Perspective'. In: D. L. CLARK, McKIBBEN, S. and MALKAS, M. *Alternative Perspectives for Viewing Educational Organizations*. San Francisco: Far West Laboratory.

CLARK, P. (1975) 'Organizational design: A review of key problems', *Administration and Society*, 7, Autumn, 153–65.

COHEN, M. D., MARCH, J. G., and OLSEN, J. P. (1977) 'A Garbage Can Model of Organizational Choice', *Administrative Science Quarterly*, 17, 1–25.

CONNOR, D. R. and PATTERSON, R. W. (1982) 'Building Commitment to Organization Change', *Training and Development Journal*, **36**, 4, 18–26.

COOKE, R. A. and COUGHLAN, R. J. (1979) 'Developing Collective Decision-Making and Problem-Solving Structures in Schools', *Group and Organization Studies*, **4**, 1, 71–92.

COUGHLIN, R. J. and COOKE, R. A. (1974) *The structural development of educational organizations*. Ann Arbor, Mich.: Survey Research Centre.

COUNTS, G. S. (1932) *Dare the school build a new social order?* New York: Day Publishing.

CRANDALL, D. *et al.* (in print). *Master Report Series of the Study of Dissemination Efforts Supporting School Improvement*. Andover. Mass.: The Network.

CRECINE, J. P. (1977) *Report of the study group on organizational changes and adaptation*. NIE conference paper concerning Research on Schools as Organizations, Washington, D.C.

CREMIN, L. A. (1965) *The genius of American education*. New York: Vintage.

CULVER, C. M., and HOBAN, G. J. (1973) *The power to change: Issues for the innovative educator*. An I/D/E/A report. New York: McGraw-Hill.

DAHRENDORF, R. (1959) *Class and conflict in industrial society*. Stanford: Stanford University Press.

DALIN, P. (1978) *Limits to educational change*. London: McMillan.

DALIN, P. (1973) *Case studies in educational innovation: Strategies for innovation in education*. Paris: OECD.

DALIN, P. (1983; 1986) *Skoleutvikling*. Oslo: Universitetsforlaget.

DALIN, P., and McLAUGHLIN, M. W. (1975) Strategies for innovation in higher education. Background document for Educational Research Symposium on Strategies for Research and Development in Higher Education, Sweden, September 1975.

DATTA, L. E. (1981). 'Changing times: The study of federal programs supporting educational change and the case for local problem-solving'. *Teachers' College Record*, pp. 101–15.

DAVIS, T. R. (1975) 'OD in the Public Sector: Intervening in Ambiguous Performance Environments'. *Group and Organization Studies*, **4**, 3, 352–65.

DERR, B. C. (1976) '"OD" won't work in schools', *Education and Urban Society*, **8**, 227–241.

DERR, B. C. and ORTON, D. A. (1975) 'Crisis and contingencies for the small private college', *Teachers College Record*, December, **77**, 2, 231–45.

DOWLING, W. F. (1975) 'To move an Organization: The Corning Approach to Organization Development', *Organization Dynamics*, **3**, 16–34.

DUNCAN, R. B. (1977). A contingency approach to designing organizations for innovation: Some implications for the organizational designer. University of Pittsburg Conference on Organizational Design, Pittsburgh, Pa.: October 1977.

DUNN, W. N., and SWIERCZEK, F. W. (1977) 'Planned organizational change: Toward grounded theory', *Journal of Applied Behavioral Science*, **13**, 2, 135–57.

ELBOIM-DROR, R. (1970) *Some characteristics of the education policy formation system*. In: POLICY SCIENCES, I. 231–53.

ENGELAND, O. (1979) From the superintendents' and principals' point of view. Conclusions from a survey of Norwegian IDP School Districts. Mimeographed paper. Oslo.

FAUCHEUX, C., GILLES, A., and LAURENT, A. (1982) 'Organizational Development and Change', *Annual Review of Psychology*, 33, 343–70.

FEITLER, F. C., and LIPPITT, L. L. (1972) 'A multi-district organizational development effort', *Educational Technology*, October, 34–38.

FREY, K. (1976) *Innovation in in-service education and training of teachers*. Federal Republic of Germany and Switzerland. A CERI case study. Paris: OECD.

FRIEDLANDER, F. (1978) 'OD reaches adolescence: An exploration of its underlying values', *Journal of Applied Behavioral Science*, **12**, 7–21.

FRIEDLANDER, F., and BROWN, L. D. (1974) 'Organization development', *Annual Review of Psychology*, **25**, 313–41.

FRYE, N., SIEFERT, G. and YANCY, S. P. (1977) 'Organizational Change Through Feedback and Research (OD) Efforts', *Group and Organization Studies*, **2**, 3, 296–309.

FULLAN, M. (1972). 'Overview of the innovative process and the user', *Interchange*, 3, pp. 1–47.

FULLAN, M. (1982). *The Meaning of Educational Change*. Toronto: OISE Press.

FULLAN, M., MILES, M. B. and TAYLOR, G. (1978) *OD in schools: The state of the art*. Final report to the National Institute of Education, United States, Contract Nos. 400-77-0051, 0052 (five volumes).

GALBRAITH, J. (1973) *Designing complex organizations*. Reading, Mass.: Addison-Wesley.

GOODLAD, J. R. (1975) *The dynamics of educational change: Toward responsive schools*. New York: McGraw-Hill.

GOULDNER, A. W. (1959) 'Organizational Analysis'. In: R. K. MERTON, L. BROOM, and L. S. COTTRELL (eds.), *Sociology Today*. New York: Basic Books, 400–28.

GRAN, B. and MARKLUND, S. (1975) 'Organization of national R&D information and communication systems'. In: *Council of Europe, education R&D information: Case studies*. Strasbourg: Council of Europe.

GREENFIELD, T. B. (1979). *Research in Educational Administration in the United States and Canada: An Overview and Critique*. A report presented in a research seminar organized by the British Education Administration Society. University of Birmingham.

GREENWOOD, P. W., MANN, D. and McLAUGHLIN, M. W. (1975) *Federal programs supporting educational change: The process of change*. Santa Monica: RAND Corporation, R-1589/3-HEW, Vol. III.

GROSS, N., GIACQUINTA, J. B. and BERNSTEIN, M. (1971) *Implementing Organizational Innovations*. New York: Basic Books.

HAGE, J. and AIKEN, M. (1970) *Social change in complex organizations*. New York: Random House.

HAMEYER, UWE. (1981) Understanding social processes of innovation development. Paper presented at the Annual IMTEC Seminar on Educational Change Strategies, The Hague, April.

HARTZ, L. (1955) *The Liberal Tradition in America*. New York: Harcourt, Brace, & World.

HOUSE, E. R. (1974) *The politics of educational change*. Berkeley: McCutchan.

HAUSSER, D. L., PECORELLA, P. A. and WISSLER, A. L. (1977) *Survey-guided development II: A manual for consultants*. La Jolla, Calif.: University Associates.

HAVELOCK, R. G. (1969) *Planning for innovation through dissemination and utilization of knowledge*. Ann Arbor, Mich.: Institute for Social Research.

HAVELOCK, R. and BENNE, K. D. (1969) 'An Exploratory Study of Knowledge Utilization'. In: WATSON, G. (ed.), *Concepts for Social Change*. Washington: NTL Institute for Applied Behavioral Science.

HAVELOCK, R. G. (1972) 'A critique: Has OD become a social technology?' *Educational Technology*, October, 61–2.

HAVELOCK, R. G. and HAVELOCK, M. G. (1973) *Training for change agents*. Ann Arbor, Mich.: Institute for Social Research.

HELLRIEGEL, D., and SLOAN, J. W. (1980) 'Assessing Organizational Change Approaches: Toward a Comparative Typology', *Group and Organizational Studies*, **5**, 1, 35–47.

HERBERT, L. (1979) *Auditing the Performance of Management*. Belmont, CA: Lifetime Learning Publications.

HEYDEBRAND, W. (1977) *Organizational Analysis: Critique and Innovation*. Beverly Hill: Sage, 85–109.

HOWES, N. J. and QUINN, R. E. (1978) 'Implementing Change: From Research to a Prescriptive Framework' *Group and Organization Studies*, **3**, 1, 71–84.

HOWES, N. J. A. (1974) *Change Factors Related to the Institutionalization of the Multi-Unit Elementary School*. Madison: Wisconsin Research and Development Centre.

HUSE, E. F. (1975) *Organization development and change*. St. Paul, Minn.: West Publishing.

INSTITUTE FOR THE DEVELOPMENT OF EDUCATIONAL ACTIVITIES (I/D/E/A) (1970) *The problem solving school: Guidelines for implementing collaborative and systematic problem solving*. Dayton, Ohio: Charles F. Kettering Foundation.

KAHN, R. L. (1974). 'Organizational development: some problems and proposals', *Journal of Applied Behavioral Science*, **10**, 4, pp. 485–502.

KOLB, D. A. and FROHAN, A. L. (1970) 'An organization development approach to consulting', *Sloan Management Review*, **12**, 51–65.

KOZOLL, C. E., MEANS, R. P. and WEICHENTHAL, P. B. (1980) 'Staff Development and Organization Development: An Analysis of their Interaction in a Community-College Setting and Resulting Changes', *Group and Organization Studies*, 5, 3, 353–67.

KRELL, TERENCE C. (1981) 'The Marketing of Organization Development: Past, Present, and Future', *The Journal of Applied Behavioral Science*, **17**, 3, 309–29.

LAKE, D. G. and CALLAHAN, D. M. (1971) Entering and intervening in schools. In: R. A. SCHMUCK and M. B. MILES (eds.), *Organization development in schools*. Palo Alto, Calif.: Mayfield.

LAWRENCE, P. R. and LORSCH, J. W. (1971) *Organization and environment*. Cambridge, Mass.: Harvard Business School Division of Research.

LAWRENCE, P. R. and LORSCH, J. W. (1969) *Developing organizations: Diagnosis and action*. Reading, Mass.: Addison-Wesley.

LEAVITT, H. J. (1974) On the design part of organizational design. University of Pittsburgh Conference on Organizational Design, Pittsburgh, Pa.: October 1974.

LEVIN, M. A. and SIMON, R. I. (1974) 'From ideal to real: Understanding the development of new educational settings', *Interchange*, **5**, 45–54.

LIPPITT, R. (1979) 'Consultation: Traps and Potentialities'. In: HERRIOTT, R. E. and GROSS, N. *The Dynamics of Planned Educational Change*, Berkeley: McCutchan Publishing Co.

LORTIE, D. (1975) *School teacher: A sociological study*. Chicago: University of Chicago Press.

LOUIS, K. S. (1977) 'Participation and the implementation of planned change'. Paper presented at AERA, New York: April 1977.

LOUCKS, S. and HALL, G. (1979). *Implementing Innovations in Schools: a concern-based approach*. ARAE.

McDERMOTT, L. C. (1982) 'The Productivity Bandwagon – The Hottest Game in Town?' *Training and Development*, **36**, 4, 68–73.

McDONNELL, L. and McLAUGHLIN, M. W. (1980) *Program Consolidation and the State Role in ESEA, title IV*. Santa Monica: Rand, (R-2531-HEW).

McGILL, M. E. (1977) Organization development for operating managers. AMACOM (Division of American Management Associations), New York.

McKEACHIE, W. J. (1970) *Research on college teaching: A review*. Washington, D.C.: ERIC Clearinghouse on Higher Education.

MANN, D. (1976) 'The Politics of Training Teachers in Schools', *Teacher's College Record*, **77**, 3, 323–38.

MANN, F. C. (1957) Studying and creating change: A means to understanding social organizations. In: ARENSBERG, C. M. *et al*. (eds.), *Research in industrial relations*. New York: Harper.

MANNING, P. K. (1977) 'Rules in Organizational Context'. In: BENSON, J. K., (ed.) *Organizational Analysis: Critique and Innovation*. Beverly Hills: Sage, 46–63.

MARCH, J. G. and OLSEN, J. P. (1976). *Ambiguity and Choice in Organisations*. Oslo: Universitetsforlaget.

MARCH, J. G. and SIMON, H. A. (1958) *Organizations*. New York: Wiley.

MARKLUND, I. (1981) 'Educational Research in Sweden: Reform Strategies and Research Policy', *International Review of Education*, **27**, 2, 105–19.

MARGULES, N. (1978) 'Perspectives on the Marginality of the Consultant's Role'. In: BURKE, W. W. (ed.). *The Cutting Edge: Current Theory and Practice in Organization Development*. La Jolla, Ca.: University Associates, 60–69.

MATHER, A. F. (1973) 'ECHO: A framework for organization development', *Training and Development Journal*, **27**, 40–46.

MILES, M. B. (1964) *Innovation in Education*. New York: Teachers College, Columbia University.

MILES, M. B. (1965) 'Planned change and organizational health: Figure and ground', In: CARLSON, R. O., *et al*. (eds.) *Change processes in the public schools*. Eugene, Ore.: Centre for the Advanced Study of Educational Administration.

MILES, M. B. (1979) 'Should We Care? Ethical Issues in OD Intervention', *OD Practitioner*, Vol. II, No. 3, Oct.

MILES, M. B. (1976) 'Critique: Diffusing OD in schools: The prospects'. *Education and Urban Society*, February, **8**, 242–254.

MILES, M. B. (1980). *Common Properties of Schools in Context: The Backdrop for Knowledge Utilization and School Improvement*. NIE.

MILSTEIN, M. M. and SMITH, D. (1979) 'The Shifting Nature of OD Contracts: A Case Study', *The Journal of Applied Behavioral Science*, **15**, 2, 179–91.

MILSTEIN, M. M. (ed.) (1980) *Schools, Conflict and Change*. New York: Teachers College, Columbia University.

MYHRE, R. (1976) *Den norske skoles utvikling*. Oslo: Fabritius.

NADLER, D. A., COMMANN, C., and MIRIUS, P. H. (1980) 'Developing a Feedback System for Work Units: A Field Experiment in Structural Change', *The Journal of Applied Behavioral Science*, **16**, 41–62.

NADLER, D. A. (1981) 'Managing Organizational Change: An Integrative Perspective', *The Journal of Applied Behavioral Science*, **17**, 2, 191–211.

NADLER, D. A. (1976) 'The use of feedback for organizational change: Promises and pitfalls', *Group and Organization Studies*, June, **1**, 177–86.

NAUMANN-ETIENNE, M. (1976) Applying organizational development techniques to in-service education. Paper presented at the annual meeting of the American Educational Research Association, San Francisco.

NEFF, F. W. (1965) 'Survey research: A tool for problem diagnosis and improvement in organizations'. In: GOULDNER, A. W. and MILLER, S. M. (eds.) *Applied sociology*. New York: Free Press.

NESS, E. (1977) A report on a Norwegian project to upgrade pedagogical skills of vocational teachers. A case study prepared for the IMTEC seminar at Cambridge, England.

NISBET, J. (1974) Strengthening the creativity of the school. *Creativity of the school*. A CERI publication. Paris: OECD.

NISBET, J. and BROADFOOT, P. (1980) *The Impact of Research on Policy and Practice in Education*, Aberdeen: Aberdeen University Press.

OECD (1974) *Participating planning in education*. Paris: OECD.

PASMORE, W. A. (1980) 'The Comparative Impacts of Socio-Technical System, Job-Redesign, and Survey-Feedback Interventions'. In: KATZ, D., KAHN, R. L. and ADAMS, J. S. (eds.) *The Study of Organizations*. San Francisco: Jossey-Bass, 523–30.

PASMORE, W. A. and KING, D. C. (1978) 'Understanding Organizational Change: A Comparative Study of Multifaceted Interventions'. *The Journal of Applied Behavioral Science*, 144, 455–68.

PERREW, C. (1973) 'The short and glorious history of organizational theory', *Organizational Dynamics*, Summer, **2**, 1, 2–15.

PINCUS, J. (1973) *Incentives for innovations in the public schools*. Santa Monica: RAND Corporation.

PORRAS, J. I. (1979) 'The Comparative Impact of Different OD techniques and Intervention Intensities', *The Journal of Applied Behavioral Science*, **15**, 2, 156–78.

RAMSTROEM, R. (1975) European contributions to organization theory. Unpublished manuscript.

ROGERS, E. M. and SHOEMAKER, F. L. (1971) *Communication of Innovation: A Cross Cultural Approach*. New York: Free press.

ROSS, F. D. and DEAL, T. E. (1977) The effects of an externally-directed organizational change intervention on the structure of a small elementary school district. Paper presented at the annual meeting of the American Educational Research Association, New York, April 1977.

ROTHMAN, J., ERLICH, S. L. and TERESA, J. J. (1976) *Promoting Innovations and Change in Organizations and Communities: A Planning Manual*. New York: John Wiley.

ROTHWELL, W. J. (1981) 'Alternatives to Organization Development', **35**, 9, 119–24.

RUST, V. D. (1973) The European educational reform process', In: W. G. THOMAS (ed.), *Issues in American education abroad*. New York: MacMillan.

RUST, V. D. (1977) *Alternatives in education: Theoretical and historical perspectives*. London: Sage.

RUST, V. D. (1968) The common school issue – A case of cultural borrowing.' In: W. CORRELL and F. SULLWOLD (eds.), *Forschung und Erziehung*. Donauworth: Auer.

RUTTER, M., MAUGHAM, B., MORTIMORE, P. and OUSTON, J. (1979). *Fifteen Thousand Hours. Secondary Schools and their Effects on Children*. Somerset: Open Books.

SARASON, S. (1971). *The Culture of the School and the Problem of Change*. Boston: Allyn and Bacon.

SASKIN, M., MORRIS, W. C. and HORST, L. A. (1973) 'A comparison of social and organizational change models: Information flow and data use process', *Psychological Review*, **80**, 510–26.

SCHEIN, E. H. (1969) *Process consultation: Its role in organization development*. Reading, Mass.: Addison-Wesley.

SCHEINFELD, D. (1979) 'A Design for Reviewing Urban Elementary Schools', *Theory into Practice*, **18**, 114–25.

SCHMUCK, R. A. and MILES, M. (1971) *Organization development in schools*. Palo Alto: Mayfield.

SCHMUCK, R.A., RUNKEL, P., ARENDS, J. and ARENDS, R. (1977) *The second handbook of organization development in schools*. Palo Alto: Mayfield.

SHIMAN, D. A., CULVER, C. M. and LIEBERMAN, A. (eds.) (1974) *Teachers and individualization: The way we do it.* An I/D/E/A publication. New York: McGraw-Hill.

SIEBER, S. D. (1980) *Incentives and Disincentives for Knowledge Utilization in Public Education*. Program on Research and Educational Practice. Washington, D.C., National Institute of Education.

SILBERMAN, C. (1970) *Crisis in the classroom*. New York: Random House.

SIMON, H. A. *The Sciences of the Artificial*. (1969) Cambridge: M.I.T. Press.

SMITH, L. M. and KEITH, P. M. (1971). *Anatomy of Educational Innovations: An Organizational Analysis of an Elementary School*. New York: John Wiley.

SPENGLER, J. J. (1961) *Theory, ideology, noneconomic values, and political-economic development*. Durham, NC: Duke University Press.

SWIERCZEK, F. W. (1980) 'Collaborative Intervention and Participation in Organizational Change', *Group and Organization Studies*, 5, 4, 438–52.

TANNENBAUM, A. S. (1968) *Control in Organizations*. New York: McGraw-Hill.

TAYLOR, J. C. and BOWERS, D. G. (1972) *Survey of organization: A machine-scored standardized questionnaire instrument*. Ann Arbor, Mich.: Institute for Social Research.

TAYLOR, W. (1973) 'The organization of educational research in the United Kingdom.' In: TAYLOR W., (ed.), *Research perspective in education*. London: Routledge and Kegan Paul.

TAYLOR, W. (1981) 'Educational Research and Development in the United Kingdom: Framework, Impact, and Future Prospects', *International Review of Education*, **27**, 2, 179–95.

TERRY, C. (1977) Deeside High School, Clwyd, North Wales: The establishment of a part-time school-based course leading to the degree of bachelor of education. A case study prepared for the IMTEC seminar at Cambridge, England, 1977.

TICHY, N. M. (1978) 'Current and Future Trends for Change Agentry', *Group and Organization Studies*, **3**, 4, 467–82.

TOFFLER, A. *Future shock*. New York: Bantam.

TUMBULL, B. J. (1974) *Promoting change in schools: A diffusion casebook*. San Francisco: Far West Regional Laboratory for Research and Development.

TUSHMAN, M. L. A. (1977) 'A Political Approach to Organizations: A review and rationale', *Academy of Management Review*, 2, 206–16.

TYE, K. and NOVOTNY, J. (1975) *Schools in transition: The practitioner as change agent*. An I/D/E/A report. New York: McGraw-Hill.

TYE, K. A. (1969) *Monitoring The Systems: Points of Entry*. Santa Ana, Calif. Orange County School Office, Supplementary Educational Centre.

WALTON, R. and WARWICK, D. (1973) 'The ethics of organization development', *Journal of Applied Behavioral Science*, **9**, 681–99.

WATSON, G. (1964) 'Resistance to change.' In: BENNIS, W. G. BENNE, K. D. and CHIN, R. (eds.), *The planning of change*. New York: Holt, Reinhart, & Winston.

WEICK, K. E. (1976) 'Educational organizations as loosely coupled systems', *Administrative Science Quarterly*, March **21**, 1–19.

WEISBORD, M. (1977). 'How do you know it works if you don't know what it is', *OD Practitioner*, **9**, 3, pp. 1–9.

WILLIAMS, R. *et al*. (1974) *Effecting organizational renewal in schools: A social systems perspective*. An I/D/E/A report. New York: McGraw-Hill.

WRIGHT, R. D. and WRIGHT, S. N. (1972) 'A plea for further refinement of the marginality theory', *Phylon*, **33**, 359–368.

WOERDEN, W. W. and KNIP, H. L. (1974) In: VERRECK, W. A. (ed.), *Methodological problems in research and development in higher education*. Amsterdam: Swets and Zeitlinger.

YUCHTMAN, E. and SEASHORE, S. E. (1967) 'A system resource approach to organizational effectiveness', *American Sociological Review*, **32**, 891–903.

ZALTMAN, G., DUNCAN, R. and HOLBECK, J. (1973) *Innovations and Organizations*. New York: Wiley-Interscience.

ZALTMAN, G., FLORIO, D. H., and SIKOVSKI, L. A. (1977) *Dynamic Educational Change Models, Strategies, tactics, and Management*. New York: Free Press.